RHETORIC, REASON
AND SOCIETY

RHETORIC, REASON AND SOCIETY

Rationality as Dialogue

George Myerson

SAGE Publications
London • Thousand Oaks • New Delhi

© George Myerson 1994

First published 1994

SAGE Publications Ltd
6 Bonhill Street
London EC2A 4PU

SAGE Publications Inc
2455 Teller Road
Thousand Oaks, California 91320

SAGE Publications India Pvt Ltd
32, M-Block Market
Greater Kailash – I
New Delhi 110 048

British Library Cataloguing in Publication data

A catalogue record for this book is
available from the British Library.

ISBN 0-8039-7766-9
ISBN 0-8039-7867-7 (pbk)

Library of Congress catalog card number 94–061372

Typeset by M Rules
Printed in Great Britain by The Cromwell Press Ltd, Broughton
Gifford, Melksham, Wiltshire

Contents

Acknowledgements

Once a brief remark was appropriate to launch a publication: 'Go, little book'. Rhetorical criteria have changed. I would like to thank the people without whose dialogues the idea of dialogue would have been baseless for me. I would like to thank you properly but this isn't really the best place, so I will just say how grateful I am, as ever, to the family of dialogues, Yvonne, Simon, Syb and Cliff. I am also grateful to dialogists within the academy, especially Yvonne Rydin, Paul Kenny, Peter Lunt. My thanks to Cliff as creative re-reader and also to Yvonne and Paul for their supportively renewable attention. Simon encouraged me by finding it so funny that there could be dialogue about dialogue about . . . . I received an essential sabbatical semester from the English Department of King's College London. Ziyad Marar has been a humane and constructive editor.

Abbreviations of Sources

Seyla Benhabib, *Situating the Self: Gender, Community and Postmodernism* (Cambridge: Polity Press, 1992): ***Situating the Self***

Michael Billig, *Arguing and Thinking: A Rhetorical Approach to Social Psychology* (Cambridge: Cambridge University Press, 1987): ***Arguing and Thinking***

Michael Billig, *Ideology and Opinions* (London: Sage Publications, 1992): ***Ideology and Opinions***

Murray Bookchin, *The Philosophy of Social Ecology* (Montreal: Black Rose, 1990): ***Social Ecology***

Murray Bookchin, *The Ecology of Freedom*, rev. edn (Montreal: Black Rose, 1991): ***Ecology of Freedom***

John S. Dryzek, 'Policy Analysis and Planning: From Science to Argument', in Frank Fischer and John Forester (eds), *The Argumentative Turn* (London: UCL Press, 1993, pp. 213–30): ***'Policy Analysis'***

Robyn Eckersley, *Environmentalism and Political Theory* (London: UCL Press, 1992): ***Environmentalism***

Jon Elster, *Ulysses and the Sirens* 2nd edn (Cambridge: Cambridge University Press, 1984): ***Ulysses***

Jon Elster, 'Economic Order and Social Norms', *Journal of Institutional and Theoretical Economics*, 144 (1988), pp. 357–66: ***'Economic Order'***

Jon Elster, *Solomonic Judgements* (Cambridge: Cambridge University Press, 1989): ***Solomonic Judgements***

Jon Elster, *Political Psychology* (Cambridge: Cambridge University Press, 1993): ***Political Psychology***

Paul Feyerabend, ***Farewell to Reason*** (London: Verso, 1987): ***Farewell***

Frank Fischer and John Forester (eds), *The Argumentative Turn in Policy Analysis and Planning* (London: UCL Press, 1993): ***Arg. Turn***

Nancy Fraser, *Unruly Practices: Power, Discourse and Gender in Contemporary Social Theory* (Cambridge: Polity Press, 1989): ***Unruly Practices***

Ernest Gellner, *Reason and Culture* (Oxford: Basil Blackwell, 1992): ***Reason and Culture***

Anthony Giddens, *The Consequences of Modernity* (Cambridge: Polity Press, 1990): ***Consequences***

Anthony Giddens, *Modernity and Self-Identity* (Cambridge: Polity Press, 1991): ***Modernity and Self-Identity***

Anthony Giddens, *The Transformation of Intimacy* (Cambridge: Polity Press, 1992): ***Intimacy***

Marjorie Harness Goodwin, 'Tactical Uses of Stories: Participation Frameworks within Boys' and Girls' Disputes', in Deborah Tannen (ed.), *Gender and Conversational Interaction* (New York: Oxford University Press, 1993), pp. 110–43: *'Tactical Uses of Stories'*

Jürgen Habermas, *The Theory of Communicative Action. Volume 1: Reason and the Rationalization of Society*, trans. Thomas McCarthy (London: Heinemann, 1984): **CA1**

Jürgen Habermas, *The Theory of Communicative Action. Volume 2: Lifeworld and System: The Critique of Functionalist Reason*, trans. Thomas McCarthy (Cambridge: Polity Press, 1987): **CA2**

Jürgen Habermas, *The Philosophical Discourse of Modernity*, trans. Frederick Lawrence (Cambridge: Polity Press, 1987): **PDM**

Jürgen Habermas, *Moral Consciousness and Communicative Action*, trans. Christian Lenhardt and Shierry Weber Nicholsen (Cambridge: Polity Press, 1990): **MC**

Jürgen Habermas, *Postmetaphysical Thinking*, trans. William Mark Hohengarten (Cambridge: Polity Press, 1992): *Postmet.*

Jürgen Habermas, *Justification and Application*, trans. Ciaran P. Cronin (Cambridge: Polity Press, 1993): *Justification*

Donna Haraway, 'A Manifesto for Cyborgs', in Linda Nicholson (ed.), *Feminism/Postmodernism* (New York: Routledge, 1990), pp.190–233: *'Cyborgs'*

Genevieve Lloyd, *The Man of Reason: 'Male' and 'Female' in Western Philosophy* (London: Routledge, 1984): *Man of Reason*

Jean-François Lyotard, *The Differend: Phrases in Dispute*, trans. Georges van den Abbeele (Manchester: Manchester University Press, 1988): *Differend*

Martha C. Nussbaum, *The Fragility of Goodness* (Cambridge: Cambridge University Press, 1986): *Fragility*

Martha C. Nussbaum, *Love's Knowledge: Essays on Philosophy and Literature* (New York: Oxford University Press, 1990): *Love's Knowledge*

Hilary Putnam, *Reason, Truth and History* (Cambridge: Cambridge University Press, 1981): **RTH**

Hilary Putnam, *Realism and Reason: Philosophical Papers 3* (Cambridge: Cambridge University Press, 1983): **R&R**

Hilary Putnam, 'Reflexive Reflections', *Erkenntnis*, 22, 1, 2, and 3 (January 1985), pp. 143–53: *'Reflexive Reflections'*

Hilary Putnam, *Realism with a Human Face*, ed. James Conant (Cambridge, MA: Harvard University Press, 1990): *Human Face*

John Rawls, *Political Liberalism* (New York: Columbia University Press, 1993): *Political Liberalism*

Richard Rorty, *Philosophy and the Mirror of Nature* (Oxford: Basil Blackwell, 1980): *Philosophy*

Richard Rorty, 'Habermas and Lyotard on Postmodernity', in Ingeborg Hosterev (ed.), *Zeitgeist in Babel: The Postmodernist Controversy* (Bloomington: Indiana University Press, 1991), pp. 84–97: *'Habermas and Lyotard'*

Amartya Sen, 'Rationality and Uncertainty', *Theory and Decision*, 18 (1985), pp. 109–27: ***'Rationality and Uncertainty'***

Amartya Sen, *On Ethics and Economics* (Oxford: Basil Blackwell, 1987): ***On Ethics***

Amy Sheldon, 'Pickle Fights: Gendered Talk in Pre-School Disputes', in Deborah Tannen (ed.), *Gender and Conversational Interaction* (New York: Oxford University Press, 1993), pp. 83–109: ***'Pickle Fights'***

Deborah Tannen, *You Just Don't Understand: Women and Men in Conversation* (London: Virago, 1991): ***You Just Don't Understand***

John Young, *Post Environmentalism* (London: Belhaven, 1990): ***Post Environmentalism***

Introduction

This book is about reason and contemporary thought; specifically, how thinkers connect reason, dialogue and communication. Reason has always been arguable, disputed, open to different views. Some people have protested against reason, others have defended it. But more profoundly, there have always been different interpretations of what reason is, what it does, where it is found, or not found. I shall examine why many thinkers now consider reason as dialogue, as communicative activity. Many perspectives are possible; there are many ways to interpret reason dialogically, communicatively. Reason remains arguable, and the argument is profound – a profound dimension of contemporary thought.

The issue is interdependence: reason is linked to other activities, not separate and superior to the rest of life. At its simplest, such interdependence implies that what one individual thinks is reasonable may be modified in a dialogue with others, modified towards a different view, or modified against compromise, given new justifications. Either way, we need avenues for communication: without interchange, reason is not dynamic, not agile, not progressive. Non-communicative reason may be oppressive even. Individuals exchange views, but general viewpoints also interact, across cultures, across systems of belief, traditions, institutions, even across times (writing and its readers). In dialogue, reason is interactive, and the interactions are limitless: direct and oblique or mediated; friendly and suspicious; adversarial and sympathetic; reluctant and fluent.

Questions arise: what kinds of interaction are rational? In which dialogues does reason thrive? Who participates in the dialogues, and why them? How can communication be inclusive, and why is it often exclusionary? How does reason relate to the non-rational in communication, to emotion and to expectation? Much is at stake: democracy, justice, fairness, hope. The debate is organic: it follows from the issues; they are worth debating. It is not a disadvantage that reason is arguable, and it is one virtue of seeing reason as dialogue that so many interpretations follow and compete.

Different kinds of approach yield different reasons, dialogic and also non-dialogic reasons. Some thinkers inherit another model: rational calculation, estimation, including successful science and cognitive instrumentality. The model contrasts with reason as dialogue, but the contrast is becoming complicated. Some thinkers have modified previous ideas about instrumental reason, scientific success: their ideas are flexible, modified alongside the dialogic interpretations. There are also anti-rationalist currents, and lately anti-rationalism has also been modified, particularly by dialogue. Views multiply, and there is no consensus about reason; indeed consensus is more remote than ever. Yet there is meaning in considering together the interpretations; they connect and contrast significantly.

Following different disciplines, many thinkers today perceive that reason, dialogue and communication have, at least, a tangential effect on each other, whether positive or negative. ~~Much fresh thinking has been modified by perceptions of the interdependences between reason, dialogue and communication, including the tensions.~~ This book is also about disciplines and interdisciplinarity among social sciences and humanities. There are deep changes occurring, changes involving new perceptions of dialogue, changes within disciplines and between disciplines. It is too early to predict outcomes, but we get glimpses, hints of new configurations. The text that follows combines sources from a variety of disciplines: philosophy, sociology, psychology, linguistics, literature.

It hardly needs to be added that in the circumstances the book is not a compendium of knowledge in all these areas, just as it does not attempt a definitive view of reason, or dialogue, or communication individually, and is concerned with these themes insofar as they interact, interlink. The theories will not synthesise, their horizon is not theoretical synthesis, but a new kind of wisdom, towards which different ideas point in their own ways. A central topic is 'the good life', and the good society, classical themes in the search after wisdom.

I start from individual contributions, particular distinctive voices. One most personal contribution is that of Jürgen Habermas, himself a philosopher, sociologist, anthropological theorist, communication theorist and many other things. He has a vision which sweeps across domains of thought: 'From physics to morality, from mathematics to art criticism, our cognitive accomplishments form a continuum within the common, though shifting, terrain of argumentation in which validity claims are thematized' (*Justification*, p. 30). Habermas is formative for current thinking about reason, dialogue and communication. I shall maintain his work is a generative source, a creative impulse; but, I shall argue, Habermas's work is less appealing as a final achievement, a venerated position, a body of theories and claims.

Of course, discussion of reason was never restricted to a Habermasian 'paradigm'; reason (and dialogue) is (are) too arguable, too profoundly arguable. Presently, the discussions are speeding away and around, spreading ever further beyond Habermas's theories. Nevertheless, Habermas is a generous provider, a great innovator, and he continues to develop and interact. He is always urgent, he has an intuition about common problems, even if his solutions are partial: 'Modern life is characterized by a plurality of forms of life and rival value convictions' (*Justification*, p. 22). Habermas is not afraid to connect theory with experience; he thinks in the world. But there have been profound developments elsewhere in the area of argument and reason, so that Habermas occupies only one space in the large area that has evolved, and continues to evolve, on the subject.

Hilary Putnam's work has been long recognised in analytic philosophy and logic, and increasingly he influences other areas. Putnam himself has consistently acknowledged that 'Habermas is pointing in the right direction' (R&R, p. 301), but he has deep differences from Habermas – and from many other prominent thinkers! Putnam is an intellectual individualist, though committed to exchanging ideas. He has a distinctive voice, a personal perspective, and he follows his own winding path. Putnam is always moving beyond every perspective, through the maps he makes and beyond. Consider his 'Reflexive Reflections'. He has been explaining an idea about logic and competence:

> The optimistic interpretation is: **Isn't it wonderful! We always have the power to go beyond any reasoning we can survey and see to be sound. Reflexive reflection cannot totally survey itself**. The pessimistic interpretation is: **How sad!** (p. 144, emphasis as original)

Putnam is an optimist, but he sees both sides of the problems he raises, and encounters paradoxes. He is always 'going beyond'. We will never define reason, not finally, Putnam believes, because we understand reason by using another reason, a reason which is beyond the achieved definition. The quest is endless, and reason has no final expression. Instead we have a dialogue, between optimist and pessimist, two characters, two voices. This book incorporates these two voices and also attempts to celebrate in reason 'the power to go beyond' reason, beyond fixed definitions of reason.

I devote attention to Habermas and Putnam, because the comparison is resonant; my theme is interaction. The conjunction is luminous, dramatic, and it makes for a good story, a story also representative of the present time. I have not interpreted each thinker so that they can then be pulled together: the interpretations presuppose each other. The story is about a hypothetical conversation, which I connect with other hypothetical conversations. Major contributors include: Michael Billig, Jon Elster, Nancy Fraser, Anthony Giddens, Genevieve Lloyd, Martha Nussbaum, John Rawls and Deborah Tannen. The encounter extends to postmodern thinking: Jean-François Lyotard, Donna Haraway, Richard Rorty. Perspectives spread from any centre, through the process of dialogue.

Of course, voices do not only 'speak for themselves' in any story: connections involve an interpretation. Every effort has been made to represent views fairly, though selection is inevitable, particularly when proposing connections in a whole dialogue. This is not just a neutral survey, there is a purpose: to reveal dialogic possibilities in contemporary thought. Dialogue is the work's guiding metaphor, as well as a central subject.

It is possible to consider dialogues in which contemporary thinkers have engaged. Indeed the dialogues have been intricate. But my perspective is different: I wish to create new dialogues, in order to reveal the inter-relations between ideas. There are several contexts for this idea of possible dialogues. One is the work of Mikhail Bakhtin and its impact on recent linguistics and cultural studies. Bakhtin stresses 'dialogism', the creativity of voice within voice. The particular influence here is his literary model of dialogic narration, telling a story through the interplay of different voices.[1]

Such a dialogic approach is also rhetorical, in a particular sense, an ancient sense: the study of argument, persuasion and argumentative reasoning. Michael Billig has shown the 'argumentative dimension' in 'ancient rhetoric' (*Arguing and Thinking*, p. 4), and he has shown specifically how rhetoric continues to be relevant when we consider argument today. Rhetoric is about 'the two-sidedness of human thinking' (*Arguing and Thinking*, p. 41), the interplay between contraries, the interdependence between antitheses. This book is itself structured by two-sidedness, a two-sidedness which can never be final, never a static opposition. Like the ancient rhetoricians, I am a party to the disputes, not a neutral. But judgement should be complex; it may be accountable to two sides, or ambiguous. Billig proposes 'a new rhetoric' of this kind, and he considers that 'the writing of a revived rhetoric might need to be different from the writing, which presently characterizes other new disciplines devoted to the analysis of communication, such as pragmatics, conversation analysis and psycho-linguistics' (*Ideology and Opinions*, p. 209). He leaves a question whether this rhetoric will be a new discipline, or an influence on other disciplines, or both. But the idea about a new kind of writing is fundamental. If we believe in the creative effect of contact and collision, connection and exchange, then we require a medium, a way of writing which will live with the impact and conflict of communication between ideas. That does not mean simplicity in presentation, style which forbids anything unfamiliar, 'alien', 'obscure'. Rhetoric has to include different voices, and it can hardly analyse voices if its own style of presentation suppresses them, drains their energy, bleaches their colours. If ideas matter, they should interact like characters in action, so that their personal qualities can be felt in the drama that follows.

Note

1 M.M. Bakhtin, *The Dialogic Imagination*, ed. M. Holquist, trans. C. Emerson and M. Holquist (Austin: University of Texas Press, 1981).

1

Rationalism Turns to Dialogue

Reason and Modern Society

Our lives are shaped by science-based technologies, and science claims to be rational. Many modern institutions claim to be rational, in different ways, for instance democratic, economic and bureaucratic institutions. Therefore, when problems arise, the question arises too: has reason caused the problems, in any or all of these areas? Is our world failing because reason was applied and failed, particularly scientific reason and economic rationality? One response to these critiques is that reason is adequate but modernity has not lived up to reason's standards, has not fostered sufficiently rational forms of life in practice. Another view is that the standards set for reason are the problem. There is a dilemma, a contemporary dilemma with ancient roots: will reason cure our ills, or aggravate the disease? Can we trust reason to improve our condition or must we look elsewhere for alleviation? How can we solve our problems if not rationally? And what is rationality: the scientific principle, the democratic principle, the economic principle, the organisational-bureaucratic principle? Or can reason be found in a new form elsewhere?

Seyla Benhabib writes of the 'current scepticism towards modernity and the developmental stage reached by modern societies' (*Situating the Self*, p. 69). People are sceptical about modern institutions, particularly about the state, and also the media. People also doubt whether society will solve environmental problems, whether global conflicts have rational solutions. And many are sceptical about reason itself. (But isn't being sceptical a form of rationalism, even being sceptical about reason?) Is this the age of counter-rationalism, the retreat from reason? Is this the post-rational age?

One reply is that science is inescapable in any adjustments we make because modern reason derives from science, and we must make the best of it. We depend on science for our way of life, and science defines reason, for practical purposes. This point of view can be called *scientific rationalism*. A strong reconstruction of scientific rationalism is provided by Ernest Gellner. Gellner identifies 'the respectable mainstream tradition of rationalism' as promoting the view of 'reason as something clear, orderly, and individualist: a kind of lucid, self-guaranteeing agency, transparently at work in self-sufficient and autonomous minds operating on their own' (*Reason and Culture*, p. 78). Science is a crowning achievement of this kind of reason, because the aim of this reasoning is 'liberation from mere non-rigorous and hence error-prone, error-perpetuating accretion and accumulation of ideas' (p. 55). The advance of science supports both rationalism and 'modern, technology-based production' (p. 24). Of course Gellner's study covers many challenges to this scientific rationalism, and he takes these challenges more or less seriously. He also recognises that this rationalism may be overcome by other forces. But he insists that hope lies in some version of this rigorous reason.

Experience and history have seemed to many people to undermine the claims of science-based reason, and its claims to improve the human lot. John Young surveys suspicions towards science and scientific reason in the context of environmental crisis. He emphasises the association in many people's minds between science and political tyranny, an association he traces to the 1920s and 1930s:

> In this period, the scientific dilemma became acute. Scientific authority rested to a large extent on the demonstrable power of science to do good things, like finding new cures for disease, and as science became more incomprehensible to the layman, so direct demonstration of utility became a more important condition for the continued social support of science, which became essential as science became increasingly expensive. But in the alarming context of totalitarianism it was not surprising that scientific disclaimers of moral responsibility, for good or evil, should grow more explicit. (*Post Environmentalism*, p. 80)

Science impressed people by improving their lives, but was science not also responsible for evils? One answer from science was to disclaim responsibility for either improvement or suffering in human affairs. But then science is diminished and offers no basis for a rational life. Young recalls that in earlier ages other models of understanding had existed:

> Faith and reason, induction and dialectics were equally valid means of obtaining a view of the many-sided, and hence apparently differently shaped, mountain on which stood the City of God. (*Post Environmentalism*, p. 78)

Should science, and reason based on science, be incorporated once again into a wider framework for a rational life, asks Young? Certainly, Young represents a challenge to scientific rationalism. Others go further, as Robyn Eckersley demonstrates in her account of contemporary responses to environmental crisis. She presents a movement of ecocentric emancipatory theory:

> The Enlightenment notion of rational autonomy – particularly the quest to overcome all natural constraints – is seen as fundamentally illusory since it denies the fact of man's embeddedness in nature. Accordingly, ecocentric theorists are concerned, among other things, to emphasize our continuity with and relatedness to the nonhuman world rather than our separation and differentiation from it. (*Environmentalism*, p. 112)

The ecocentric approach may not be anti-rational, but it certainly rejects the suggestion that reason can be defined by science.

Environmental crisis also stimulates science to produce new ideas, as I will show in later chapters. But the anti-scientific impact of perceived environmental deterioration is considerable. Other factors also challenge science as the basis for reason. So many discoveries seem ambiguous, partly hopeful, partly destructive. And it seems science itself does not determine whether the outcome is to be hope or destruction. People also associate science with particular contexts, specific institutions and groups, which favour some interests over others, some hopes over others, some lives over others. Therefore must there not be another form of reason to which science is linked, or even subordinate? Insofar as science responds to these criticisms, it draws on non-scientific sources to defend itself. And insofar as science is localised in its method and premises, there needs to be an alternative reason which is less localised, which can connect science to diverse forms of life.

Scientists are experts. Other experts also claim to be rational, specifically rational: for instance, in economics, management, therapy. Is rationality about expertise? Particularly, is rationality defined by effective interventions in areas wider than science and the achievement of goals by specialised techniques? In many practical contexts, the model of expertise applies. But there are many disappointments for experts. Economic theory intervenes in the real economy, but in diverse ways, with mixed results. In personal relations, therapies multiply, and again expert solutions succeed only to various degrees and in particular circumstances.

Another common model of reason deals with individuals pursuing their aims, an instrumental model, in practice close to scientific reason. The criterion of reason is successful intervention, efficiency, impact. Recent thinkers have extended this concept of instrumentalism, as we shall see: but the basic idea is simple and pervasive. It is rational to pursue aims effectively, it is rational to succeed, and this appears in the way 'rationalisation' is now applied to institutions and enterprises.

There are alternatives to defining reason through science and expertise, individual calculation and effective technique. Reason can be found in human interaction, humane interaction, and dialogue is the overt expression of reason in this form. Accepting this formulation of reason has profound ethical, social and imaginative implications. The very definition of modernity is involved in this relation of reason and dialogue. And beyond modernity, there is also a hope for the future, a hope for alleviating problems through reason in dialogue, particularly if dialogue is available to all. Many of the sources presented here inspire this hope of rational dialogue, without belittling the obstacles.

Seyla Benhabib and Richard Rorty feature in this account and, in their different ways, offer overviews of the debate about reason; Benhabib's assessments, in particular, are a recurrent point of reference and inspiration, while Rorty provides an inescapable challenge to any ready-made view of reason. The question of reason and dialogue bounces around among different viewpoints and experiences, and among different disciplinary contexts, particularly philosophical, sociological, political and literary contexts. I shall propose *rhetoric* as one important resource for coping with these expanding differences about reason, a proposition which draws upon much enabling work, particularly the initiatives of Michael Billig in '*rhetorical psychology*'.

Dialogic Rationalism

Humanising Rationalism

This book is about *dialogic rationalism*, reconstructing reason as dialogue. Dialogic rationalism connects reason with interaction between people, and is sympathetic to democratic reason, but also includes science as one requirement of social progress, though not the dominant one. Dialogic rationalism is not a finished project. No single movement embodies it, nor any single discipline or text. Diverse thinkers are relevant to its emergence, and they have many aims:

1   To defend reason, as an essential requirement for democratic progress. The challenge is to re-imagine reason with a democratic imagination.
2   To recognise science, and the benefits it confers, together with risks, and to interpret reason so that it is not the property of science.
3   To apply a dialogic principle: *reason is good dialogue*; to show that understanding reason means interpreting rational dialogue. A search for good dialogue makes argument central, for different ideas impinge on each other at the heart of reason.
4   Rational disagreement is the path to a good society, and makes a good society sustainable.

This book represents a search for dialogic rationalism, amongst many contributions, tendencies, allies, echoes, prefigurations. The search derives from a dilemma: accepted rationalism is overshadowed by so many disasters, failures and disappointments which appear to have followed in its wake or which rationalism could not prevent. From the dilemma, there emerges a motive for a new orientation. The search does not uncover a philosophical school or tradition, but an idea emerging in different places, an idea of conceiving reason as dialogue. The idea has different contexts, disciplines and political sources, different accents, inflections, potentialities, and an attempt is made in this book to represent them all as far as possible. It would be self-contradictory for one theory to represent a dialogic tendency, and these different voices are often directed at each other's positions, or are aligned to each other. The resulting discourse is here called 'dialogic rationalism'.

Habermas and Dialogic Rationalism

Jürgen Habermas is a major source for this new approach to reason. His work has derived from critical theory, diversifying from the Frankfurt School, in which Horkheimer and Adorno produced their dialectic of enlightenment, partly redemptive, partly devastating. Habermas has recreated critical theory, and his critical theory is a source for a new rationalism, known as communicative reason, one version of reason as dialogue, which has promoted reason as interaction using communicative rationality, especially since *The Theory of Communicative Action*. His position is polemical in *The Philosophical Discourse of Modernity*, elaborated in *Justification and Application*, adjusted in *Postmetaphysical Thinking*. Habermas emerged from debates about positivism, social sciences and legitimation with a vision in *The Theory of Communicative Action*, a vision of hope, and also a critique of the wrongs of our time. The central moment is:

> This concept of communicative rationality carries with it connotations based ultimately on the central experience of the unconstrained, unifying, consensus-bringing force of argumentative speech, in which different participants overcome their merely subjective views. (CA1, p. 10)

The principles are:

1   argumentative speech is central to rationality;
2   argument is interactive, it has a dialogic structure;
3   the interaction leads towards agreement when it is understood;
4   the achieved agreement is the foundation of a good society;
5   these requirements are compatible with science, but not reducible to the methods or conclusions of science.

In 'The Unity of Reason in the diversity of Its Voices', a striking essay from a later collection of work, *Postmetaphysical Thinking*, Habermas reassesses contemporary disputes about reason:

> I have gone into this controversy with the intention of rendering plausible a weak but not defeatistic concept of linguistically embodied reason. (*Postmet.*, pp. 115–148, 142)

His concept of reason is 'communicative' (p. 146) and 'weak' means limited as compared to earlier rationalism, which proposed attaining absolute truth independent of specific viewpoints and admitting only one description. But he intends communicative reason to be powerful, insofar as it will settle issues, particularly about ethics:

> . . . this idea . . . contains no more, but also no less, than the formal characterization of the necessary conditions for the unforeseeable forms adopted by a life that is not misspent. No prospect of such forms of life can be given to us, not even in the abstract, this side of prophetic teachings. (*Postmet.*, pp. 145–6)

Only communicative reason adjudicates how 'a life. . . is not misspent', and so his theory of the rational comes near to prophetic authority; as we shall see, this summation has a limiting effect on the theory's ability to sustain dialogues with other theories seeking solutions in the same field, though it never detracts from the original viewpoint of the vision. I shall argue that his approach tends towards becoming monologic and definitive. Moreover, dialogue is integral to seeing reason as dialogue. The project must be a dialogue between participants looking at reason from different perspectives, if dialogue is central to reason. To illustrate this requirement, I now juxtapose Putnam with Habermas.

Putnam and Dialogic Rationalism

Another move towards dialogic rationalism appears within analytic philosophy and liberal theory in the work of Hilary Putnam, during the late 1970s and 1980s and into the 1990s. Putnam developed in the American analytic tradition, and also within the influences of liberal theory. He has produced a major theory of science. He is also a professor of modern mathematics. For a time, Putnam was notorious for the idea that the human mind is comprehensible as a computer. Putnam is a changing proposition! Introducing a volume of his essays, *Realism and Reason*, he describes how he has changed his ideas. He used to believe that language corresponds to reality, a complex correspondence, multiple and diverse. The change that followed is subtle. He has not reversed the view, he still connects language, thought and reality; the correspondence does not seem 'exactly wrong' to the new Putnam writing in 1983 (R&R, p. vii). Now the problem is more difficult: there is a real world, and we know about it, language and thought apply to it, but the relationship is trickier. Putnam describes his previous view as 'my hard-line "realist" position' (R&R, p. viii). He is still a realist, he thinks, but not 'hard-line'. Being Putnam, he tells a story about the differing applications of language, in fact a 'parable'.

The parable begins with Kierkegaard and his God. Kierkegaard believed that 'God is subject to recurrent boredom' (R&R, p. ix), and each time He is bored, He changes the universe. First, there is the world, then Adam, then Adam was bored too, so along came Eve. Putnam likes the story so far, Kierkegaard's creation myth. But he adds an episode. God watched people, and it was boring, so He did something new. He decided to make language more interesting, an episode recorded as the Tower of Babel. He made sure people spoke different languages, but, according to Putnam, there was another trick. Different languages are livelier than one language, more varied, less monotonous. But within each language, the old boring unity might return. So He transformed the notion of language altogether, to make sure that perceptions appeared various. Within every language, He introduced a secret variation, one invisible even to the speakers of the language. The trick was clever, to 'play around with the satisfaction relations, the "correspondences" upon which the words – world connection depends' (R&R, p. ix). He unhinged the relation between language and reality. Of course, words do still relate to reality, but they relate in contrasting ways; they do not scoop up reality in one net, they do not reflect reality in one mirror. But the contrasts are hidden, concealed in the language.

The parable is elaborate. Suppose that English was spoken. Putnam proposes two relations between English and the world, two sets of connections between the language and reality. Each connection implies a model of English, a way of understanding the language in relation to experience. Both connections work, and they work equally well in practice. Men use English with one model, women with the other! Out there, God can see, are some objects which men refer to as 'cats'. And other objects which women refer to as 'cats*'. The objects are not identical. But the uses of cats/cats* always coincide. Whatever sentence is true of 'cats' is also true of 'cats*'. Therefore, no one can ever realise the difference, that men are referring to a 'cat' and women to a 'cat*'. Whatever the difference is, it is not observable by comparing things men say about 'cats' to things women say about 'cats*'.

Yes, words refer to reality, but reference is a problem, not a solution. The approach is characteristic of Putnam: lively, provocative, disturbing. The parable continues:

> It amused God for a while to see men and women talking to each other, never notic-
> ing that they were almost never referring to the same objects, properties and relations,
> but then, once again, inevitably, He became bored, so He invented philosophers.
> (R&R, p. x)

But philosophers only make the plight of language more problematic, in some ways. They are not above language, and so they perpetuate the divisions within its usage, the secret bifurcations of reference. They try to talk about language and reality. But they use language to do so, and so they also enact the problem which they are discussing: the problem of how words apply to reality.

I shall be exploring Putnam's work from 1981, the new Putnam, or Putnams, none of whom is a 'hard-line "realist"', none of whom is happy to say firmly that language corresponds to reality, not without many qualifications. A major source will be *Reason, Truth and History*, a dramatic story about reason, reality and culture. I shall also refer, if one may use the word, to essays from *Realism and Reason* and *Realism with a Human Face* and to *The Many Faces of Realism*. Putnam has many themes. His approach affects logic, science, mathematics. He also has an idea about reason and argument. It is this idea which is central for present purposes.

In and after *Reason, Truth and History* he shifts towards dialogic rationalism, and so arises the potential for a connection with Habermas: a central consideration of this book. Putnam believes that knowledge depends on values:

> Our views on the nature of coherence and simplicity are historically conditioned, just as our views on the nature of justice and goodness are. There is no neutral conception of rationality to which one can appeal when the nature of rationality is itself what is at issue. (*Human Face*, pp. 138–9)

In contrast with Habermas, there is no guiding model of rationality, no model of what rationality should be above the fray. Yet Putnam also converges with Habermas in valuing argument:

> I see the idea that the only purpose or function of reason itself is prediction (or prediction plus 'simplicity') as a prejudice – a prejudice whose unreasonableness is exposed by the very fact that arguing for it presupposes intellectual interests unrelated to prediction as such. (*Human Face*, p. 140)

There are some who consider that the function of reason is to make prediction possible, but reason is more than prediction, more than science, in which prediction is a basic value. When people argue that reason is scientific prediction, argument becomes primary, prediction is secondary. You cannot establish a prediction without arguing for it. But there is this difference from Habermas: the arguing is controversial, perpetually. There is no sense that the arguing leads towards resolution, which is the value of argument for Habermas. Rationality is more polemical, it is about maintaining a position critically and assertively:

> . . .the idea that science (in the sense of exact science) exhausts rationality is seen to be a self-stultifying error. The very activity of arguing about the nature of rationality presupposes a conception of rationality wider than that of laboratory testability. (*Human Face*, p. 140)

Again, Putnam makes the characteristic twist: if someone is arguing that reason defines science, then arguing comes first, before science. The wider 'conception of rationality' is argument itself! But argument is understood as being open to multiple interpretation. For Putnam, argument is more open-ended than for Habermas: the boundaries are not definite. Above all, differences are unbridgeable in a more profound sense than in Habermas, so argument does not lead towards agreement, but – and this is the essence of Putnam – over time there is a possible advancement of arguing, and rationality corresponds closely with that advancement.

Putnam conjures up dialogues between irreconcilable points of view, such as Rudolf Carnap and Cardinal Newman, to whom he allows different kinds of rationality and elaborates debates, debates whose point is that they are unresolvable (RTH, p. 136). For Putnam, rationality is involved with argument, he does not concede that rationality can arise equally from any argument; he defends impartiality, critical judgement, imagination, as the personal attributes which enhance an argument and lead towards greater rationality.

In an important essay called, 'Why reason can't be naturalized', Putnam defends his rationalism against rivals. The dispute is complex, and I will return to the essay several times. At one point, he describes W.V. Quine's work, to which he is centrally replying. Quine has a difficult philosophy, says Putnam, 'a large continent, with mountain ranges, deserts, and even a few Okefenokee Swamps' (R&R, pp. 229–247, 240). Personally, I find few deserts in Putnam, his continent seems perhaps more inclined to jungles, but then we now know it is rainforests that are the lungs of the earth. I do not propose to deforest this territory, to trim away the undergrowth, to disentangle all the creepers. Putnam is not dogmatic about answers, certainly not definitive answers. He has views; they are serious. But when he characterises his art, he thinks of questions. Philosophy is on the defensive, he believes, on the defensive against many sceptics. Past solutions do seem dubious: 'But the questions are deep, and it is the easy answers that are silly' (R&R, p. 236). Putnam stands for questions. His is a questioning voice. And from these questions, tensions arise.

This book is structured by the tension within dialogic rationalism, between reason and dialogue. There are problems to be focused:

1   How far can rationality be defined in advance of dialogue?
2   To what dialogue does reason gravitate: consensus-seeking or controversy-based? Can both models contribute to rationality?

Extending the Conversation among Contemporary Theorists

One main platform in this book will be shared between Habermas and Putnam, presenting their viewpoints about reason and argument. Other viewpoints intervene, and increasingly transform the context. Anthony Giddens also values dialogue, but he does not propose argument as a model dialogue. Instead he favours romantic dialogue, or post-romantic dialogue. Giddens sees intimacy as the source of alternative values for the future in a new democracy. Yet Giddens supports reason; he is not saying that good dialogue is emotional instead of rational. He requires dialogue to have a rational structure, a form, an order. He advocates fair interaction, respect for the other, open communication, requirements for a dialogue that overlap with those of Habermas and Putnam, even when suffused by emotion. Therefore Giddens is another source for dialogic rationalism. However, the tone is different, from Habermas, and even from Putnam, who also stresses the importance of supportive feeling. Giddens begins his approach to rationality from emotions, emotional attitudes, orientations to a proper life more basic than reasons. Dialogue is important in social relationships, reason is also important, but not dominant. Giddens provides a romantic context for dialogic rationalism:

> Intimacy is not being absorbed by the other, but knowing his or her characteristics and making available one's own. Opening out to the other, paradoxically, requires personal boundaries, because it is a communicative phenomenon; it also requires sensitivity and tact, since it is not the same as living with no private thoughts at all. The balance of openness, vulnerability and trust developed in a relationship governs whether or not personal boundaries become divisions which obstruct rather than encourage such communication. (*Intimacy*, p. 94)

The subject is central to dialogic rationalism: ideal communication, openness, free interaction, mutual respect. But Giddens affirms intimacy (a great theme of Sartrian existentialism). The model is still rational, because an intimate relationship is balanced, ordered, dynamic, fair. But though reason contributes to intimacy, reasoning is not supreme in human affairs. The model for humane conduct is dialogic, dialogues are a creative principle of authentic society; but the best dialogue is romantic, rather than critical. Giddens promotes dialogic romanticism, within a rational framework. He regards dialogue as a path towards a better world, and looks for a connection between interpersonal enrichment and political development:

> A symmetry exists between the democratising of personal life and the democratic possibilities in the global political order at the most extensive level. (*Intimacy*, pp. 195–6)

Giddens is a social theorist. Yet his tone is personal, direct, provocative: he challenges citizens to find a democratic context as authentic as true intimacy.

Genevieve Lloyd applies critical theory to philosophy and the history of reason in philosophy. Her critical approach is feminist. Lloyd raises the question of gender and reason. She argues that reason must mean the same for women and men: 'It seems highly implausible to claim that what is true or reasonable varies according to what sex we are' (*Man of Reason*, p. viii). But reason is also cultural, an idea, an ideal, a value. Particularly, reason applies to people, as well as to claims:

> There is more at stake in assessing our ideals of Reason than questions of the relativity of truth. Reason has figured in western culture not only in the assessment of beliefs, but also in the assessment of character. (*Man of Reason*, p. ix)

People, as well as ideas, are called 'rational' or 'irrational'. Rational character has a history, and Lloyd shows the history is complex; she also shows it is persistently biased to favour men and disadvantage women. Sometimes the bias is direct, propagandist; sometimes, it is indirect, inadvertent; and sometimes good intentions have bad outcomes.

The perspective is complex:

> Augustine attempted to articulate sexual equality with respect to Reason, while yet finding interpretative content for the Genesis subordination of woman to man. (*Man of Reason*, p. 29)

Augustine is contradictory: he believes in sexual equality, equal reason in the sexes, but he also endorses hierarchy of male over female. Again, Aquinas denies that men are more rational: 'For Aquinas, then, woman does not symbolise an inferior form or lesser presence of rationality' (*Man of Reason*, p. 36). But the negation is revealing, not being lesser is a limited equality, an equality despite gender, rather than in gender:

> These early versions of woman's relations to Reason presented her, in some manner or other, as derivative in relation to a male paradigm of rational excellence. (*Man of Reason*, p. 37)

The interpretation is twofold. There persists an ideal, that reason is indifferent to gender. But the ideal is never realised, because bias distorts each theory, other motives creep in, other discourses influence the thinkers.

Lloyd's approach is important to the search for dialogic rationalism, the exploration of how reason appears in dialogue, how far rational dialogue may re-create reason. The question is whether dialogic views will contribute to the unbiasing of reason, reason as a cultural influence, a view of character. The problem is: will interactive reason also encourage bias? Answers cannot be confident, complacent. But Lloyd also cautions against despair:

> Can anything be salvaged of the ideal of a Reason which knows no sex? Much of past exultation in that ideal can be seen as a self-deceiving failure to acknowledge the differences between male and female minds, produced and played out in contexts of real inequalities. But it can also be seen as embodying a hope for the future. (*Man of Reason*, p. 107)

A question arises about 'differences' between male and female minds, and also about social contexts. Difference can be neither ignored, nor enshrined in another kind of reason. Lloyd encourages criticism and openness to differences between men and women, to individual differences and differing contexts. Difference itself varies, and cannot be formulated abstractly. Often difference is slanted, rigged to fit preconceptions; but difference may also be compatible with 'the ideal of a Reason which knows no sex'. Difference may also mean connection, interconnection, since there cannot be interconnection without difference. The proposal is balanced: a search for reason, open to contradiction, at the same time critical of injustice. Above all, Lloyd warns that ideas of reason have effects; they are influences on how people think and relate. They matter.

Lloyd is a rationalist when looking towards the future. She considers the Hegelian idea that 'the real is the rational and the rational the real' (*Man of Reason*, p. 107). Does the idea not serve merely 'as a dubious rationalization of the status quo'? Partly, perhaps mainly in context. But not necessarily: 'it can also be taken as the expression of an ideal – as an affirmation of faith that the irrational will not prevail', but that reality will, and with it, reason. Perhaps 'naïve', but an ideal held in good faith; and so her critical theory motivates the search for a better reason, a better account of reason.

Political theory is rich in reinterpretations of reason and dialogue. John Rawls has been liberalism's leading political theorist since *A Theory of Justice* in 1971. His recent work endorses political liberalism, and also rational dialogue. Rawls is a rationalist who believes in common human reason, a reason which has affinities with science:

A way of reasoning, then, must incorporate the fundamental concepts and principles of reason, and include standards of correctness and criteria of justification. A capacity to master these ideas is part of common human reason. (*Political Liberalism*, p. 220)

This view of reason is less dialogic than Habermas or Putnam, for it sees reason as a personal capacity. But its 'justification' requires dialogue, so he includes interaction in his requirements for reason, even if it is secondary to a capacity to 'master' ideas. In practice, Rawls examines dialogue carefully. He is preoccupied by differences of opinion, their risks and value. Rawls links consensus with social order, and to that extent he resembles Habermas:

. . . let us suppose first the ideal case: the society in question is more or less well ordered. Its members recognize a firm overlapping consensus of reasonable doctrines and it is not stirred by any deep disputes. (*Political Liberalism*, p. 248)

However, Rawls is more qualified about consensus. He seeks 'overlapping consensus', not deep agreement. People will not really agree over rooted beliefs:

Political liberalism assumes that, for political purposes, a plurality of reasonable yet incompatible comprehensive doctrines is the normal result of the exercise of human reason within the framework of the free institutions of a constitutional democratic regime. (*Political Liberalism*, p. xvi)

People use reason differently. Reason creates differences, it does not resolve them. Like Putnam, Rawls begins a consideration of dialogue from disagreement and he assumes people will seek to perpetuate disagreement. But he is less confident than Putnam that differences can lead to useful developments: he hopes for compromise. Rawls looks for a minimal agreement between views which otherwise differ: while differing in other respects, they may agree about the political system, the public debate, the rules. His problem is to combine consensus with division.

Thinking Dialogically and Rhetorically

The above thinkers, and others to be considered, represent a new way of approaching reason, which in each case features dialogue. I recognise a way of considering reason – a tone of caution and qualification in talking about it, but the caution of thinkers trying not to discredit reason; on the contrary, these thinkers defend reason powerfully with new approaches. Fundamentally, these thinkers are rationalists, who want to approach human problems through reason, though they accept in varying degrees that reason cannot always solve them. But they discard what they see as previous definitions of reason, and particularly definitions which are exclusively scientific or privilege strategic calculation.

One of the main claims in this book is that dialogic rationalism implies divergent opinions, and that this could be a strength. But there is this shared message within the diversity: *there is more to reason than science or strategy*, though science is a high point of human reason, perhaps *the* high point, and effective calculation is also rational. Reason is part of human character, it is active in the conduct of our lives and it is integral to our interactions with other people. Further, it is dangerous to ignore these *lived* dimensions of reason, and dangerous to focus too exclusively on specialist activities involving reason, however spectacular may be their impact, as in the case of science. Such reconsideration of reason is 'dialogic' as well as rationalist, when dialogue is the basis for lived reasoning. Then reasonable dialogues are the epitome of rational character.

A key point in considering dialogic rationalism concerns form, for such a viewpoint needs to be expressed in dialogue, so that the perception does not reduce to one or other position held by its proponents, and the dilemma arises: how to convey the theory in dialogic form. More care goes into making theories rational; less care has gone into making theory itself dialogic. Do not some thinkers use monologue to deny monologue and stress the value of dialogue?

My purpose is to present dialogues about dialogic rationalism, which I see as irreducibly dialogic in form and content, as compared to 'essentially contested', ambiguous, undecidable. Yet the most relevant theorists represented have not invented a form which corresponds to the principle of dialogue in conveying their ideas. Of course they face other demands – to be rigorous, comprehensive, consistent enough, systematic – and these demands lead to an internalisation of their approach, and an attempt to achieve complete formulation.

Paradoxically, what they have in common is the view that too often in the past reason has been identified with one voice, one viewpoint, one party even. Gestures towards debate between different parties have often been unconvincing, given the prior emphasis on their own viewpoint as the rational one. But sharing reason is a necessary element for a constructive outlook on the human future: partly because reason is integral to our problems, reason will need to be an aspect of the future response, and we must respond to it where we find it with dialogue. Taken in its diversity, with all its different accounts of reason, dialogic rationalism keeps reason on the contemporary agenda.

I shall also propose an alternative to the focus on argument provided by individual thinkers: by applying *the concept of double arguability*, the internal formation of an argument through the interaction of the people taking part in it, which includes many components, including emotional ones, such as liking, or mutual dislike and suspicion. It becomes relevant what their motives may be for arguing: in short, what kind of people they are, and *how* they live, and what place the argument has in their lives. As we continue to examine established approaches to argument, the need to consider double arguability will become ever more apparent.

This reveals a need to enhance the imaginative potential of the theory so as to take in all the human aspects of disagreeing which feature under argument. The text develops *the concept of argumentative imagination*, which attempts to conceive the whole setting of argument, to account for the views expressed and the way disputants behave.[1] We are going to need voices which assert the whole situation in imagination, and fill it out with motive and action; voices which connect theory with experience, including experience imagined in everyday life and in literature. Indeed the expansive theories of Habermas, Putnam and Giddens can be shown to *possess* far more imaginative energies than are usually drawn from them; they feature aspects of argumentative imagination, ideas which can only be grasped when they are represented concretely with a full complement of characters and settings, except that the terms of their proposals sometimes disguise the imaginative element in their discourse.

Dialogic Relativism

An important challenge to rationalism comes from relativism, represented influentially in the work of Lyotard. In this book, it will be observed that Lyotard's theories of incommensurability nevertheless derive from a consideration of dialogue and the possibilities of interaction, and he is therefore considered as a dialogic relativist, in which form his objections to dialogic rationalism demand respect and attention, a model in which dialogue subverts reason. Dialogic relativism denies that dialogue is a basis for reason, or even for shared reasoning: instead, for Lyotard, dialogue represents the irreducible diversity of thinking and judging, and his view is notably effective in challenging scientific rationalism and the new rational initiatives towards dialogue.

This is the principle from which Lyotard's speculations arise:

> There are as many universes as there are phrases. And as many situations of instances as there are universes. (*Differend*, p. 76)

How could there be general laws, or formulations of the truth, if people lived in 'as many universes as there are phrases'? Any proposition applies to only a small fraction of the situations in which people live: Lyotard claims to prevent the encroachments of comprehensive theory on particular worlds.

Beyond dialogue, Steven Connor finds a further relation between Habermas and Lyotard:

> It may seem unpromising, given the bitter and unyielding antagonism between Lyotard and Habermas, to look for points of convergence between them. Surprisingly, perhaps, such points of convergence are evident. For one thing, Lyotard and Habermas have in common a conviction of the centrality of discursive ethics to moral and political reasoning in general, and share a remarkable tendency to translate political into linguistic questions.[2]

There is a common focus on discourse and in particular on discursive *interactions*, and a common need to judge those interactions, not merely to 'describe' them. The criteria of the judgements conflict, their objectives overlap.

Lyotard is so threatening to dialogic rationalism because he, too, thinks of interactions between differing parties as fundamental to the human condition. He even conceives his text in interactive terms, more profoundly than Habermas and at least as profoundly as Putnam. But his view of interaction is different. For Habermas, interactions are rational when the parties aim at consensus. And for Putnam, many interactions are unresolvable, though there are rational responses to that predicament. Lyotard thinks encounters are unbridgeable at a more basic level of communication:

> Why these encounters between phrases of heterogeneous regimen? Differends are born, you say, from these encounters. Can't these contacts be avoided? – that is impossible, contact is necessary. (*Differend*, p. 29)

Contact is forced on people but in many cases there is no common ground for evaluating its effects. Lyotard sees no scope for transcending differences. They are always widening beyond our comprehension. The fundamental issue between dialogists is the nature of dialogue, or 'the dialogical principle'.[3] Who has the most accurate interpretation of dialogic interaction: the rationalists, with their coherent models, or Lyotard with his relativist model?

A Guide to the Book

This text reaches towards a new intellectual culture by rearranging existing voices. Inspiration for this approach comes from the work of Bernstein and Connor in juxtaposing some voices in contemporary thought.[4] Meanings develop as ideas collide, compete, displace each other or coincide: each answer makes most sense interacting with other answers. It is important for dialogic rationalism that there are alternative sources within it, and concern with an interaction across boundaries, a challenge which cuts across the division between 'Continental' and 'Anglo-American' thought, a challenge advanced by diverse commentators such as Bernstein, Benhabib and Schrag.[5] Alongside the fundamental contributions of Habermas and Putnam, Giddens, Lloyd, Rawls and others enter into the conversation, which focuses on the dialogue about reason and dialogue. Then come other challenges: an alternative rationalism from the new instrumentalists, Elster and Sen, and the deliberative ethics of Nussbaum; followed by the challenge from Lyotard and postmodernism. Finally, there is an analysis of a famous argument in literature, from Galileo's *Dialogue Concerning the Two Chief World Systems*, in which some new terms are applied, in the hope of bridging some gaps between rationalists and relativists.

One feature of these various contexts is that they derive from different disciplines: Putnam's work from philosophy, though consciously directed outwards to the cultural area in this case; Benhabib's from politics and philosophical ethics; Lyotard's from cultural theory and philosophy; the text of Galileo pointing towards the history of science, and the interpretative approach to it pointing towards literary studies. Of course Habermas's work is already interdisciplinary, with references ranging from philosophy and sociology to anthropology and psychology. In common with other influential theories of our time, Habermas's theory has a complex, multiple life, and naturally enters other discussions. Therefore visualising new interdisciplinary relations is developing a principle inherent in the work under consideration.

The framing issue for this book is intellectual practice itself. Zygmunt Bauman analyses contemporary academic and intellectual life and he remarks that we have lost confidence in the power of ideas, particularly the power of ideas to change society. He sees academics and intellectuals searching for identities that are adapted to this lower confidence. In his view, the intellectual identity of 'legislator' is giving way to the new identity of 'interpreter': intellectuals mediate between worlds, they do not transform *the* world.[6] But, though the context is chastened, we continue to give a high status to the activity of theory: could the status of ideas possibly be higher than the current status of some theories? We have several theories which are as comprehensive as any theory could be! Sometimes, as with Lyotard, the claims of theory are inclined to be negative, and deal with the limits of truth or of action; but, even so, the scope of theory has surely *not* been diminished, in a context of reduced confidence. Perhaps we do see theory in more personalised terms than previously, when movements seemed to embody theories: we identify ideas with particular theorists, rather than with general movements. In current debates, one theory may contribute to several movements of thought, or a theory may resist identification with collective movements altogether. So we are increasingly preoccupied with the thought of a contested list of exemplary figures, full of dynamic possibilities for the interaction of ideas if the individual elements are not hardened into stasis. We mediate between them in different ways, for differing purposes. We seek the historical significance, the sources, of a theory. We analyse and criticise these great networks of propositions. We use them to reflect on the times, and, particularly, on the difference between our intellectual context and previous contexts. These theories define academic and intellectual identities in diverse ways, and nourish them. And we can also transform the theories we are given, extending their terms of reference, so as to advance our own interpretations of the questions with which they deal. For in my view, it is interpretation which makes theory signify.

Notes

1 George Myerson, *The Argumentative Imagination* (Manchester: Manchester University Press, 1992).

2 Steven Connor, *Theory and Cultural Value* (Oxford: Basil Blackwell, 1992), p. 111.

3 Tzvetan Todorov, *M.M. Bakhtin: The Dialogical Principle*, trans. Wlad Godzich (Minneapolis: University of Minnesota Press, 1984).

4 Connor, *Theory and Cultural Value*, especially Chapter 5, 'The Ethics of Discourse', pp. 102–32, and Chapter 7, 'Feminism and Value', pp. 158–81. Richard Bernstein, *The New Constellation* (Cambridge: Polity Press, 1992), especially Chapter 2, 'The Rage against Reason', pp. 15–30.

5 Richard Bernstein, *The New Constellation*, p. 4 and a number of essays notably 'Rorty's Liberal Utopia', pp. 258–92; Seyla Benhabib, *Situating the Self*, especially 'Feminism and the Question of Postmodernism'; Calvin O. Schrag, *Resources of Rationality* (Bloomington: Indiana University Press, 1992), especially Chapter 6, 'Transversal Rationality', pp. 148–80.

6 Zygmunt Bauman, *Intimations of Postmodernity* (London: Routledge, 1992), pp. 1–25, notably p. 14: 'The deepest cause of the gradual dissolution of modern self-confidence can be, arguably, traced back to the slow but steady disengagement between the intellectuals, as collective guardians of societal values, and the modern state.'

2

Resituating Reason

Stories of Reason

What has led thinkers towards dialogic rationalism? I want to explore some of their accounts of reason in our time, and their defence of reason, through stories which reveal the essential rationale for integrating reason with dialogue and the central role of *argument*, a concept understood in different ways. Thinkers differ about history, about reason's history, and about human relations: hence, they give *different interpretations of argument*, as part of their different worldviews. Different though they are, however, Habermas and Putnam seek a positive model of argument, as the bridge between reason and human interaction. There will also be an account of Giddens's critical perspectives and alternative models of reason, including the feminist work of Lloyd, Elster's view of strategic reason and the environmentalism of Bookchin. The stories are also about intellectuals, theorists, thinkers in society and in history.

Habermas's Tale of Two Reasons

Enlightenment

> The nineteenth century is remarkable for triumphs of science, enterprise and perseverance over great and acknowledged difficulties, and for the solution of problems, practical and theoretical, sought in vain or despaired of in former ages.
>
> (The Westminster Review, June 1846)

In *The Theory of Communicative Action* (CA), Habermas presents a historical account of reason, a story of progress, but flawed and incomplete progress. 'Enlightenment' is the central term for the progress of reason through history. 'Enlightenment' gives Habermas's theory a broader sweep than science, but science is central to the meaning of enlightenment. For Habermas, 'enlightenment' covers a phase of Western history, from the later eighteenth century to the present, a period in which science becomes a dominating influence not only on human hopes but also on social organisation. Habermas tends to attribute this historical story of enlightenment to other sources, but he does so in ways which imply at least partial endorsement. For instance, he abstracts an enlightenment story from the sociologist Talcott Parsons:

> His [Parsons's] basic assumptions regarding evolutionary theory become clearer if one looks at the status he accords to the Reformation and Renaissance, those two major

events of the early modern period. They are the precursor revolutions that made the transition to the modern age possible by unleashing the cognitive potentials contained in the traditions of Christianity and of ancient Rome and Greece – but previously worked up only by cultural elites in monastic orders and universities – and by allowing them to exert an influence on an institutional level. (CA2, p. 286)

Here the phrase 'unleashing the cognitive potentials' signals Habermas's own involvement with the progressive story, a story in which human reason advances towards the centres of cultural power. Habermas elsewhere refers to 'an unfolding of the potentials residing in culture' (CA2, p. 298) as part of his own perspective on human development. 'Enlightenment' also indicates the continuing advancement of reason, as the imagery of 'potentials' implies.

Habermas does not merely reproduce stories of enlightenment. He is also exploring the ambiguities inherent in many of the enlightenment narratives. Probably his major source here is Max Weber, whose key terms for Habermas are 'rationalization' and 'rationalism'. Habermas summarises Weber's version of Western progress through reason, a progress in which science is central and scientific attitudes more generally influential:

> The list of original achievements of Western rationalism is long. Weber points first to modern natural science, which puts theoretical knowledge in mathematical form and tests it with the help of controlled experiments; he adds to this the systematic specialization of scientific activity in university settings. He mentions . . . the institutionalization of art . . . harmonious music . . . scientific jurisprudence, institutions of formal law . . . modern state administration . . . calculable commerce. (CA1, p. 157)

Here the achievements of Western society derive from 'purposive rationality' (CA1, p. 167). This rationality considers means and ends, and the correct calculation of methods to gain results. Purposive rationality has flourished under the patronage of science. The advancement that follows in thought and society is 'a rationalization process' (CA1, p. 167). The story clearly has a negative aspect: here is the enlightenment which ends so *badly* in many stories, particularly stories of environmental crisis introduced above, where science and its cultural beneficiary or ally, calculation, have been *too influential*, leading to disaster by repressing other human potentialities. Probably the darkest of the dark narratives of reason, and the most influential, is the narrative of 'the dialectic of enlightenment', told by Adorno and Horkheimer, in which 'reason itself has become the mere instrument of the all-inclusive economic apparatus'.[1] Habermas includes these dark plots in unfolding his story of 'enlightenment'. He incorporates Lukács's version of enlightenment where in this total rationalisation all is lost except the spirit of the basest calculation, whose embodiment is the rule of money (CA1, pp. 371–2). He also includes Adorno and Horkheimer whom he quotes at their darkest:

> Man's domination over himself, which grounds his selfhood, is virtually always the destruction of the subject in whose service it takes place. (CA1, p. 380)

So at the centre of the theory there is the story of a process turning on itself, an enlightenment made tragedy.

Habermas is ambivalent about humanity's development, its would-be progress.

He shares the sense of implicit disaster with Adorno and Horkheimer. But he also admires the dynamic in these developments. We can see the ambivalence when he discusses early heroes of enlightenment such as the eighteenth-century 'philosophes', whom he admires for their intellectual courage at the same time that he treats science as a major problem. For instance, towards the late eighteenth century he finds an 'institutionalization of science' which gave rise to the hope 'that the organization for the discovery of truth can become a model for the organization of state and society' (CA1, p. 146). Enlightenment is to enable the *social* triumph of expanding knowledge, 'a bridge between the idea of scientific progress and the conviction that the sciences also serve the moral perfection of human beings' (CA1, p. 147). But the disaster is immanent where the hopes overreach.

If enlightenment is about 'counting on the empirical efficacy of an ever-improving theoretical knowledge' (CA1, p. 150), then enlightenment cannot be ours any longer, as events of our time show. The ending story closes in with the militarisation of technology, the enhanced effects of nuclear weapons, social chaos, economic instability and pollution. But Habermas wants to begin another story, a story which takes him towards the position which I am reinterpreting as dialogic rationalism. In the new story of reason, there is a potential that was present in the old story, and that potential can never be subdued. Enlightenment may renew itself by recognising this undying potential, just as the old hopes are losing their fire.

Communication

In the new story, rationalisation would mean something different: 'The rationalization of society would then no longer mean a diffusion of purposive-rational action' (CA1, p. 339). The source of hope is not correct calculation, not theory used to engineer effects. Indeed that kind of rationality has suppressed the real potential, by imposing 'a transformation of domains of communicative action into subsystems of purposive-rational action' (CA1, p. 339). It is communicative action which is the new source of our hopes and that communicative action requires a changed view of rationality, not as rationality operated in purposive-rational action or instrumental actions, but as rationality linked to human interaction. Habermas seeks to give rationality a new centre:

> The point of reference becomes instead the potential for rationality found in the validity basis of speech. (CA1, p. 339)

Here is the heart of the vision, for a vision is what it seems to be, a vision of reason emerging creatively from general communication and interaction, which is the essence of dialogic rationalism. According to Habermas, this is a new way of seeing action, but it was always possible to adopt such a perspective. This new rationality does not entirely discredit Weberian rationalisation, because that earlier process was necessary for 'releasing communicative action from traditionally based institutions' (CA1, p. 341). As Stephen K. White puts it, the Habermasian project aims to remedy an imbalance in rationalisation, rather than to reject it altogether.[2] But purposive rationalisation functioned at a cost: the triumph of purpose over communication. The rationalising process freed society in one way from more primitive natural and social constraints, only to impose its own constraints on human interaction. The key to appropriate advancement is the *communicative* power of reason, reason freed from purposive bias. True enlightenment is possible and 'puts the cognitive-instrumental aspect of reason in its proper place as part of a more encompassing communicative rationality' (CA1, p. 390). Therefore Habermas frequently distances himself from thinkers who assume that the failures of enlightenment are total and irreversible, as in his response to Alasdair MacIntyre (MC, p. 43). Instrumental reason is not the end of the story of enlightenment.

How does Habermas conceive this alternative enlightenment? His conception develops through a complex of terms; and the basic term, foundation of this enlightenment, is *argument*, twinned with *consensus*. They appear to be incompatible, but for Habermas argument and consensus are united in his vision of rationality because people argue rationally only when they seek consensus. Striving towards consensus, we enter the area of reasonable behaviour, rational character and rational interaction with other people. I will pursue this theme of argument and consensus throughout the present book, but a strong flavour can be tasted from such assertions as the following passage where Habermas proposes a universal principle to link argument with agreement:

> I will introduce the principle of universalization (U) as a bridging principle that makes agreement in moral argumentation possible. The version of the principle that I will give excludes any monological application of this rule for argumentation. ('Discourse Ethics', in MC, pp. 43–115, p. 57)

Habermas's 'discourse ethics' is still sustaining his story of enlightenment and rational hope, and based on the linkage of argument with at least the possibility of agreement.

Communicative Evolution

To grasp the nature of Habermas's challenge, his creative achievement, it is necessary to see the scale of the founding stories. There is not only enlightenment and modernisation. Habermas tells several stories about the past, linked stories. Closely related is a story of how language itself began, a more general story! Habermas tells his stories by reinterpreting previous theories, particularly sociological theories. The account of language starts with a story that uses the theory of G.H. Mead, but grips that theory firmly in Habermasian terms. Mead's ideas appear in a story with two actors in the first scene:

> The model from which he starts is not the behavior of an individual organism reacting to stimuli from an environment, but an interaction in which at least two organisms react to one another and behave in relation to one another. (CA2, p. 4)

These organisms may be very primitive. One makes a move; the other responds:

> He views the *conversation of gestures* found in developed vertebrate societies as the evolutionary starting point for a development of language. (CA2, p. 5)

First come signals: a gesture arising out of their situation. This move brings about action. Signals prompt joint action, organisms respond together to problems. But signals are appropriate to the specific situation: they only mean something in that situation. Signals perform a function of language, because they help organisms to act together, but they are tied to particular contexts, unlike proper language:

> Signals are embedded in interaction contexts in such a way that they always serve to coordinate the actions of different participants. (CA2, p. 6)

Habermas uses this narrative to reinforce the idea that communication is founded upon consensus, indeed unanimity. He is reconfirming his defence of authentic communication or of illocutionary acts, as he also terms them, adapting terminology from Austin's speech act theory. He is demonstrating 'that the use of language with an orientation to reaching understanding is the *original* mode of language use' (CA1, p. 288). These cohesive signals given by the primitive organisms do not remain limited to specific contexts, and as they move beyond the contexts, language evolves from signalling. In Habermas's retelling, the signals become symbols, which transcend the local context, and apply outside the particular situation in which they arose. Habermas sees his theoretical task as 'reconstructing the emergence of this early stage of languagelike communication' (CA2, p. 8): in turn, this 'reconstruction' justifies the definitions required for his own systematic theory. The central terms are already present for rational consensus: 'conversation', 'interaction', 'to coordinate actions'. The central *problem* for his theory is also present in the terms of the story: 'embedded in . . . contexts' explains the need for the communication, and it also explains why the communication is only 'languagelike'. Communication begins with contexts, and then matures until communication is not merely 'embedded' in its situation.

For Habermas, it is crucial to explain 'the genesis of meanings that are the same for at least two participants' (CA2, p. 11). If he can explain how meanings are 'identical' in different situations, he can show how communication transcends particular contexts: in the story, both organisms would take away the same meaning; the stable meaning would then be in circulation. Habermas then focuses on another of Mead's ideas, with an ancient background in rhetoric, 'the model of thought as an inner dialogue' (CA2, p. 10). He examines Mead's use of 'inner dialogue' for further elaboration of his story. According to the story, as a result of acquiring symbols, each organism replays the whole interaction internally, in conceptual fashion, as it tries to comprehend the response of the other. An organism can then gesture in anticipation of the response, a response appropriate for its needs, and it identifies that response through inner dialogue which is a simulation of outer dialogue. Habermas is half-satisfied with this formulation. He approves the notion of organisms becoming able 'to understand the meaning of their own gestures in the light of the expected responses of others' (CA2, p. 12). But he wonders why the two organisms arrive at 'the *same* meanings' – not just meanings which are similar or compatible. *Similar* meanings are not enough for Habermas, because true consensus requires a full understanding between these organisms.

Next Habermas must attempt an authoritative account of the pre-primitive origin of understanding. He reconstructs the episode in which the first true understanding occurs, then adds a level, responding to problems remaining for his theory with a more complex narrative. The organism advances from 'reacting to its own gesture'; it sees itself 'addressing a gesture to an interpreter' (CA2, p. 13). The crucial step is the idea of address. Another key idea follows smoothly from address: misunderstanding. Once the organisms are addressing each other, each realises that the other is actively interpreting its own address, and as a result come:

> the responses through which ego and alter mutually express disappointment at misunderstandings. In adopting toward themselves the critical attitude of others when the interpretation of communicative acts goes wrong, they develop *rules for the use of symbols*. (CA2, pp. 14–15)

We arrive at 'meaning conventions'. 'Convention' could be arbitrary, but Habermas means that conventions governing meaning come about by a rational process. Language itself originates in rational interactions leading to understanding, leading in turn to co-ordinated action. Once rational communication has penetrated language, universal validity is possible. The story historicises Habermas's definitions of communicative rationality, of argument leading to consensus, of reason beginning in contexts which it then transcends. The narrative structure supports the prior conceptual requirements. The theory re-creates itself as a historical story.

Further, Habermas's story of communicative development elides with one of the grandest of the grand narratives, Darwin's story of evolution by natural selection. Contrary to one myth, Darwin's story is not necessarily about conflicts between individuals. Darwin himself proclaimed firmly that:

> In social animals, [natural selection] will adapt the structure of each individual for the benefit of the community.[3]

Habermas reconstructs Mead, and uses the outcome to reconstruct Darwin. Communication becomes the central theme of evolutionary narrative in a new phase. Darwin's views are taken up in the Habermas system but, like other views, they are also always *contained*, made to serve the larger enterprise. The problem of introducing rationality leads all the way back to the great evolutionary story, where it is resolved in a narrative image. Evolution then comes to the rescue of the concept of rational consensus: organisms interact; gradually, they learn to anticipate responses to gestures; they learn that the other is actively interpreting, not merely reacting automatically; and so they learn to agree about symbols for what is happening and for what they wish to happen. In this image, this metaphorical episode, language is the original consensus, the prior agreement behind all the others, the agreement on the scope and use of the symbol.

The Communicative Self

Habermas reappropriates Mead to extend his problem-solving narrative: how does the self evolve? In their joint story, there first comes a stage analogous to that of primitive organisms acquiring reasoned language, a stage of expectations and responses: 'particularistic expectations that are "clustered", that is to say, conditionally connected and complementarily related to one another' (CA2, p. 33). The child realises that certain things are expected or required, without knowing *why*. The child is not yet inside the social world. The child advances towards social being. Habermas focuses on *communication* to explain this advance. He takes as his central example of communication in childhood the function of imperatives. The child

> learns to follow imperatives not only in connection with positive and negative sanctions but in a context of caring and of the satisfaction of his own needs. (CA2, p. 33)

Already, the child progresses beyond complying uncomprehendingly with external expectations, as it satisfies its own needs. The next move comes from the parent, who now 'no longer connects his announcement only with individual imperatives'. Instead, the parent introduces a 'generalized expectation': the child will 'exhibit a willingness to obey', in return for 'the care he receives'. There is a negotiated progress, a developmental dialogue in which the parent's utterances get more complex, as the child gains responsive insight.

Next the child begins to enter the wider social world. The child starts by 'anticipating the sanctions', the reactions of others (CA2, p. 38) in the social world which are immanent in the imperatives of its parent; the child then has a rather negative relation to this wider sphere. Things progress in the social world, rather as they did with the parents, as the child experiences that social world less as an external force, and connects its demands with an interior voice, which represents its own needs: a phase of 'internalizing the power of the social group' (CA2, p. 38). Once the child has elided the social voices with its own voice, any valid imperative will be experienced as if from within. Social voices speak from within the child, who enters the world of the norm:

> ... generalized behaviour patterns acquire for him the authority of a 'thou shalt!' – no longer in an imperativistic sense – and thus that kind of normative validity in virtue of which norms possess binding force. (CA2, p. 38)

The concept of 'validity' is crucial, for it rationalises the theme of prior consensus. At first, children are forced to obey the rules. But then they learn that these rules represent 'the validity of norms'. They share in 'a normative consensus among members of the group' (CA2, p. 39). They comply because they accept the norm from inside, not merely because someone imposes it on them. They belong. They understand the benefits of belonging. The child's acquisition of norms is a reasoning experience, an experience involving assent and dissent, not merely submission and recalcitrance.

There is a metaphorical echo of the evolutionary story in the acquisition of norms. These analogies are powerful. They close the structure, making every part cross-refer to every other part. But what about the hope of dialogue, indeed the *test* of dialogue? Nothing could be less prepared for dialogue than this type of self-supporting structure of analogies criss-crossed with each other and based on prior definitions. Again, though, the judgement is necessarily complex: the creativity of the theory is always present in its limitations; what is self-contradictory from one perspective, insofar as the theory of dialogue is hardly adjusted to dialogue, is energising from another point of view, since so many themes are being inter-related. There is real excitement in the theorising process, profound intellectual alertness in the interconnections, and a true shaping imagination in the narration.

Habermas is conscious that the theory makes norms ambiguous.[4] He acknowledges 'the repressive character evinced in the fact that norms, demanding obedience, take effect in the form of social control' (CA2, p. 39). He keeps open a space: the norms are under social control, they are not *the same as* social control. Habermas distinguishes the norms from the way they are implemented. The integral *authority* of norms could be different from the way the actual *authorities* use them, which involves the judgement and assent of individuals. Drawing on Mead's story, Habermas insists that 'the social control exercised via norms that are valid for specific groups is not based on repression *alone*' (CA2, p. 39).[5]

The outcome of all this dynamic thinking is finely poised. To belong is more than to obey – to belong is to agree, in some intermediate sense, to a consensus which potentially requires rational assent. Habermas sees a 'two-sidedness' to normative requirements (CA2, p. 39). This 'two-sidedness' is required to hold the construction in place while recognising the uncertainties it contains. There is 'a concrete group's power to sanction', a power which the new member internalises. Is this not to be absorbed by power – to be constructed from outside by something overwhelming, basically threatening? No, Habermas insists, at least not entirely, for, the story adds,

> that same moment of generality also already contains the claim – aiming at insight – that a norm deserves to be valid only insofar as, in connection with some matter requiring regulation, it takes into account the interests of everyone involved, and only insofar as it embodies the will that all could form in common. (CA2, p. 39)

First, Habermas tells of the agreements of language which contain criticism; then he tells of the agreements of norms to which adherents remain half critical.[6] Together, language and norm support the new interactions, where people begin to reach their own understandings. If norms were merely enforced, then the social context would inhibit the process of coming to terms. Habermas concludes that social norms have the potential to be true agreements. But in his own terms, how could they *not* be reconcilable with true understanding, since language conveys norms, and language itself begins in true understanding?

The stories of human and linguistic evolution echo back to the account of social rationalisation where Habermas ruled that:

> Processes of rationalization can attach to societal orders of life only because the stability of legitimate orders depends on the de facto recognition of validity claims that can be attacked internally, that is, shaken by critique, new insights, learning processes, and the like. (CA1, p. 192)

Because we inherit traditions with some rational bases, we can revise those traditions along more rational lines. The evolutionary stories lead into an account of religious authority which again stresses some consensual element:

> Nothing is depicted in ceremonies of this kind; they are rather the exemplary, repeated putting into effect of a consensus that is thereby renewed. (CA2, p. 53)

Modernisation can be reappraised, as a process which loosens the normative consensus. On the one level, the new order is provided by complex and impersonal systems, but on another level, the result is 'successive releases of the potential for rationality in communicative action' (CA2, p. 155). Communicative rationality is inexhaustible, because the species itself presupposes it:

> Even within formally organized domains of action, interactions are still connected via the mechanism of mutual understanding. If all processes of genuinely reaching understanding were banished from the interior of organizations, formally regulated social relations could not be sustained, nor could organizational goals be realized. (CA2, p. 310)

Yet the interplay of institutions does threaten communicative rationality, 'they do disempower its validity basis' (CA2, p. 311). The narrative is poised and subtle: Habermas has told one of the great stories about reason, a story leading towards his idea of rational communication. Does Habermas also create space for dialogue, dialogue about his vision? Could he have created more space? Or has he reached one limit of dialogue in presenting communicative reason?

Putnam's Story of Reason and Science

The Spell of Science

Putnam takes a different path towards dialogic rationalism. His way leads through debates about reason and rational method, rather than through stories about historical advancement. Sometimes, Putnam tells stories about faith in science, almost mechanical faith. At a party, someone says 'science has taught us that the universe is an uncaring machine' ('Beyond the Fact – Value Dichotomy', in *Human Face*, pp. 135–41, 135). The implied contrast is Islam. Putnam objects:

> Our modern revelation may be a depressing revelation, but at least it is a demythologizing revelation. If the world is terrible, at least we know that our fathers were fools to think otherwise, and that everything they believed and cherished was a lie, or at best superstition. (*Human Face*, p. 136)

Science endorses a deadly universe, or so it seems – but science is of our making, we are superior to those without it:

> This certainly flatters our vanity. . . . I think that this consolation to our vanity cannot be overestimated. Narcissism is often a more powerful force in human life than self-preservation or the desire for a productive, loving, fulfilling life. (*Human Face*, pp. 136–7)

The resort to psychology is characteristic of Putnam. He diagnoses the predicament of people who believe rigidly in science:

> In fact, I suspect many of us will stick with the scientistic view even if it, at any rate, can be shown to be inconsistent or incoherent. In short, we shall prefer to go on being depressed to losing our status as sophisticated persons. (*Human Face*, p. 137)

Therefore, Putnam is aware of our over-scientific limitations. But in *Reason, Truth and History*, he also engages with contemporary scepticism about science and rationality. He begins by acknowledging that there have always been good grounds for not trusting human reason. But they lead to an immediate problem: if reason is discarded, what alternative source could there be for human understanding and human integration? For these purposes, many alternatives to reason have been proposed, from revealed truth to inspired imagination, from experience to intuition, from instinct to tradition. But there is an irony about these proposals to replace reason: don't the reasons for not trusting reason come from reason? Putnam focuses on the irony, which, being a logician, he calls 'a trap':

> . . . the temptation is to fall into the trap of concluding that all rational argument is mere rationalization and then proceeding to try to argue rationally for this position. (RTH, p. 162)

'Rationalization' here does not refer to a sociological process of the Weberian kind that manipulates reason for profit; instead it means that proffered reasons are really masks for the irrational. Putnam is challenging this assumption, namely that we are only superficially rational, and that, therefore, reason *cannot* be our central resource. He suggests that this position is self-contradictory, because it can only be maintained through reasons. Those who attack reason still believe their own views should abide by virtue of superior reasoning. They rarely concede defeat against reason's pervasive action in defining and countering differences: reason's reason. Reason's proscription is less complete in practice than in theory. Nevertheless, there always has been a problem about how much credence to give reasons, and, like Habermas, Putnam recognises that this problem has grown more acute recently.

Putnam knows that there *are* now good reasons to doubt the utility of reason, particularly when reason is understood in certain modern ways. He is more forthright on his doubts about reason than Habermas, more robust in recognising justifiable motives for anti-rationalism. If reason were *identical* with science, Putnam concedes, then who would *not* have reservations? He puts it graphically: if 'the hero is Science' (RTH, p. 176), as has been common in the recent past, then the story of reason would be impressive, but it will be clouded with tragedy and foreboding:

> And if what impressed the Few about science from the start was its stunning intellectual success, there is no doubt that what has impressed the Many is its overwhelming material and technological success. We are impressed by this even when it threatens our lives. (RTH, p. 176)

There follows the dialogic rationalist turn: Putnam insists that reason is *not* the same as science, although science is one of the achievements of human reason.

Putnam is defending reason in a *contemporary* climate. He defines this contemporary context by saying that until recently reason *would* have been defended in the name of science, by 'philosophers who did not seriously doubt that "science" exhausts reason' (RTH, p. 187). In the contemporary situation, reason can no longer be defended simply by pointing to science. To us now, it seems that there has been in the culture . . . a philosophical tendency which was hypnotized by the success of science to such an extent that it could not conceive of the possibility of knowledge and reason outside of what we are pleased to call the sciences. (RTH, p. 185)

What 'hypnotized' so many people so that they identified human reason with science? Putnam gives two explanations:

> I am suggesting that the high prestige of science in the general culture is very much due to the enormous instrumental success of science, together with the fact that science seems free from the interminable and unsettleable debates that we find in religion, ethics and metaphysics. (RTH, p. 185)

Science was so effective at doing what they wanted that people forgot about all the other aspects of human reason. The second explanation is more complex. Science seemed to solve questions, whereas other disciplines seemed only to discuss them endlessly. People valued science as an alternative to endless arguments. Science meant certainty, though it is now obvious that science unrestrained will deliver horrors as well as blessings. The instrumental success is compromised. But perhaps almost paradoxically, Putnam also defends endless arguments, indeed his defence of engaging in arguments when they are unresolvable will be a main theme of my account. Argument, in his view, is the basis of reason, and it turns out that, in his exposition, argument is necessarily endless, and there is no escape from endless argument in the pursuit of reason.

Argumentative Reasoning

Putnam does not counterpose *science* to anti-rationalism; instead, to anti-rationalism he opposes *argument*, argument between people. We can see how he values arguing in the sequel to his warning about 'the trap':

> If all 'rational argument' were mere rationalization, then not only would it make no sense to try to argue rationally for any view, but it would make no sense to hold any view. (RTH, p. 162)

Putnam is making several connections: he is identifying rationality with 'rational argument', meaning argument *between* people with differing views; he is also connecting 'sense' with rational argument, because he is claiming that the views we hold only make sense in relation to rational argument about them. To say that people hold a comprehensible view is to say that they could defend that view in a rational discussion. Most notably, Putnam does not say that the discussion needs to be resolvable in order to be rational. What matters is the way people argue, and not the prospect of consensus.

Not that Putnam thinks a static discussion is good enough. He believes that when people argue properly about an issue, they will improve their understanding of it. In practice, we continue to discuss even the claims against reason as if that could advance our understanding:

> None of this would make the slightest sense if we did not think that these practices of discussion and communication, and these virtues of criticism and impartiality tend to weed out irrational beliefs, if not at once, then gradually, over time. (RTH, p. 163)

A number of questions arise: is 'impartiality' universally required? What is the scope in argument for someone who is not impartial, someone hurt by criticism? Would it always be best to argue impartially? What would be the role of emotion in human communication, in this view? Putnam's definition makes one wonder what *positive* role feeling would have in discussion seeking the truth. Again, the dilemma: could the approach be more dialogic? The effect is eloquent, in upholding reason, and giving it some autonomy from science, by calling up the ancient spirit of *argument* to rescue reason. Is the eloquence dialogic? Could it be more so? Or has Putnam reached one limit of dialogue and its potentialities in establishing his ideas about endless argument and the improvements that follow from it?

Habermas and Putnam

Both Habermas and Putnam focus on argument, as the central way of integrating reason with dialogue, and advancing reason beyond the requirements of science and strategic calculation. Argument becomes the cornerstone of Habermas's social and ethical theory, and of Putnam's theory of ethics and understanding, a theory which also has profound social resonances. They are not neutral about argument; their models of good argument differ from each other, and from many familiar conceptions of argument. By good argument, they intend more than coherent chains of reasoning, though they may include such logical chains in their requirements. Dialogic rationalists apply 'argument' to an *interaction between people*. Reason is more than the strong case, defence and criticism; reason is the criterion for the way people relate to others in a worthwhile way, particularly to those with different views. Dialogic rationalists insist that being rational is primarily a matter of how we respond to the views of others, and particularly how we respond to views which are critical of our own. Have they embodied the criteria for reason in this way?

It is important to realise that dialogic rationalism has landed on an unstable term in selecting 'argument'. For it is a matter of common understanding that 'argument' has other connotations than rational discussion. Argument can refer to something disruptive, something heated and messy, even violent. Certainly argument can refer to emotive and passionate conflicts. Some dialogic rationalists try to exclude these experiences of conflict from their account of reason, or to limit their intrusion: we shall see that Habermas tends to do so. Such thinking suggests that emotional reactions interfere with rational communication. Other thinkers, such as Putnam, recognise that the problem of thinking and feeling goes deeper, because there is a close connection between the rational dimension of argumentative dialogues and the heated and messy aspects of conflict in general. As Michael Billig has suggested, in *Ideology and Opinions* (p. 44), the ambiguities of the word 'argument' are fruitful, rather than disruptive, if we consider them deeply enough. The problem then is how to evaluate different types of dialogue and interaction so as to recognise the 'mixed' quality of human relations.

Giddens on the Experience of Modern Reason

Giddens overlaps Habermas and Putnam. Like them, he accepts that the modern world, as an irreversible reality, is not anti-scientific, nor anti-modern. But he believes opportunities for better worlds have slipped by, and he hopes others will be taken in the future. Giddens sees modernity from a more psychological point of view. The modern world is a psychological disaster:

> Personal meaninglessness – the feeling that life has nothing worthwhile to offer – becomes a fundamental psychic problem in circumstances of late modernity. We should understand this phenomenon in terms of a repression of moral questions which day-to-day life poses, but which are denied answers. 'Existential isolation' is not so much a separation of individuals from others as a separation from the moral resources necessary to live a full and satisfying existence. (*Modernity and Self-Identity*, p. 9)

In modern society, reason tests claims, we demand evidence, we reject mere assertions: Giddens believes that in science critical reason is constructive, new theories emerge, new evidence is found; but in daily life this critical approach uproots old beliefs without replacing them. Critical reason triumphs, and the triumph creates a crisis:

> Modernity is a post-traditional order, but not one in which the sureties of tradition and habit have been replaced by the certitude of rational knowledge. Doubt, a pervasive feature of modern critical reason, permeates into everyday life as well as philosophical consciousness, and forms a general existential dimension of the contemporary social world. (*Modernity and Self-Identity*, pp. 2–3)

Yet after critical reason comes a new order, if we choose, if we struggle, if we are lucky.

Where is the hope in modern developments? One hope is enlightenment. Giddens defines enlightenment as emancipation: the struggle against oppression, blind tradition. Enlightenment is vital. However, enlightenment is only one hope: Giddens also has another hope, a new politics, a politics distinct from enlightenment. After the enlightenment, Giddens discerns life politics:

> Emancipation, the general imperative of progressivist Enlightenment, is in its various guises the condition for the emergence of a life-political programme. (*Modernity and Self-Identity*, p. 9)

Life politics complements enlightenment, it is not anti-enlightenment. Enlightenment causes emancipation, and life politics is about how to use emancipation, what to choose or reject. Life politics promotes 'reflexivity' and self-construction to give meaning to emancipation, because specific choices are important to determine how we will live after enlightenment: choice presupposes life politics. Life politics offers Giddens a dialogic hope, a hope to set alongside dialogic rationalism's faith in argument.

Life politics is already present, and nothing can suppress it. (See below, Chapter 4, for life politics and social renewal in Giddens.) Like Habermas, Giddens sees the new world emergent inside present society: a potential for other societies within our own that is irreducible and encouraging. But for Giddens, rationality is not the main factor in the emergent society. He starts with basic trust:

> Trust, of varying sorts and levels, underlies a host of day-to-day decisions that all of us take in the course of orienting our activities. (*Modernity and Self-Identity*, p. 19)

Life is impossible without trust, and we learn trust as children, if we are fortunate. Trust may be rational, sometimes, but the ability to trust comes before reasoning. And trust is necessary for life politics, in making choices and assessing risks. People could not tolerate choice if they could not trust, trust others and also trust the world, not naïvely, but consciously. Giddensian trust is a virtue, a virtue which complements hope:

> The trust which the child, in normal circumstances, vests in its caretakers, I want to argue, can be seen as a sort of emotional inoculation against existential anxieties – a protection against future threats and dangers which allows the individual to sustain hope and courage in the face of whatever debilitating circumstances she or he might later confront. (*Modernity and Self-Identity*, p. 39)

Trust is basic, other virtues follow from it, particularly courage and hope. Giddens's theory is emotional, existential. The future means choice, doubt, decision; and we could not bear that future without trust. With trust, the future is significant:

> Creativity, which means the capability to act or think innovatively in relation to pre-established modes of activity, is closely related to basic trust. Trust itself, by its very nature, is in a certain sense creative, because it entails a commitment that is a 'leap into the unknown', a hostage to fortune which implies a preparedness to embrace novel experiences. (*Modernity and Self-Identity*, p. 41)

These terms are romantic, profoundly so: 'creativity', 'embrace novel experiences'. But Giddens also analyses society objectively, as far as possible; then the vocabulary is often scientific.

Giddens's story is both rationalist and romantic. His work extends the conversations about reason and hope. In Giddens's view, emotion is central to human relations and social development: the quest for self-identity is primary in any situation that is also socially creative, and trust is the nurturing connection between self and society. Trust is the heart, and trust is also the precondition for reason. Trust is interactive, dialogic. So Giddens sees hope in human interaction, and the interaction is communicative. In this way, he complements dialogic reason, though he subordinates reason to trust, as a source of hope. He does not subvert rational dialogue: he provides qualifications for supporting it.

Lloyd and the Image of Reason

Genevieve Lloyd tells a story about reason and gender, which, in the present context, poses a question: when stories lead towards dialogic reason, how do they influence assumptions about gender? For instance, like Habermas, Lloyd also discusses reason as purposeful and power-centred:

> Rational knowledge has been construed as a transcending, transformation or control of natural forces; and the feminine has been associated with what rational knowledge transcends, dominates or simply leaves behind. (*Man of Reason*, p. 2)

But reason is changeable, mobile, ambiguous. Even purposive reason varies, modulates. Metaphors keep shifting, and domination takes many forms. Sometimes power is overt, sometimes oblique. Any formulation can have many effects, since metaphors are complex, multivalent. One implication is: do not assume that egalitarian statements are self-fulfilling. Consider Descartes and his influence, argues Lloyd. Descartes presents 'reason as methodical thought' and he claimed to make the method universally accessible. He wrote in the vernacular, he avoided restrictive terminology, he addressed humanity. Nevertheless, suggests Lloyd, 'Something happened here which proved crucial for the development of stereotypes of maleness and femaleness, and it happened in some ways despite Descartes's explicit intentions' (*Man of Reason*, p. 39). The project was revolutionary, and the revolution aimed at 'a new egalitarianism in knowledge' (p. 44). The ideal was sincere, in good faith. The theory demanded 'no differentiation between male and female minds' (p. 48). But the language used still 'provided a basis for a sexual division of mental labour' (p. 49), and, crucially, an exploitative division. The problem arose in how the theory was interpreted, how it was connected with other images and ideas. Reason belonged to mind, mind transcending body, senses, the physical. Due to other influences, and despite Descartes, Lloyd tells how: 'Women have been assigned responsibility for that realm of the sensuous which the Cartesian Man of Reason must transcend' (p. 50). The ideal was progressive, the effect was repressive.

The moral is cautionary: do not underestimate the potential for different interpretations of a theory, a story. Why assume that contemporary theories are immune where Descartes was vulnerable? Out of regard for the past, we must not overestimate the present. The answer is not to disavow the past, for then we risk repetition. Rather, it is to develop potential, to reinterpret, to redefine, reinvent. Lloyd is concerned with philosophy specifically, but her approach applies to every rationalist project:

> . . . criticisms of ideals of Reason can in fact be seen as continuous with a very old strand in the western philosophical tradition; it has been centrally concerned with bringing to reflective awareness the deeper structures of inherited ideals of Reason. (*Man of Reason*, p. 109)

Perhaps an answer is critical dialogue, new dialogue, though that dialogue must be vigilant, sceptical. There are 'resources for critical reflection' (p. 109), as well as exclusionary prejudices. The problem is to discover new ways of conducting the dialogue without reanimating old prejudices.

The remedy lies in the imagination. Considered from the perspective of gender and inequality, we can still perceive the enlightenment motive, the ideal that 'we must see human history as a gradual progression towards the full realization of human capacities for Reason' (*Man of Reason*, p. 65). And we can see in retrospect that 'human history' is open to many interpretations, so that a liberating doctrine becomes oppressive and is often widely influential in that form. Enlightenment may not have advocated injustice, but it cannot avoid responsibility for the attitudes that followed. For instance, Lloyd suggests that Hegel presents a 'pattern' which 'lends itself to the accommodation, containment and transcending of feminine consciousness' (pp. 72–3), as when Hegelian influence 'functions as a rationalization of women's exclusion' (p. 84). To deal with the corrupting of effect in philosophy, the approach should be dialogic, a complex dialogue, 'to confront past ideals with perspectives drawn from the present' (p. 110) – neither constraining the present, nor reducing the past. The dialogue is open, in the sense that we cannot foresee how it will go. The point is to pursue the dialogue with hope but critically, not to settle for false solutions.

Elster and Rationality as Success

These are good stories contributing towards dialogic rationalism, including borderline stories such as told by Giddens. There is space for conversation: about enlightenment, about where dialogue meets reason, about the type of dialogue which encourages progress. The voices play against each other, and the effect is rich. Other stories enter the discussion, stories in which reason is independent of dialogue. I want briefly to consider some of these views about reason, non-dialogic rationalisms. Chapter 5 will examine how complex the non-dialogic views can be; here I wish to suggest the basic contrast with dialogic tendencies to show why the dialogic tendencies are important.

The major alternative to dialogic reason is the monologic model of 'the rational agent', the calculating individual seen as a singular unit of reasoning. The basic model is presented by Elster:

> Rational action is concerned with outcomes. Rationality says: If you want to achieve Y, do X. ('Economic Order', p. 357)

The rational agent pursues goals in the way most likely to succeed. The issue is efficiency, and depends on the choice of means. In fact, Elster is giving a critique of the simple model of rational choice, and he belongs to a tendency to be considered as new instrumentalism. Nevertheless, he starts from the basic model, which is pervasive today in economics, in public debate, in the discourses of self-help and advice. The model is 'instrumental', and it is effective because it is clear, and tells hard-edged stories: people pursue their interests, using reason. Advice is forthcoming:

> A prudent person avoids making a transaction with someone he suspects will be unreliable. Therefore, people seek information about the reliability of those with whom they deal. Reliability, however, is not an inherent personality trait. A person is reliable only if it is more advantageous to him than being unreliable. . . . A basic hypothesis of this approach is that someone is honest only if honesty, or the appearance of honesty, pays more than dishonesty. Hence, if someone thinks he can gain by dishonesty with impunity then he will be dishonest.[7]

The model is rigid: only one motive, basically, and individuals as distinct, preformed, calculative vehicles.

Elster identifies 'the unique human capacity for strategic behaviour' (*Ulysses*, p. 2), and exemplifies the instrumental model as a core vision of human development:

> I believe . . . that rational behaviour must be reduced in two steps: first by subsuming it under the general capacity for rational problem-solving and secondly by explaining that general capacity by the workings of natural selection. (*Ulysses*, p. 3)

Elster tells a story where evolution favours rational problem-solving, and where humanity embodies that trend. Evolution acts efficiently, like a business organisation, a rationalised institution:

> Optimal budgeting, linear programming, profit maximization and cost minimization are now as much part of evolutionary theory as of economics. (*Ulysses*, p. 8)

Could it be no coincidence? Is economics not being justified by the analogy?

Habermas's evolution story envisages two organisms communicating in their development; Elster's scenario is different:

> In a first evolutionary stage both predator and prey follow the simple strategy of direct pursuit and evasion. In a second stage the predator evolves the indirect strategy of path interception. In a third stage the prey evolves the protean counter strategy, and in a last stage the predator responds with the waiting behaviour of sub-optimal pursuit speed. (*Ulysses*, p. 15)

Humanity emerges from the stories about problem-solving agents as the embodiment of problem-solving:

> . . . globally maximizing behaviour in man is immediately explained by his ability to relate to the future and the merely possible. He can choose the globally best alternative. . . . We may say that in creating man natural selection has transcended itself. (*Ulysses*, p. 16)

And then comes the twist. Elster addresses the problem of co-operation, as a sub-theme of strategic rationality, and finds it a better way to pursue strategies: 'A necessary (but insufficient) condition for collective rationality is the transition to strategic thinking' (p. 18). Elster never reduces co-operation directly to individual strategic purposes – they are inter-related but not identical; indeed, he offers conditions for true co-operation, conditions not unlike communicative rationality: 'Only in a fully transparent situation will the actors converge upon the collectively rational behaviour' (p. 21). Communication once again is integral to true collective rationality, though communication is secondary to the role of individual rational agents who are the basic units of reason. In rational choice terms, a classic case concerning rationality and communication is the 'prisoner's dilemma'. Two parties face the same choice: to act or to refrain from action. If both choose to act, they will succeed: that is the optimal outcome. But if only one acts, then the action fails, to the particular detriment of the agent. Therefore, it would be best to refrain if you thought the other party was not going to join in. The problem is that they cannot communicate. Therefore, they are likely to refrain from acting: it is safest, since neither can be sure of the other's participation. Yet the optimal outcome depends on both acting. In the prisoner's dilemma, communication is the key to a rational outcome.

Instrumental rationality has powerful allies, notably in contemporary economic theory. Economics is scientific only if people are predictable, and the rational agent is more predictable than many other human characters:

In order to be able to arrive at generalisations, economists have to assume that individual behaviour follows some regular pattern, that all actions possess a common structure, however different the individual motives behind them might be. Generality is attained by modelling individuals as rational decision-makers.[8]

The key is 'individuals as rational decision-makers': individuality is absolute, interconnection is incidental. The story is historical, as well as general. Whole societies evolve out of cumulative rational decisions, patterns of individual choice.

Bookchin, Reason and Ecology

One particular rationalist tells a story directly relevant to the account of dialogic rationalism, relevant because of overlap and also of conflict. Bookchin is an ecological rationalist with a dialectical approach to reason, an approach which, however, does not call for dialogue, and which is dealt with here as a further approach to reason. Bookchin's view of reason also connects with richer developments in ecology, dialogic developments, which are considered more broadly in Chapter 5.

He tells an ecological story against instrumentality, purposive reason, calculation, and proposes a better alternative:

Today, sensitive people in growing numbers feel betrayed by the centuries-long glorification of reason with its icy claims to 'efficiency', 'objectivity', and freedom from ethical constraints – in short, an everyday form of reason that has nourished particularly destructive technologies like nucleonics and weaponry. Such popular reactions are understandable. But in swerving away from the misuses of a very specific form of reason that is largely manipulative, instrumental, and coldly analytical, we face problems that are no less disturbing than those from which we are seeking refuge. (*Social Ecology*, pp. 9–10)

Modern life is the outcome of instrumental reason, and reason shrinks to 'efficiency'. 'Objectivity' sounds better, but is also amoral and unethical. Modern reason threatens the environment, and humanity as part of the environment. Bookchin warns us that

we may overlook other forms of reason that are organic and yet retain their critical qualities; developmental and yet retain their analytical insights; ethical and yet retain their contact with reality. (*Social Ecology*, p. 11)

Ecological values are implicit in terms like 'organic'; 'contact with reality' links humanity and nature. Bookchin advocates dialectical reason as the alternative to instrumental reason:

I refer specifically to the great tradition of dialectical reason. . . . Dialectical reason acknowledges the developmental nature of reality. (*Social Ecology*, pp. 12–14)

Dialectic means super-logic, extra logic, logic beyond contradiction, compared with the logic in 'conventional reason' (p. 17).

Bookchin's dialectic means reason from above – potential discovered, released and directed to human requirements:

> Reason has the obligation to explore the potentialities that are latent in any social development and educe its authentic actualization, its fulfilment and 'truth' through a new and more rational social dispensation. (*Social Ecology*, p. 32)

Reason is heroic, actualising the future.

Bookchin also includes communication in his story, as an ally of rationality. Communication is a gift, of our 'first nature' acquired in evolution:

> ... and 'first nature' exhibits a high degree of orderly continuity in the actualization of potentialities that made for more complex and more self-aware or subjective life-forms. Insofar as this continuity is intelligible, it has meaning and rationality in terms of its results: the elaboration of life-forms that can conceptualize, understand, and communicate with each other in increasingly symbolic terms. (*Social Ecology*, p. 41)

Communication is part of reason, though reason is originally conceptual, not communicative. To rediscover our relation to nature, we must restore our powers of conception and communication. The dialectic lends support to communication, though the support is qualified by other priorities.

Questions

A pressing question is: what is the role of the intellectual, the role in relation to society, to experience? Is it possible to play a dialogic role as well as propounding a dialogic theory? And how should dialogic theories engage with less dialogic neighbours? In the next chapter, I consider the central issue, argument itself. How should a dialogic approach develop, in form and in content? How should a dialogic approach express the potentialities of argument for establishing rational views and rational conduct? How should a dialogic approach regard the limitations of argument as a medium for rationality? How can a theory of rational dialogue be itself rational and dialogic? And what are the comparative merits of different models for rational dialogue? For dialogic rationalism to progress, the models must be persuasive indeed, given the entrenched views on alternative kinds of rationality.

Notes

1 Theodor Adorno and Max Horkheimer, *Dialectic of Enlightenment*, trans. John Cumming (London: Verso, 1979), p. 30.

2 Stephen K. White, *The Recent Work of Jürgen Habermas: Reason, Justice and Modernity* (Cambridge: Cambridge University Press, 1988), p. 58: Habermas aims to enhance 'the realization of a rational potential which is always present in all communicative action but only realized in the modern world'.

3 Charles Darwin, *The Origin of Species* (Harmondsworth: Penguin, 1968), p. 135.

4 Others see the problem of norms less ambiguously. Michael Waltzer in *Interpretation and Social Criticism* (Cambridge, MA: Harvard University Press, 1987) addresses the question of moral critique and speculation. He sees new values as rooted in existing traditions (p. 17): 'We have to start from where we are. Where we are, however, is always *someplace of value*, else we would never have settled there.'

5 A major critique is Nancy Fraser, 'What's Critical about Critical Theory? The Case of Habermas and Gender', in *Unruly Practices*, pp. 113–43, notably pp. 120–1: 'Consider that Habermas

subdivides the category of socially integrated action into two subcategories . . . normatively secured . . . reflectively achieved consensus. . . . What is insufficiently stressed, however, is that actions co-ordinated by normatively secured consensus in the male-headed nuclear family are actions regulated by power.' In Fraser's view, the term 'normative' is obscuring power relations, which are not consensual at all.

6 Waltzer does not attempt the assertion of rationality as emphatically as Habermas does, but he has a vivid picture of how norms arise, analogous to these stories of communicative action (Waltzer, *Interpretation and Social Criticism*, p. 24): 'They are, in fact, however, the products of many people talking, of real if always tentative, intermittent, and unfinished conversations.'

7 L.G. Telser, 'A Theory of Self-Enforcing Agreements', in *The Journal of Business*, 53, 1 (January 1980), pp. 27–44, 28–9.

8 Cristina Bicchieri, 'Rationality and Predictability in Economics', in *The British Journal of the Philosophy of Science*, 38, 4 (December 1987), pp. 501–13, 502.

3

Argument in Theory

The Concept of Argument

The concept of argument is deeply ambiguous: is arguing a problem, or a solution? Have things gone wrong when people begin to argue? Does arguing put things right? The questions make immediate sense, they proceed from our understanding of what argument involves. Furthermore, it is hard to imagine a time when this dichotomy between the constructive and destructive effects of argument was not significant: Billig, notably, has explored the ancient origins of these conceptual ambiguities (*Ideology and Opinions*, pp. 46–53). In our own time, argument is again a pressing theme, grounds for trouble and for hope, a source of thought, as well as a scene of thinking. In this chapter, I examine the different ways in which Habermas and Putnam have considered argument, with all its problems, as a basis for redeeming reason. Then I consider alternative theories, from different disciplines and political perspectives: Michael Billig's rhetorical psychology, the liberal theories of Rawls, Giddens's theory of life politics and intimacy and theories of dialogue and gender from Deborah Tannen, Amy Sheldon and Marjorie Harness Goodwin.

Habermas and the Dialogic Theory of Argument

Argumentative Speech

Habermas frames his theory of argument with his even larger theory of rationality, which is in turn supported by the theory of argument. He has given his work 'the goal of formally analyzing the conditions of rationality' (CA1, p. 2): to determine what it means for people to act rationally, under what conditions they can do so, what prevents people from acting with reason. Ultimately, he proposes to define the type of social development which promotes rational action. Habermas accepts that being rational is a corollary of knowing things. But he makes a big leap from this connection simply by saying that being rational is not identical with knowing the answers. This step suggests that rationality is dynamic, it has 'less to do with the possession of knowledge than with how speaking and acting subjects *acquire and use knowledge*' (CA1, p. 8). Clearly, on this view, people who know the facts can still act irrationally; people who do not yet know the facts can take reasonable decisions. More resonantly, a society can master much knowledge and still govern itself unreasoningly, if it does not use knowledge constructively. Regarding knowledge, he has already moved away from other definitions towards a dialogic rationalist definition. Reason cannot be simply a better knowledge, nor can reason be reduced to an instrument for collecting more and more advanced knowledge. To define reason fully, it is then necessary to explain how people use knowledge in their dealings with each other, how people live and why they behave as they do.

After considering the role of knowledge, Habermas moves towards his consideration of argument by asking how *language* impinges on rationality. How does rationality show itself in what speakers say? He avoids the idea that a rational statement is true, properly informed. He proposes instead a dynamic model, 'basing the rationality of an expression on its being susceptible of criticism and grounding' (CA1, p. 9): so that words are used rationally in utterances which are open to argument, utterances that people address to each other. Positively, we are prepared to justify our views; negatively, we are not suppressing criticism, when being rational. And it must follow that our actions are rational if they, too, are open to such defence and criticism, if our actions are appropriately influenced by other views. Thus, he reaches experience.

Experience is the basis of Habermas's theory, however grand and abstract the terms.[1] He appeals to experience when introducing his major themes. Above all, his reinterpretation of reason derives from a specific experience, one which Habermas appeals to readers to validate by acknowledging it from their own lives. Instead of presenting a recipe, or a formula, for rationality, leading to instant identification, he refers us to scenes from life, asking that we share his own fundamental recognition:

> This concept of *communicative rationality* carries with it connotations based ultimately on the central experience of the unconstrained, unifying, consensus-bringing force of argumentative speech, in which different participants overcome their merely subjective views and, owing to the mutuality of rationally motivated conviction, assure themselves of both the unity of the objective world and the intersubjectivity of their lifeworld. (CA1, p. 10)

The whole theory grounds itself 'ultimately on the central experience' of a certain quality in discussion. The moment is moving and exhilarating, and it is characteristic of Habermas, his approach, tone and originality, and the range and sweep of his conceptions which give his theory its strength. Habermas locates the centre of his rationalism in an appeal to an experience, at least to a potential in experience. But questions arise: what identifies the experience; and to whom is it central?

The experience seems to be that of participating in an argument. But more than that: it is participating in an argument which leads towards *agreement*. It seems to me that once the subject is an experience, the experience must entail a story. We could unpack the story in these terms: we differ, we encounter the other view, we assess our own view again, we are absorbed into the exchange and we discover a new union of views and of parties. Not only do we resolve the specific dispute, we also affirm a sense of sharing a world. In fact, we share two worlds: a world out there and a world inside. The key result of this exchange is 'unity'. We differ but when we resolve the dispute we reaffirm a common world. Only if we resolve the argument with reasons can we affirm our shared world and our congruity with each other and the requirements of that world. Otherwise, we can never be sure what that world is, and what we are. Habermas sometimes puts the case for argumentative consensus in analytic terms, as above; but he is also capable of presenting it as an ethical and political imperative; 'what is needed is a "real" process of argumentation in which the individuals concerned cooperate' ('Discourse Ethics', in MC, p. 67). Habermas both depicts and prescribes the argumentative pursuit of consensus.

Clearly questions arise about the definition which unites consensual experience with argument. Even if we acknowledge the importance of this 'unifying' moment of arguing, what about the experience of argument as conflict? Conflict is implied: otherwise there is no place in the sequence for defence or criticism. But the *experience* is not conflict, except as a precondition for resolution and union. The experience is considered to be unambiguous. Can we recognise all argument in such an experience? If not, Habermas has a definition of argument that is narrow in form, though powerfully focused. The ambiguity of argument has been lost in consolidating the theory. Habermas is enriching because he points towards experience: he takes us into an ambiguous world of lived arguing, but then ignores the ambiguity. The implications of this flaw in Habermas's fundamental model are not entirely negative, as a superficial reading might suggest: on the contrary, his most complex ideas develop from his struggle to relate his definition of argument to experience and to match ideal requirements with the complexity of experience, of which he is well aware. Furthermore, the tension gives us scope to develop dialogues with the theory, and extract a rationality from argument, from argument as a process.

Unresolved tensions could be integral to a successful dialogic rationalism, fully realised without being final. Perhaps the most disappointing feature of Habermas's presentation is that he seems unaware that incompleteness and tension in his work can lead to a wider process of discussion with all the advantages that argument can have in its widest applications. I would contend that the main flaw is *not* that Habermas's theory is strained and contains gaps; it is that he tries to resolve all the tensions that his investigations throw up within his own terms, to close the gaps within the limits of his own perception: too little dialogue, too much rationalism. Habermas has not trusted in dialogue, as his own tenets require. His statements remain self-sufficient and comprehensive, almost autonomous. This problem is generated in the construction of the theory: for Habermas works in definitions. This is a self-defeating strategy, and self-contradictory, for he is the great proponent of open argument, and what is more binding than a definition?

Irrationality

Consider how Habermas defines argument itself:

> We use the term argumentation for that type of speech in which participants thematize contested validity claims and attempt to vindicate or criticize them through arguments. (CA1, p. 18)

Conflict is irreducible in the words: 'contested', 'vindicate' or 'criticize'; and yet, by this definition, argument corresponds to the 'central experience' of a 'unifying' process. There is a gap between definition and experience, in these terms. And, more basically, does *this* method satisfy the criteria for being rational which are being asserted in this very passage? It seems that in this vital area concerning argument Habermas prefers logical consistency to dialogic address. He continues definitively:

> Corresponding to the openness of rational expressions to being explained, there is, on the side of persons who behave rationally, a willingness to expose themselves to criticism and, if necessary, to participate properly in argumentation. (CA1, p. 18)

For Habermas, it seems, one thing that is not arguable is the definition of being rational. To be rational is to argue properly, according to his criteria, or to be ready to argue properly when challenged. But anyone who rejects this definition of rationality is automatically barred from arguing about it because we have to accept this principle in order 'to participate properly', to enter the discussion. 'Properly' by whose requirements? If anyone refuses to accept that argument is the proper test of rationality, Habermas can label them 'irrational' and disqualify their contributions to the subject. Indeed in an essay on Habermas, Putnam hints at this irony. He wonders what Habermas will do about those who know their own ethical beliefs are *not* rational.[2] The problem comes back to having an argument where there is no ambiguity. Habermas wants argument without the ambiguity. No-one can argue who does not accept the basic procedures. Not surprisingly, conflict is muted, and argument is much more the solution than the problem in disagreement.

Habermas is clear about his right to label and negate 'types' who fail to satisfy his definitions of rationality: 'Anyone who systematically deceives himself about himself behaves irrationally' (CA1, p. 21). Such a person is contrasted with 'one who is capable of letting himself be enlightened about his irrationality'. A comparable definition of rationality has even been employed in an experimental study of argumentation by Deanna Kuhn, who assessed 'people's ability to envision conditions that would falsify the theories they hold, that is, their ability to generate a counterargument to the theory and supporting evidence that comprise the primary argument'.[3] But the tension is sucked out of the need for argument and the scope of arguments by Habermasian and other prescriptive definitions. If people deceive themselves about themselves, they are excluded from argumentation. They are impossible and there is no need to argue with them. If people think they are calm and considerate, and are actually heated, if they think they are open to criticism and are dogmatic, they are ruled out of the argument. But don't these conditions describe much of our actual experience of arguing, our experience of the way we argue and the way others argue too?

The Unified Diversity of Argument

Having used argument to define rationality, Habermas defines proper arguing. He wants to demonstrate that all proper arguments have the same 'form'. Since arguments convey rationality, he will then be able to show that all rationality is interconnected in the form taken by the argument from which rationality emerges. The content of argument varies, but they all take one form:

> What is common . . . is the form of argumentation: We try to support a claim with good grounds or reasons; the quality of the reasons and their relevance can be called into question by the other side; we meet objections and are in some cases forced to modify our original position. (CA1, p. 31)

Claims to validity occur in innumerable contexts and instances; the procedure for testing claims is a constant. The issue may be legal or ethical or scientific or musical, but the process for testing claims about them is the same. What counts as a good reason for believing an argument about them will depend on the type of discussion, but rationality supplies coherent ways of resolving disagreements, ways which lend themselves to rational agreement.

Being rational in a discussion of science is the same as being rational about ethics, allowing for differences of genre and context. Here is the *strength* of Habermas: he broadens the area which counts as rational, and connects the parts coherently. Indeed Habermas himself sees his model of argument precisely as having a connective function. From Weber, he derives the idea of 'an antagonism between cultural value spheres with their own linear logics' (CA2, p. 304). Habermas denies that such antagonism is necessary. He replies that 'In principle, when substantive reason comes apart into its different moments, reason can retain its unity in the form of procedural rationality' (CA2, p. 304). In other words, the process of argument is common to contexts which are otherwise divergent or even conflicting.

To me, the model *is* appealing, particularly by contrast with *scientific* rationalism. We are not required to dismiss as irrational large territories of human practice and their accompanying defence. We need only consider the form taken by the argument on their behalf to decide whether claims on their behalf are rational. But the problem is that Habermas has provided a narrow definition of argument in order to make arguing so central in deciding whether a claim is acceptable. Emotion is marginalised by the definition, and therefore 'emotional claims' are left out: feeling is largely a source of bias. But many claims for attention and justice derive from feelings; they are presented emotionally, and rouse emotions. Fundamentally, many arguments are full of emotions; they do not reduce to trying 'to support a claim with good grounds or reasons'. In practice, we recognise arguing in all kinds of incidents which fail the test of 'good grounds and reasons' and accept the right to argue such cases without prejudice. But if Habermas were to admit that argument is so complex, he could not use argument to support his unified definition of rationality for different subjects. The crucial point is that argument is too diverse for Habermas's purpose, which is to define reason and present authentic exchange in a unified form. He is too anxious about keeping reason pure to engage wholeheartedly with the twin concept of dialogue in a robust dialogic rationalism. Dialogue is subordinate to reason: dialogue is the means and reason the end. Even when Habermas does attribute more positive roles to emotion, he does so cautiously and under the supervision of reason:

> Emotional responses directed against individual persons in specific situations would be devoid of moral character were they not connected with an impersonal kind of indignation over some breach of a generalized norm or behavioural expectation. It is only their claim to general validity that gives an interest, a volition, or a norm the dignity of moral authority. ('Discourse Ethics', in MC, p. 49)

Sometimes emotion in an argument is inevitable; but even where emotion is inevitable, it is only impersonal criteria which provide validity, not the emotion itself. Argument refers personal emotions to general standards, and not the other way round. As we shall see in the next chapter, Habermas works hard to establish a link between cultural norms of behaviour or judgement, which might include emotion, and rationality.

Habermas relates his theory to intellectual traditions of argument. He is aware of the relevance of the classical syllabus of rhetoric, logic and dialectic, since each analysed argument, and he links his theory to the whole 'trivium', the threefold discipline:

> Rhetoric is concerned with argumentation as a process, dialectic with the pragmatic procedures of argumentation, and logic with its products. (CA1, p. 26)

But the definitions are too convenient. In most views, a rhetorical analysis of arguing would not deal with the 'process' purely in terms of reasons; from the time of Aristotle's *Rhetoric*, emotions are as relevant as reason in a rhetorical analysis. Habermas is referring to 'the Aristotelian canon', but he then simplifies the parts. Aristotle's rhetoric is precisely about the problem of integrating emotion and reason. When Habermas connects logic with rhetoric, he creates an opportunity to widen his theory, at the cost of making it less watertight. He could have acknowledged that rhetoric is less purely about reasons than is logic, and then he could have used that moment to invite speculation about the ambiguities in the nature of argument. The result could have been a dialogue with the past, one revealing and exploring tensions and even contradictions; instead Habermas makes the past conform to his definitions, and in doing so evades a dialogue in the present.

Dialogics of Theory

Yet dialogue is still integral to the method. Habermas elaborates his theory by commenting on other modern views of argument. For instance, he addresses Toulmin's model, which puts more emphasis on the different fields of argument. According to Habermas,

> [Toulmin] doesn't draw the proper lines between accidental institutional differentiations of argumentation, on the one hand, and the forms of argumentation determined by internal structure, on the other. (CA1, p. 35)

Here is the idea that all arguing shares a certain 'structure', the pattern of claim, reason and counterclaim leading towards mutual understanding and agreement by modification. For Habermas, this structure is more important than the differences between one argument and another due to local requirements:

> Thus *all* arguments, be they related to questions of law and morality or to scientific hypotheses or to works of art, require the *same* basic form of organization which subordinates the eristic means to the end of developing intersubjective conviction by the force of the better argument. (CA1, p. 36)

'Eristic' refers to the classical arts of persuasion. These arts are 'means', which should serve to reach true agreement. People try to persuade each other by eristic

means, until they recognise which is the 'better argument'. The crux is 'require':
'all arguments . . . require . . . '. Habermas means that the arguing process makes
people follow these patterns; almost, the language itself follows a relentless
course towards resolutions of differences. The techniques of argument take over
from the other motives, liberating the participants from their more partisan or
strategic aims. Habermas's theory contributes a perspective towards dialogic
rationalism because he has founded it on this model of arguing. But even where
he is more dialogic in his method, there is still a disturbing gap between the theory and the practice. 'Eristic' is *defined* as 'subordinate' or secondary to the
organisation of the argument; but is that definition not a most persuasive device,
a most eristic manoeuvre, a means of seeming authoritative? Moreover, Toulmin
serves more as foil than as partner in the development of the argument.

Nevertheless, in another way, Habermas's method does humanise rationalism. Although he tends to evade dialogue, he breathes *imaginative* life into theory.
As we read on, the model becomes more emphatic, not more qualified. And we
begin to feel the true quality of the mind. True, the manner is careful, to the point
of closure. But the project is full of vision, as dialogic rationalism must also be if
it is to be true to its own criteria. For imagination is allied to personal experience,
and what one person's imagination proposes, only the imaginations of others can
grasp. Habermas's project is more humane than its definitive form suggests; the
substance is often personal, and addresses us individually in what must be a dialogue of imaginations.

The climax to which this visionary thesis of valid argument leads is the idea of
'universal validity claims':

> Only the truth of propositions and the rightness of moral norms and the comprehensi-
> bility and well-formedness of symbolic expressions are, by their very meaning,
> universal validity claims that can be tested in discourse. (CA1, p. 42)

All proper claims for attention depend on propositions about truth or analogous
assertions about norms or about meanings; and these claims are entitled to be
heard in argument and to participate in this argument with other claims. Each
claim may be modified; consensus can follow, a movement towards agreement.
There are no contexts, it seems, where such claims are not relevant. Different cultures or ages frame their claims differently. But wherever humans use language,
these claims are heard and they can contribute to argument and, ultimately, to
agreement.

Habermas insists that hearers must respond, because they have a definite
choice for doing so:

> Whether the speaker raises a validity claim implicitly or explicitly, the hearer has only
> the choice of accepting or rejecting the validity claim or leaving it undecided for the
> time being. The permissible reactions are taking a 'yes' or 'no' position or abstaining.
> (CA1, p. 38)

'Permissible' refers to the use of language itself and the sense it conveys.
Habermas means that these 'yes/no' reactions follow naturally from a proper
understanding of what was said. Alternatively, in the absence of these responses,
there has been no understanding of what the speaker means. Understanding means

responding 'yes' or 'no' or 'we'll see . . . either yes or no'. And Habermas pushes further his view of understanding. Saying 'yes' or 'no' means thinking of reasons. Having no reasons to take a stand equals not understanding the words of a claim. It is that fundamental. If you have not thought of reasons for or against a claim, you cannot have understood its meaning. Furthermore, some claims are inescapable: 'it is true that . . . '; 'it is right to . . . '; 'these words say this'. If some claims are inevitable, and claims demand that we think of reasons, then some types of reasoning must also be inevitable. The theory makes language itself determine some kinds of fundamental reasoning. And here comes the link between 'dialogue' and 'reason'. To respond ('yes' or 'no' or – temporarily – 'yes or no') is to be a potential partner in a dialogue. *The basic act of the understanding is both rational and dialogic.*

Of course, Habermas knows that many 'yes' and 'no' reactions do not concern reasons: they are 'expressions of arbitrary choice' (CA1, p. 38) in a world influenced by arbitrary power: 'I must do what you say'; 'I refuse, I cannot challenge your power'; or 'I am strong enough to resist'. No reasons are given, and so, in Habermasian logic, no real communication has occurred either, just the exercise of power, an exercise that may sometimes involve words, incidentally.[4] Does Habermas underestimate this admission? He is satisfied with defining the nature of power corrupted responses; but we could ask: how does he know where the corruption stops and the authentic responses begin? On the one hand, his vision is impressive: we feel an imagination stretching its own concepts to match the unevenness of experience. On the other hand, could a more dialogic mode have turned the complications into advantages?

The foundational model of proper argument ends with another definition. Again, Habermas delimits categorically the field of true argument, another self-threatening moment:

> I shall speak of 'discourse' only when the meaning of the problematic validity claim conceptually forces participants to suppose that a rationally motivated agreement could in principle be achieved. (CA1, p. 42)

And just here, the ambiguity of argument reappears, the ambiguity which began with the awareness that argument is a field of conflict, and passionate conflict, as well as of concurrence and arbitration. Consider the tension involved in 'conceptually forces participants to suppose'! Are these free agents or not? Communication demands that these people conceive that agreement is possible, agreement derived from reasons. It is the 'yes/no' moment in action. As they perceive the meaning of words, they realise that they *must choose*: the moment where choice becomes necessity reveals another ambiguity, one concerning the nature of the agreement which ends an argument.[5]

In arguing, people realise that they have choices; in arguing, they discover that they must take one of these choices. And then they realise that the other side is in the same position, exposed to the same choices and forced to choose. Therefore, theoretically, they could end by choosing the same response. They could agree, if the circumstances were conducive, and they could also fail to agree. For Habermas, when participants realise that they might agree, a gap closes, a gap between the possible and the actual, between the present and the future. Arguing is predetermined, according to Habermas, in the sense that there are fixed 'structures' for its proper development. But, as we have just seen, he has also acknowledged a moment between the possible and the actual, when the outcome depends on personal factors. And one could take this uncertainty further, by adding that human reactions are unpredictable, which is common experience. Habermas tries to reconcile determinism and uncertainty, by separating the structural possibilities, which are determined, from the specific outcomes, which are not. The determinism is strong: an argument presents a definite vista of choices which lead to agreement when appropriate procedures are followed. But then he realises that the future is also *indeterminate*: there is a moment of decision when circumstances matter, and circumstances vary.

Experience is reviewed until it poses problems which the theory cannot reconcile. Habermas concedes that agreement is likely 'if only the argumentation could be conducted openly enough' (CA1, p. 42). But will it be open? How damaging is this sudden qualification? The problem here is that Habermas has defined argument so as to *require* openness. Surely for Habermas an exchange cannot really *be* argument at all if it is not open? After all the tight definitions, the motives and reactions of the participants appear from experience as unpredictable factors in argument. And their appearance is a valuable addition to the theory. But one must ask whether the theory does more than acknowledge its own limits once it acknowledges experience in its indeterminacy.

Habermas constructs a complex system which derives from considering it rational to be open to criticism. There is some tension between openness to criticism and the closed system itself, between the fixed limits of argument and the need for change in response to criticism. He applies his system to experience again and again, partly because the world is open and it is necessary to meet the challenge of change in an open world, and partly to pre-empt the challenge of such differentiation. His work exhibits the tension between definition and experience, between the fixed categories of argument and the limitless response of life: always just behind the reference to experience lies a narrative. Habermas cannot prevent this overlap between definition and narrative in an area where definitions lose their distinct application. Starting from definitions, the thesis spills over into the world of experience, a world which demands *narratives* – for only narrative can contain the motives of the characters, or portray their reactions to each other and to their circumstances. The tension in this project goes back to Aristotle and it appears in any major project on argument, except pure logic. Habermas tends to defend argument *against* the incursions of narrative, so that he criticizes Heidegger for adopting a concept in which 'Being can only be meditatively expressed and presented narratively, but not argumentatively retrieved and explained' (PDM, p. 152). But narrative returns within the attempt to represent argument with a theory.

Narrative is necessary to elucidate argument, though the basic question is: how *far* can narrative convey the nature of argument? Will narrative even express our whole view of argument? Further, a related problem is that in any given situation where people hold differing views, argument itself may be a debatable resort, and then there may be stories to be told about how argument came to be chosen or refused. Habermas's system reaches out to narrative and then cannot tolerate its uncertainty.

Defending Argumentative Consensus

Ironically, Habermas tells a story about his theory, a theory which achieved:

> the transition to a new paradigm, that of mutual understanding. Subjects capable of speaking and acting who, against the background of a common lifeworld, come to an understanding with each other about something in the world, relate to the medium of language both autonomously and dependently. (*Postmet.*, p. 43)

His summation is compelling:

1   The theory is a new paradigm of reason.
2   The paradigm is intersubjective and relational, interactive and dialogic.
3   Reason is unifying, because the good dialogue achieves consensus. The theory is consensus-grounded, which leaves scope for dispute about how exactly the consensus arises, and how far people actually achieve consensus in practice.

The narrative summation confirms how Habermas bases his theory on language:

> On the one hand, these subjects always find themselves in a linguistically structured and disclosed world; they live off grammatically projected interconnections of meaning. To this extent, language sets itself off from the speaking subjects as something antecedent and objective, as the structure that forges conditions of possibility. On the other hand, the linguistically disclosed and structured lifeworld finds its footing only in the practices of reaching an understanding within a linguistic community. (*Postmet.*, p. 43)

Again, the self-narration is illuminating:

1   Habermas has a philosophy of language, a philosophy about how linguistic structure conveys individual interactions.
2   The analysis claims objectivity: language is a framework, objectively analysable and knowable.
3   But Habermas recognises local contexts: 'reaching an understanding' is specific, active, free, within the structure.

Habermas continues to narrate communicative action as a theory about how language imposes rationality. Rationality means reaching understanding, using the structures of language:

> In this way, the linguistic formation of consensus, by means of which interactions link up in space and time, remains dependent upon the autonomous 'yes' and 'no' positions that communication participants take toward criticizable validity claims. (*Postmet.*, p. 43)

Some control themes are here concentrated:

1   True consensus is linguistic, people achieve it by communicating. True consensus is not the result of social forces or institutions.
2   Key terms are 'yes'/'no' and 'criticizable'. People make claims, language compels us to make claims when we speak. Claims require a response: yes or

no. Argument is diffused through communication, diffused explicitly or implicitly. Claims invite criticism. Yet true criticism has a purpose: to further the interaction, to implement an understanding. Genuine arguments lead towards agreements. The parties wish to agree, even if agreement is difficult, apparently impossible. Communicative reason contrasts with power, inequity, interactions between unequal parties. Saying yes and no is not always rational, it may be forced by power.

The 'new paradigm' defends consensus, and here Habermas recognises it is open to challenge. The story elaborates, as communicative action accommodates further inflections. Habermas stresses how consensus allows individuality:

> The intersubjectivity of linguistically achieved understanding is by nature porous, and linguistically attained consensus does not eradicate from the accord the differences in speaker perspectives but rather presupposes them as ineliminable. (*Postmet.*, p. 48)

Here he is trying to realign his theory to allow for differences. Argument is the model: yes/no and criticism. But argument's goal is consensus. Is consensus not anti-individual? The reply is that consensus does not eliminate differences. But it must surely alter them, reduce them, integrate them?

Habermas presents his theory responding to new pressures, including new demands about individuality and difference. He remarks upon 'the postmodern mood' which 'is making its mark':

> Repulsion towards the One and veneration of difference and the Other obscures the dialectical connection between them. For the transitory unity that is generated in the porous and refracted intersubjectivity of a linguistically mediated consensus not only supports but furthers and accelerates the pluralization of forms of life and the individualization of lifestyles. More discourse means more contradiction and difference. (*Postmet.*, p. 140)

The theory explicitly tries to value contradiction and difference, within the context of 'consensus'. Responding to a 'mood', Habermas recognises difference. But is a difference supported by consensus enough to satisfy autonomy, self-identity, even if the consensus is porous? The recent defences are revealing: Habermas trying to resolve a tension, which keeps eluding his solution, a tension between differing and agreeing.

Putnam and the Dialogic Theory of Argument

The Argumentative Quest

As we saw, Putnam approaches dialogic rationalism by a different route from Habermas. He is more immediately concerned with knowledge and method, particularly scientific method. Putnam develops a model of argument. He perceives argument differently from Habermas; both use a conception of argument to formulate a theory of rationality, and the contrast reveals much about the wide scope of dialogic rationalism. Putnam is more cautious about the outcomes of argument, and particularly he is sceptical that we can *resolve* our differences by arguing. *For Putnam the central instance which represents reason is an argument which is unresolvable, whereas for Habermas the central embodiment of reason is an argument leading to agreement.* Yet Putnam is more optimistic than Habermas: he accepts that there will be irreconcilable differences, and that rationality itself will be open to disagreement, and he is still confident, his outlook is eager rather than pessimistic. He believes we don't *need* to resolve our differences in order to live reasonably, though agreement is often helpful. Does Putnam avoid the strains in Habermas's theory by accepting irreducible disagreement in the pursuit of reason? Or has he lowered the requirements of reason too far, so that his approach would make dialogic rationalism too limited if it were the dominant model?

Putnam does not offer a comprehensive view of rationality, like Habermas, though he can see that a comprehensive view is a *temptation*:

> It is tempting . . . to say that what determines whether a belief is rational is not the norms of rationality of this or that culture, but an *ideal theory* of rationality, a theory which would give necessary and sufficient conditions for a belief to be rational in the relevant circumstances in any possible world. (RTH, p. 104)

In Putnam's terms, Habermas's theory is 'an ideal theory of rationality', based on a universal standard. Putnam's theory has no definitive criterion for what is rational, and accepts there will be 'the norms of rationality' which flourish in different contexts. If there are different norms of rationality, then rationality varies more than Habermas admits.

Putnam knows that other thinkers hope for an ideal theory of rationality but considers this a forlorn hope as 'the prospects for actually *finding* powerful generalizations about all rationally acceptable beliefs seem so poor' (RTH, p. 104). Putnam's *own* theory of rationality follows from his view of all theories: no theory is absolute, no single theory can apply in all situations, but there are some basic theoretical virtues, and they are:

> (1) the desire that one's basic assumptions, at least, should have *wide* appeal; (2) the desire that one's system should be able to withstand rational criticism; (3) the desire that the morality recommended should be *livable*. (RTH, p. 105)

Rationality appears as a *critical* force in human affairs, since every rational system should respond to criticism; it is similar in that respect to Habermas's rationality. But the story is different, because Putnam requires 'basic assumptions' which possess 'wide appeal' in the first place, so it is easier for them to face criticism. Moreover, beliefs should be 'livable'. These standards are 'the desiderata for a methodology or a system of rational procedure in any major area of human concern' (RTH, p. 105). The result is that what is rational is never divorced from human experience, which it may seek to transform but never to ignore. Putnam's 'rational procedure' overlaps with Habermas's communicative rationality because critical discussion is central to both. But 'wide appeal' makes Putnam's model more thoroughly dynamic, more active, more likely to be argued over itself, so that his model *impacts*. The slightly puzzling term 'livable' is also dynamic: people may make a belief livable, depending on how they use it. These concepts make 'rational procedure' experimental, provisional, almost tentative, thereby avoiding the tensions in Habermas's system, since Putnam's founding model of rationality is attuned to indeterminacy in experience.

Yet Putnam, too, is seeking a definition of 'rational procedure'. In one way, he is more definitive about rationality than Habermas. He begins from a positive position:

> The view which I shall defend holds, to put it very roughly, that there is an extremely close connection between the notions of *truth* and *rationality*; that, to put it even more crudely, the only criterion for what is a fact is what it is *rational* to accept. (RTH, p. x)

Putnam aims to define 'what is a fact' and he risks becoming rigid and fixed, less dynamic, but there is an immediate disclaimer:

> I do not believe, however, that rationality is defined by a set of unchanging 'canons' or 'principles'; methodological principles are connected with our view of the world . . . and change with time. (RTH, p. x)

In Putnam's view, rationality determines what is to be a fact, and facts appear fixed in their cultural and historical contexts; but he considers that rationality changes. He is attempting to bridge the gap between the view that there are always going to be diverse perspectives in human experience and the view that some truths are reliable. Putnam provokes us with paradoxes and near paradoxes, which display and control conceptual tensions at the same time.

Putnam and Habermas offer different conceptions of communication and indeed of human interaction. Putnam returns constantly to the *unresolvable* dispute or debate. Why is that unresolvedness not counterproductive in his theory of communication? Can he provide a dialogic rationalism where agreement is not fundamental, where arguments are constructive even though they could never end in consensus? Putnam shows how he conceives of unresolvable arguments by considering imaginary disagreements. One of the most tantalizing is imagined between Cardinal Newman, the Victorian religious writer, and Rudolf Carnap, the twentieth-century logician:

> The conception of rationality of a John Cardinal Newman is obviously quite different from that of a Rudolf Carnap. It is highly unlikely that either could have convinced the other, had they lived at the same time and been able to meet. (RTH, p. 136)

Putnam re-imagines Carnap and Newman in an essay entitled 'Beyond Historicism' (R&R, pp. 287–303). The essay explains further why the disagreement is unresolvable, and also why unresolvable disagreement is compatible with truth and reason. Putnam is expounding why positivism is inadequate. He shows how positivism fails to overcome Catholicism in a dialogue, a generalised dialogue like Carnap versus Newman. The issue is language, rather than character. There are two languages, formalised and systematic: Lrc and Lp. In Lrc, there is a true sentence, 'God exists'. The positivist language excludes the sentence 'God exists', and the positivist tries to win the game. The positivist accepts that Lrc says 'God exists', and that Lrc has rules to explain the meaning. But the positivist believes 'God exists' is 'vacuously confirmable' (R&R, p. 289), an empty definition, because there are no sense data to support it. The Catholic replies that sense data are not required, not under the Catholic system: positivist procedures only apply to positivist claims. No rule is 'applicable to all language systems'. Putnam intervenes to support the Catholic, negatively. No-one is forced to accept someone else's rules as neutral, as universal: 'There is no reason for the Roman Catholic, speaking his language, to "admit" that "God exists" means what the positivist says it means.'

The dialogue continues. Now the positivist replies that Catholic ideas are 'not clear'. But clarity is not neutral; it depends on your whole approach. Clarity is 'being persuasively redefined' by the positivist. Then the roles reverse, and the Catholic advances. He has an aim, serving God. The positivist is baffled, since the aim 'isn't expressible' according to positivism, it makes no sense. But it makes sense for the Catholic. The disagreement is unresolvable, and, specifically, positivism fails to refute Catholicism, positivist language cannot incorporate Catholicism, and, therefore, Catholicism is not refuted by an idiom which fails to comprehend it.

Isn't the upshot relativism, that each idea exists in its own language? Not so. Absolute verdicts are impossible, but criticism is practicable. Positivism has unrealistic expectations. No-one can refute another view satisfactorily if refutation must be absolute, based on uncontestable rules. But refutation need not be so grand, so final. The rules will be part of the dialogue, not outside the dialogue. And we can evaluate ideas as they interact. Of course, the evaluation will not bring agreement. It does not make sense to ask these parties to seek agreement, nor will anyone reconcile them. The viewpoints are disjunct, legitimately. But we can judge the people who hold them from the way they hold them. We can make a judgement of human characteristics like consistency and balance, attentiveness and coherence. A viewpoint may excite unbalanced propositions, it may make its protagonist impatient towards information. Then we can criticise, we can look elsewhere for a reliable standpoint. But we will not be applying a rule, internalised by reason, particularly not a rule above the perspective of human interaction. On the contrary, we will be employing psychological intuition as well as logic. And these judgements lead towards truth, another step, a hint, a hope.

Habermas prohibits this quandary by indicating a procedure for participants to follow in rational discussion. But Putnam sees a deeper problem for the discursive resolution of controversies:

> The question: *which is the rational conception of rationality itself* is difficult in *exactly* the way that the justification of an ethical system is difficult. There is no *neutral* conception of rationality to which to appeal. (RTH, p. 136)

Rationality is fundamentally contested in Putnam's theory. There is no external model to determine what is rational in any disagreement where rationality itself is disputed. Yet we have seen that Putnam endorses the validity of 'facts' and 'truth', and he is optimistic about the function of argument itself. Putnam is no relativist, despite his conception of unresolvable disputes.

He considers some compromises where disputes will not resolve, only to dismiss them:

> One might attempt various conventionalist moves here, e.g. saying that 'justified/Carnap' is one 'property' and 'justified/Newman' is a different 'property', and that a 'subjective value judgment' is involved in the decision to mean 'justified/

> Carnap' or 'justified/Newman' by the word 'justified' but that no value judgment is
> involved in stating the fact that a given statement S is justified/Carnap or
> justified/Newman. But from whose standpoint is the word 'fact' being used? (RTH, p.
> 136)

He is pondering the possibility that each might determine what the facts are from
one viewpoint, within a larger definition of fact. A kind of objectivity would
emerge, an objectivity about the identity of each system. But Putnam resists this
compromise: who is to decide on this larger definition of a fact? There cannot be
a neutral description of the two viewpoints.

Putnam's theory rests on the denial of neutrality in the conception of rationality. Since different viewpoints exist irreducibly with their differing claims to
rationality, the story has to be told in terms other than an omniscient, impartial
narrative:

> . . . we are left with the necessity of seeing our search for better conceptions of ratio-
> nality as an intentional human activity, which, like every activity that rises above habit
> and the mere following of inclination or obsession, is guided by our idea of the good.
> (RTH, pp. 136–7)

There must be a 'search for better conceptions of rationality', a search which
requires competition between diverse models. True, we cannot absolutely resolve
these conflicts, but they form part of a process of the dialogic testing of rationality itself. The conception of rationality emerges from the complex process of
exchange, rather than acting as a general framework for the particular exchange.

In Putnam's view, reason is capable of being re-shaped and developed within
the search, the debate, even the collision of different views, though this does not
mean that reason can take *any* shape:

> . . . there is no fixed, ahistorical organon which defines what it is to be rational; but I
> don't conclude from the fact that our conceptions of reason evolve in history, that rea-
> son itself can be (or evolve into) *anything*. (RTH, p. x)

Rationality is the goal, and the search for rationality is endless. Yet Putnam is certain that real advances occur in understanding, real progress is made in
knowledge:

> Rationality may not be defined by a 'canon' or set of principles, but we do have an
> evolving conception of the cognitive virtues to guide us. (RTH, p. 163)

'Virtues' brings us to the heart of Putnam's theory, his contribution towards dialogic rationalism. Rationality is not necessarily an orientation towards
agreement – as Habermas would have it – but there are virtues which supply the
proper conduct of rational discussion. That conduct includes the way to argue,
even if it cannot be properly defined. Putnam mentions as possible virtues 'criticism and impartiality', but he is not specifically prescriptive. We *learn* to prefer
some outcomes and the virtues on which they depend.

Putnam picks out strengths and weaknesses in each case:

> Most of us think that Newman's Catholicism was somewhat obsessive; and most
> philosophers think that, brilliant as he was, Carnap employed many weak arguments.
> (RTH, p. 163)

These judgements are provisional. They imply that each party has strengths and limitations, even if neither will admit it. Putnam knows that most people expect a decisive verdict on a polarised argument like that between Newman and Carnap. He insists that we do have relevant standards for judging arguments, but we cannot determine an absolute outcome:

> That we make these judgments shows that we do have a regulative idea of a just, attentive, balanced intellect, and we do think that there is a fact of the matter about why and how particular thinkers fall short of that ideal. (RTH, p. 163)

The very terms of the judgement are provisional; we possess an 'idea' for considering arguments, not an absolute criterion for deciding them; the idea is regulative, not prescriptive. The idea is for an attitude which is 'just', 'balanced' and 'attentive', each term being itself open to discussion. Moreover, each term brings moral and psychological considerations into judging an argument. For Putnam, our standard of rationality derives from such complex values as justice and consideration for others, values which hardly permit sweeping verdicts.

Ambivalence and Intellectual Virtues

Characteristically Putnam admits an objection to his own views on argument which do not lead to a general formula for making judgements:

> Some will say, 'So what; we are no better off when it comes to resolving an actual dispute than if there were no notion of rational acceptability external to the views under debate to which we could appeal!' (RTH, p. 163)

Putnam does not promise to solve the problems of disagreement, and particularly he offers no resolution that depends on being rational. He concedes that many individual disputes are unresolvable, yet these disputes are still potentially meaningful. He makes a paradoxical observation about these disputes:

> This is true when it comes to any one unresolvable dispute such as the Carnap–Newman dispute just imagined; but it is not true that we would be just as well off in the long run if we abandoned the idea that there are really such things as impartiality, consistency, and reasonableness, even if we only approximate them in our lives and practice. (RTH, pp. 163–4)

When many exchanges have occurred, there are cumulatively better outcomes, shifts of emphasis, changes of tone and balance. The presentation of cases may progressively improve. From the unresolved contests, facts do emerge, and Putnam is emphatic about the impact of facts, denying categorically

> the view that there are only subjective beliefs about these things, and no fact of the matter as to which of these 'subjective beliefs' is right. (RTH, p. 164)

Continuing disagreements do not subvert the concept of facts; on the contrary, disagreements help to teach us to take facts seriously, since we need them to present our case and criticise the other view. We learn to respect facts and judgements of facts. It is a long process, but ultimately facts and judgements constitute human truth.

Putnam follows the case of Newman and Carnap with an example from personal experience. He describes the dispute between himself and Robert Nozick, a Harvard colleague, about welfare benefits and the state. Putnam is liberal, he supports state benefits; Nozick objects to the state intervening in those personal areas and maintains it has no right to do so. Putnam describes the impasse with relish:

> In *my* view, *his* fundamental premises – the absoluteness of the right to property, for example – are counterintuitive and not supported by sufficient argument. On *his* view I am in the grip of a 'paternalistic' philosophy which he regards as insensitive to individual rights. This is an extreme disagreement. (RTH, p. 164)

He acknowledges the emotive force of 'the fundamentals on which one cannot agree' – and here emotion becomes central. But there are still possibilities for constructive conduct in a debate which is unresolved provided that 'one sensitively diagnoses and delineates the source of the disagreement' (RTH p. 164). Constructive conduct becomes essential in a situation fraught with ill consequence where

> Each of us regards the other as lacking, at this level, a certain kind of sensitivity and perception. To be perfectly honest, there is in each of us something akin to contempt. (RTH, p. 165)

Putnam concedes that this feeling – so 'akin to contempt' – 'is a painful thing to explore'. The dialogue between Putnam and Nozick is partly rational, insofar as each party presents reasons and faces criticisms. But the reasons involve feelings, which are intense and not easily manageable. Their connections and associations permeate our being, and we can no more separate ourselves from them than we can recapitulate and change the experiences that gave rise to them in the first place. High in the order of this emotional system is self-respect and self-value which motivates us to present our arguments in competition with the arguments of other people. In other words, there is no purely rational solution to such differences as those between Putnam and Nozick – in Putnam's view – and for this very reason emotions must be recognised in the dialogue, because *other emotions* are the main counterbalance to the contempt and dislike that accompany passionate disagreement:

> There is no contradiction between having a fundamental liking and respect for someone and still regarding something in him as an intellectual and moral weakness. (RTH, p. 165)

Liking is the only balance to contempt: neutral reasoning will be insufficient. That is, the best supports during critical disagreement are personal affection, kindness, respect for the other as a person. Putnam sees the dialogue as a *whole relationship*: the parties react to each other as whole individuals, not just as voices speaking for differing views.

Putnam returns to the subject of the virtues required in argument, virtues which will ultimately give the disagreement, among many disagreements, rational significance:

> I want to urge that there is all the difference in the world between an opponent who has the fundamental intellectual virtues of open-mindedness, respect for reason, and self-criticism, and one who does not. (RTH, p. 165)

Even these virtues cannot make deep disagreement comfortable or purely friendly. But if each adversary sees the other as 'an opponent who reasons carefully' instead of one who 'merely gives vent to his feelings' (RTH, p. 166), then they may contain their negative feelings. The ideal is not neutrality, certainly not pure acceptance, but manageable ambivalence:

> And the ambivalent attitude of respectful contempt is an honest one: respect for the intellectual virtues in the other; contempt for the intellectual and emotional weaknesses (according to one's own lights of course, for one always starts with them). (RTH, p. 166)

For Putnam, it is *psychologically* implausible for deep-seated disagreements to be *resolved* through dialogue, because of their emotional sources. But because of this limitation he regards careful reasoning, attempted impartiality and critical judgement as all the more important in argument. These are the virtues that Putnam makes mandatory, and without them there is no hope of any progress at all in disagreement; with them, it is possible to advance understanding. Ambivalence remains the key theme in Putnam's story of argument, which implies a complex interplay of different factors, not a simple contradiction of reason and feeling. Putnam must avoid an antithesis between reason and feeling, having proposed that such feelings as liking and respect support the rational progress of the dialogue.

Dialogue and Truth

I have considered the way Putnam treats unresolvable dialogue on one level only, one which can be observed directly in individual confrontations. But there are factors of a more general and all-embracing kind behind the inability to agree. Ultimately Putnam thinks that it is the nature of knowledge itself and of human language which make our differences insurmountable. For the present context, it is sufficient to consider the fundamental principle that shapes knowledge according to Putnam, a principle which he calls 'internalism':

> Internalism does not deny that there are experiential inputs to knowledge; knowledge is not a story with no constraints except internal coherence; but it does deny that there are any inputs which are not themselves to some extent shaped by our concepts, by the vocabulary we use to report and describe them, or any inputs which admit only of one description, independent of all conceptual choices. (RTH, p. 54)

'Facts' are embedded in ways of thinking; they do not, therefore, settle differences of view. But, once again, it is necessary to add that Putnam is not – for this reason – a relativist, in his own judgement. Ways of thinking are ingrained and there is something irreducible about differences between these ways of thinking, but Putnam believes *some* errors arising from ways of thinking *are* demonstrable:

> Denying that it makes sense to ask whether our concepts 'match' something totally uncontaminated by conceptualization is one thing; but to hold that every conceptual system is therefore just as good as every other would be something else. If anyone really believed that, and if they were foolish enough to pick a conceptual system that told them they could fly and to act upon it by jumping out of a window, they would, if they were lucky enough to survive, see the weakness of the latter view at once. (RTH, p. 54)

Simple experience exposes many errors of thought. Nevertheless, we cannot adjudicate neutrally between rival ways of thinking with knowledge based on experience because knowledge is always acquired using specific vocabularies.

Putnam thinks some judgements are better, some worse; although even where the facts seem clear to 'us', he sees why it may be difficult to convince the other side. We can still advance understanding, though differences are not settled in the process. Coherence and rational acceptability are core values, as long as we also recognise the nature of 'values':

> Our conceptions of coherence and acceptability are, on the view I shall develop, deeply interwoven with our psychology. They depend upon our biology and our culture; they are by no means 'value free'. (RTH, p. 55)

There is no value-free ride to understanding, a premise which has a positive application – constructive and humane values will support us in the quest for understanding – and a cautionary application – our claims to know will never be absolute, in the sense that they cannot transcend our general point of view. Putnam believes in growth through the relevant application of values; of this growth and improvement in understanding he is optimistic, but his optimism is inseparable from conflict:

> We agree with Aristotle that different ideas of human flourishing are appropriate for individuals with different constitutions, but we go further and believe that even in the ideal world there would be different constitutions, that diversity is part of the ideal. And we see some degree of tragic tension between ideals, that the fulfilment of some ideals always excludes the fulfilment of some others. (RTH, p. 148)

Putnam has many voices, not contradictory but complementary, various. The effect is complex, mixed, with different tones and colours. For instance, he does not regard differences as bridgeable, he does not see major conflicts leading towards agreements between the parties. But he does not deny connection, or belittle co-operation. On the contrary, Putnam is as aware of the possibilities in co-operation as Habermas. But he has a more ironic idea about human co-operation. In 'Philosophers and Human Understanding' (R&R, pp. 184–204), he paints a picture of co-operation and conflict. He starts from an older picture, by the philosopher Neurath, who likened science to being in a boat and reconstructing it as you go. Putnam looks beyond science, and he sees reason as 'a fleet of boats' (R&R, p. 204). The fleet co-operates, partly. Some people 'are passing supplies and tools'. People communicate between the boats. Crucially, they are 'shouting advice and encouragement (or discouragement)'! Sometimes people decide to leave one boat and join an alternative. Discouragement may be necessary, if the boat is worthless, and anyway, people just do disagree, so the scene is 'a bit chaotic'. However, the activity is also communicative, dialogic: 'no one is ever totally out of signalling distance.' Anything more orderly, and there are illusions of absolutism; but the fleet is not at war with an enemy fleet, for instance, or among itself. It may not be unified, but it's all one expedition.

To ask for more regularity, means imposing unity on an enterprise which is diverse. Reason is not a unifying force, instead it plays several roles, we can imagine, on its expedition. Reason helps people send signals which can be understood; it provides new ideas; it is both encouraging and discouraging, both connective and disjunctive. What reason cannot do is settle the differences, or become the boat we are all in together. We do not want to be all in the same boat, the good ship *Reason*. And that's because we all think our boat is reason, or many of us do, and we have our reasons. Sometimes one vessel is obviously leaky, and another seems to be heading backwards. Some do move faster, others seem shaky. But there's no big ship *Reason* with the Grand Admiral in it.

Putnam does want reason to resolve differences. He is not being negative, complaining that there is no unifying paradigm to settle disputes. On the contrary, being grown up means having the chance to decide about reason for yourself. If we are supplied with a view of reason, a fixed view, then we are prevented from developing our ideas independently. And independent ideas lead to new advances, as well as disasters or mishaps. To define reason means to pre-empt growth: 'Consensus definitions of reason do not work because consensus among grown-ups presupposes reason rather than defining it' (R&R, p. 240). We may work out some agreements about reason, but only as part of the ongoing search for growth, and against limiting definitions.

So because the argument is about reason, reason cannot resolve the argument. In fact, if we did not have reason to argue about, our differences would be poor, thin soil for new ideas. Which does not mean that some arguments aren't weak, others strong, but it means that we cannot pre-empt the process of sorting out arguments, we cannot establish definitions beforehand that foreclose on thinking. Putnam still believes in truth: some views are true, others are false. Truth must be conceivable, otherwise how do we even know there is an argument going on! Truth is 'a limit verdict' (R&R, p. 246), it makes the difference between a journey with wrong turnings, many routes, and just wandering around. But we can't pre-empt truth, and we can't be sure how reason will develop on the way. We can be pretty sure, Putnam thinks, how reason will not develop, and we have good guidelines; but there is no formula, and it would be reductive to keep seeking agreements on the way.

Conversations about Argument and Dialogue

The Conversation between Habermas and Putnam

Dialogic rationalism identifies a central tendency in the work of both Habermas and Putnam, a tendency and also a common hope. Both theorists defend reason against alternatives such as traditional authority, pure subjectivity and mere opinion. Both hope for rational progress, progress in understanding and in society. Neither thinks that *science* defines reason: science is not the model for rationality in all areas of life. Both Habermas and Putnam deny that science has guaranteed a privileged and exclusive status for strategic calculation or instrumental rationality. They consider dialogue and argument better models for general reasoning than science, though both have a high regard for science as *part* of reason.

In Habermasian terms, Putnam's answer is too provisional, leaving too many unanswered questions. In Putnam's terms, Habermas's answer is too comprehensive, leaving too few problems visible. But both thinkers are bringing dialogue to the rescue of reason; they are both central to a search for dialogic rationalism. The basic source of the difference is their conceptions of *dialogue* and the potentialities in dialogue for agreement, rather than differences in their conception of reason. Each endorses the progress of modern rationality, with similar reservations. Each distinguishes logical criteria and also criteria of practical effectiveness. Both then refer to dialogue as a more humane basis for reason than science or instrumental calculation. Habermas offers a rigorous, a definitive, model of dialogue, one in which language itself constrains the participants to be rational through the requirement of 'yes/no' responses. Putnam offers looser observations, centring on the theme of unresolvable disputes. His terms are more psychological than linguistic.

Dialogic rationalism has diverse sources, conflicting sources even. In my view, this diversity gives strength and adds potential. Rationalism need not be one programme, a fixed prescription. Dialogue opens rationalism to different possibilities. Dialogic rationalism cannot be reduced to a monologue itself, or a single formula, without being self-denying. It necessarily leads to diversity. However, this diversity is not always recognised by individual contributors, nor always acceptable. Habermas contributes the most comprehensive vision to dialogic rationalism; but he also offers complete solutions, which is inconsistent with the central premise of dialogic rationalism, that rationality is a composition of differences, a balanced interaction, an ongoing exchange. If it were possible to develop one unitary system, then the dialogue would be secondary, reduced to explanation and persuasion. But Habermas's own model implies that dialogue is primary: knowledge does not precede the discussion, it is the outcome. Why then should the theory be an exception? Certainly he acknowledges other viewpoints, but he often uses them so that they no longer serve the purpose for which they were proffered.

Putnam's model of dialogue and argument does not privilege agreement. His theory recognises unresolved problems in his own account of the world. Indeed his writings seem to evolve from dialogues between opposing viewpoints. He represents other viewpoints without adjusting them to his own premises. But he underrates some of the concessions he makes, and the damage and difficulty they cause for his case, particularly when allowing for psychological influences on argument. Is there no other way except to acknowledge feeling as a particular force, for good and for ill, on belief and conduct? Is it not possible to escape from the reason–emotion dichotomy? The dialogue on the nature of argument may extend beyond the limits Putnam has assigned to it!

Habermas and Putnam both privilege argument, and argumentative dialogue. But Habermas interprets argument in terms of agreement, and Putnam interprets argument in terms of irreconcilable division. Putnam also gives emotion a more central role in argument. Dialogic rationalism would develop differently in response to Habermas or to Putnam. However, there are also the other alternative sources for dialogic rationalism, and also neighbouring theories. The search must span disciplines and values, from sociology to ethics, from critical theory to liberal theory.

Billig's Rhetorical Psychology of Arguing

Michael Billig is a critical theorist, as well as a rhetorician and psychologist. In an essay on 'Politics and the Revival of Rhetoric', he proposes 'formulating a critique of present styles of arguing and thinking' (*Ideology and Opinions*, pp. 195–214, 212). Billig values Habermas highly, for recognising 'that any account of communicative action needs to include an adequate theory of argumentation' (*Ideology and Opinions*, p. 206). Billig sees how radical Habermas is, how his theories point to a different world, a world of free arguments. But in other ways, Billig is closer to Putnam. For instance, Billig celebrates Plato's dialogues because the participants do not resolve their differences, and they do not try to agree. Not only do they 'seldom, if ever, resolve anything', but they may show frustration, irritation, human annoyance. Sometimes, the disputants agree a point, but the agreements are temporary, 'what seemed to be agreed upon earlier becomes, at a later point, a topic of dispute' (*Arguing and Thinking*, p. 24). Yet Plato's dialogues present profound theories, theories which thrive amidst unresolved differences.

Billig proposes 'rhetorical psychology', he connects modern theories to classical rhetoric. Rhetorical psychology is about argument, from many points of view: how people argue with others, how thinking is argumentative, why arguments occur, how society relates to argument. Billig illuminates the psychology of unresolved disagreement. He retells a story from the *Avodah Zarah*, a text which is part of the Jewish Talmudic tradition. The Jewish Elders are arguing with the Romans. The issue is idolatry, favoured by Roman religion and prohibited by the Ten Commandments. The Romans begin the debate, by asking 'the reasonable, but tricky, question: Why, if God so disapproves of idolatry, does He not destroy all the idols?' (*Arguing and Thinking*, p. 100). If He is omnipotent, and He is against idol-worship, then surely He should show His power in this way? The Elders reply that God cannot destroy the idols without ending the world, because the idolaters worship 'the sun, moon, stars and planets'! Replies spring to and fro. The rhythm is lively, the reverses are acute.

Of course, the Romans are not converted. They have another question. Admittedly, some idols are also necessary objects; but others are just statues or whatever. Can't God leave the planets alone and just eliminate the statues and dispensable idols? But, reply the Elders, how would idolaters interpret the selective destruction? They would say it proved their point!

> If God destroyed your useless idols, but kept the sun, moon, stars and planets, what would you say? You would, of course, say that these were the true deities, because they had been untouched by the destruction of the idols. (*Arguing and Thinking*, p. 101)

God would have proved the Romans were right! The stroke is brilliant, because the Elders have used the other side's perspective to promote their case. They argue from how the Romans would react to the selective destruction of idols, not how the Jews would react. Billig applies the Renaissance term 'witcraft' to applaud both sides of the argument, and particularly the latest twist.

The Hebrew text ends with the Romans silent. They have nothing else to say. But surely the Romans are not persuaded – not even the source credits the Elders with that victory, making the other side agree. In fact, agreement is completely implausible in the dispute. The views are too systematic and too different – one thinks again of Newman and Carnap. Billig notes that the Elders 'would not have entertained the hope, nor even the wish, that they might convert the Romans' (*Arguing and Thinking*, p. 106). Nor are the Romans interested in persuading the Elders. There isn't the faintest hint of any 'orientation to agreement', however idealised or remote. There isn't even any tendency to force the other side to agree! It is as if Newman and Carnap met, and debated without even wanting to convince each other, like Lp and Lrc in Putnam's essay.

Billig speculates that the Romans would have told another story. They would have had more to add. He also wonders whether the Roman was woken next night by awkward insights, too late as usual to carry the argument: 'Why did I not reply: if your God does not wish to destroy the useful or the useless idols, then why, oh why, does He not destroy us useless idolaters?' (*Arguing and Thinking*, p. 109). The fantasy is familiar, all too familiar; I *should* have said it. But even the fantasy of verbal cunning does not add: and then the other side give in. Billig is celebrating a dispute, unresolved by agreement, which could not conceivably lead to understanding. No-one is really trying to understand the other side, only to invent a quick reply. No-one imagines agreement, compromise, even convergence.

In fact, agreement would be a huge disappointment, no more chance to invent new arguments. Like Putnam and Nozick, they have ambivalent feelings towards one another, liking and contempt. Could people find each other so challenging and not have some liking, suppressed perhaps? Certainly, the two sides seem to respect each other: 'Neither side is accusing the other of being illogical' (*Arguing and Thinking*, p. 101). Moreover, neither side resorts to 'specialist knowledge' (p. 103): no-one says, we are better than you, we know more, and that's that: they would lose the opportunity to think of a really good reply.

The argument is an opportunity, to think new ideas, to display 'witcraft'. Billig illuminates the motives for arguing when no agreement is possible. The Elders and the Romans are both seeking 'for the last word' (*Arguing and Thinking*, p. 106), at least to let the other side not have the final say! The last word becomes a criterion of value. But of course, there is no last word. The arguing is a paradox, a psychological paradox: the harder the Romans and Elders try to have the last word, the more difficult it gets to end the argument. The Talmud lets the Elders have the final line, but the Romans would not agree. We can tell that from the rhythm, the pattern, the energy in their replies. Maybe not today, but tomorrow, they will be back: you know you said that, well what about this? The last word is 'an unending pursuit' (p. 110). Another Talmudic text re-examines the Elders' last word against the Romans: good enough for the occasion, but there are other ideas (p. 109). Billig's psychology of the last word is important: he gives psychological meaning to unresolvable arguments, meaning which complements and deepens Putnam's examples.

Dialogic rationalism needs to consider psychology: why people argue, why they differ, when they might agree and when they will never agree. Neither Habermas nor Putnam is a sufficient source for psychological insights of that quality: the paradox of the last word is one significant contribution to the psychology of argument. Of course, there can be no single psychology of argument. As Billig also says, arguing has many motives, many emotions are relevant, many relationships develop. Pride and conceit may determine responses, so may fear, or love, as Giddens shows. Sometimes, there is 'ill-will' and 'such feelings give rise to sharp debates' (*Arguing and Thinking*, p. 84); but anger also ends arguments, doors bang, and worse may follow. No formula accounts for the reasons why people argue, nor for the ways they argue. Indeed motives can be part of the argument, a subject of dispute: Newman might accuse Carnap of vanity or arrogance, Carnap might accuse Newman of dismissing science because it is new, demanding, difficult.

Dialogic rationalism must tell good stories about argument, plausible and also gripping stories: otherwise the point of argument is lost. Further, reason cannot be endorsed by overlooking emotions. Reason may influence dialogue, but the dialogue must also be human, and accessible to the range of motivation. Putnam is good at stories of argument which convey the sense of people in their situation, and Billig's story of the Jews and the Romans resonates profoundly with everyday experience.

Argument can still involve truth. There is no need for story to exclude truth, even stories about emotional motives and disagreements. Psychologically, no word is the last word: the other side can always invent new arguments. In an essay on 'Ideology, Rhetoric and Opinions', Billig recalls Protagoras, the Greek sophist, who observed that 'On every issue, on which opinions are put forward, a counter-opinion can be formulated with equal rhetorical force as the original view' (*Ideology and Opinions*, p. 24). We need not assume the views are equally valid. Certainly, the arguers assume the very reverse: they believe some views are true, others are false. Indeed the reversals have no meaning, unless one side might be right, the other wrong, or at least some ideas better and others less good. The point of the stories is that we may discover the truth, that is why we keep following. Psychologically, arguing has no last word; but truth may be part of the process, the search.

Psychology will not settle questions which are otherwise insoluble. To see argument psychologically makes things more complex, more interesting, more human. As Billig observes, psychology is arguable itself, and he advises 'if one psychological principle appears reasonable, then try reversing it, in order to see whether its contrary is just as reasonable' (*Arguing and Thinking*, p. 11). The principle applies well to Habermas and Putnam on arguing! The only problem with either view is if it seeks to exclude the other.

Rawls and Disagreements

Putnam is a liberal. The contrast with Habermas is partly a contrast between liberalism and critical theory. Habermas emphasises social forces. He also concentrates on alienation, on the deep-rooted ills of modernity. Putnam is dialogic, but also more individualistic. Some liberals contrast with Putnam, notably Rawls who advocates neutrality because disagreement is unresolvable, the issues are too profound. Rawls proposes contexts which are neutral, contexts where disputes are regulated by neutral standards. The result is *neutral liberalism* as a basis for 'political culture'. 'Culture' suggests unity, but 'political' suggests diversity, difference and, indeed, Rawls balances unity and difference:

> The political culture of a democratic society is always marked by a diversity of opposing and irreconcilable religious, philosophical and moral doctrines. Some of these are perfectly reasonable, and this diversity among reasonable doctrines political liberalism sees as the inevitable long-run result of the powers of human reason at work within the background of enduring free institutions. (*Political Liberalism*, pp. 3–4)

Some views are not reasonable. The unreasonable views cannot participate constructively in democratic discussion, which makes Rawls's conception of argument much narrower than Putnam's. Putnam emphasises the gaps between conceptions of rationality itself. But Rawls thinks reasonable views do overlap, not in their conclusions but in their ways of being reasonable. And there are enough reasonable views to sustain a political culture, in a healthy society, enough people who share the same reasonable procedures.

Rawls aims to connect the reasonable views. He hopes reasonable people will converge towards a common ground. He hopes to reduce disagreement within a charmed circle that circumscribes reasonable opinion, and this has political consequences:

> The aim of justice as fairness, then, is practical: it presents itself as a conception of justice that may be shared by citizens as a basis of a reasoned, informed, and willing political agreement. It expresses their shared and public political reason. (*Political Liberalism*, p. 9)

Reason is interactive, reason is shared. But the model is only minimally dialogic. There is little to say about differing as a process, except curtail it:

> . . . we hope we can gain the support of an overlapping consensus of reasonable religious, philosophical, and moral doctrines. (*Political Liberalism*, p. 10)

Rawls is worried about disagreement, particularly as regards its political consequences. Consider the language, 'we hope . . . gain the support': Rawls knows enlightened parties must be persuasive, and his advice is to be persuasive quickly.

Yet Rawls is important to the conversation about reason and dialogue, about argument. He seeks rational interaction; reason is shared, overlaps individuals and parties, connects differing viewpoints. He is interested by disagreement, though anxiously: 'how might reasonable disagreement come about?' (*Political Liberalism*, p. 55). The tone is puzzled: because Rawls believes reason is constant, continuous, there are basic rules for it, he is genuinely perplexed by the fact of reasonable views which differ from one another. Why should the same reason produce different answers?

> Let's say that reasonable disagreement is disagreement between reasonable persons . . . they share a common human reason, similar powers of thought and judgment: they can draw inferences, weight evidence, and balance competing considerations. (*Political Liberalism*, p. 55)

Rawls sees difference as awkward, though natural. If reason were more comprehensive, differences would shrink. Dialogue fills in the gaps, where reason is insufficient to resolve issues. He puts the question negatively. Instead of asking why dialogue is constructive, he asks why disagreement is endemic and dialogue necessary: 'What, then, goes wrong?' What is 'wrong' is partly that the world is too complicated for human reason:

> a. The evidence – empirical and scientific – bearing on the case is conflicting and complex, and thus hard to assess and evaluate.

Reasonable people can fail to understand the facts, and so they disagree. The facts are ambiguous, science is limited. Moreover, people are subjective. They apply values to the facts:

> b. Even where we agree fully about the kinds of considerations that are relevant, we may disagree about their weight, and so arrive at different judgments.

Rawls is also fascinated by the ills of reason, the gaps in reason. The causes of reasonable disagreement are many:

> c.´ To some extent all our concepts, and not only moral and political concepts, are vague and subject to hard cases . . .
> d. To some extent (how great we cannot tell) the way we assess evidence and weigh moral and political values is shaped by our total experience. (*Political Liberalism*, pp. 56–7)

The list is long, the slippages are endless.

Rawls concedes that argument is inevitable. But he hopes to limit public argument. He does not believe in suppression or repression: on the contrary; but he believes public argument will not solve problems, and he fears too much argument may undermine political stability. He wants people to privatise their disagreements. Let individuals, groups and factions work out their differences outside the public arena. The state must not be a forum for dispute. The point is to establish a firm consensus among those who have reached reasonable positions, and let the differences play round it.

Rawls's problem is how to achieve the 'firm overlapping consensus' between those who have achieved reasonable positions. He seems to think the consensus is natural: reasonable views just do overlap, by being reasonable. But he also thinks one group ('we') must 'gain support' for the consensus, though he denounces rhetoric and mere persuasion. Should he not take argument more seriously, since his proposals point towards it? He could be more constructive about disagreement when it is required in his analysis. At the least, he could consider how to gain support without disrupting social amity by challenging other viewpoints. Rawls contributes a caution: disagreement is risky, as well as animating. But the caution is taken to excess, because disagreement is regarded as too uniformly dangerous to the public peace.

Giddens on Argument and Dialogue

In the previous chapter, dealing with reason, Giddens appeared as a thinker who valued enlightenment, but who was also conscious that a scientific and critical attitude has severe limitations. Giddens introduced a need for trust, and he endorsed the emergence of life politics to connect new interpersonal trust with new social structures. He seeks to humanise reason, and he also values dialogue, as a source of improvement in human affairs. But for Giddens, argument is not the model dialogue, though arguments are important. For him, dialogue is underpinned by relationships.

Giddens advocates 'the pure relationship'. He does not mean traditional 'purity', and he uses 'pure' provocatively, to challenge tradition. Traditionally, individuals are 'pure' if they are innocent, free from 'stain'. Conventional purity is about being separate, apart, out of contact. Giddens reinterprets purity to mean a good interaction, not an individual merit: purity becomes dialogic. The irony is profound. Giddens takes the virtue which meant 'apart', 'above', 'untarnished', the purity which meant not-related, and changes 'pure' to mean 'involved', 'engaged', 'open'. Purity comes of age as interaction, in Giddens's language, and the result is dialogue. When is a relationship pure? When the dialogue is intimate, an ideal communication, through loving contact. The 'pure relationship' is not the antithesis of romance, it has romantic origins:

> The rise of romantic love provides a case-study of the origins of the pure relationship. . . . Romantic love presumes that a durable emotional tie can be established with the other on the basis of qualities intrinsic to that tie itself. It is the harbinger of the pure relationship, although it also stands in tension with it. (*Intimacy*, p. 2)

Romantic love embodies the romantic movement. Romantic love is problematic, it is contradictory, yet also hopeful. The hope is 'a durable emotional tie . . . with the other', a tie which is self-sustaining, 'on the basis of qualities intrinsic to that tie itself'. The self-sustaining relationship is valid, though the nineteenth-century ideal of romance was flawed. Romantic love prefigures the ideal communication, the intimate dialogue. Ideal exchange is a remedy for thwarted lives, an ideal with roots in psychological history. Putnam is about how people disagree; Giddens is about how people are different. Yet Putnam's disagreements involve psychological differences, and Giddens's trust can withstand disagreements.

Giddens thinks dialogically: he starts with interaction, relationship. Virtue is discovered in relationships. But individuality is central even in the relationship. For Giddens, a keyword is 'autonomy': people need to be autonomous within personal relationships, within dialogues. Autonomy requires the self-aware construction of identity; a person is autonomous who exercises reflexivity, who lives through self-reflectiveness. But autonomy is the basis for a good interaction, not isolation. The autonomous self is integrated, and a true individuality is expressed by inter-relation.

Autonomy also has social and cultural aspects. People can be autonomous only in a favourable culture:

> Autonomy means the capacity of individuals to be self-reflective and self-determining: 'to deliberate, judge, choose, and act upon different possible courses of action'. . . . Clearly autonomy in this sense could not be developed while political rights and obligations were closely tied to tradition and fixed prerogatives of property. Once these were dissolved, however, a movement towards autonomy became both possible and seen to be necessary. (*Intimacy*, p. 185, citing Held)

If choice is impossible, autonomy is impossible. Choice derives from society, from institutions, from values. For Giddens, choice is rational: 'deliberate, judge, choose . . .'. And rationality is interactive, rationality is about association between people:

> An overwhelming concern with how individuals might best determine and regulate the conditions of their association is characteristic of virtually all interpretations of modern democracy. (*Intimacy*, p. 185)

In an authentic democracy, individuals create rational associations, and rational associations encourage free individuality. The model is the 'pure relationship', the intimate democracy. Autonomy is the lesson which personal experience makes available to politics. Politics needs to recognise autonomy. Authority must respect people: only respectful power is legitimate. Often, respect is lacking: powerful politicians are bullies, institutions are sinister. Giddens believes we should demand autonomy as a missing right, and not accept public treatment violating our autonomy, our selfhood, the 'project of the self'. So authority must justify itself anew, to autonomous and self-reflexive individuals. Giddens proposes to renew democracy on the basis of the pure relationship, and its deepest dialogue.

Therefore, in Giddens's view, argument is not the first term, the starting-point for responding to differences. Yet pure relationships are about difference, different identities in harmony. Politically, argument is central to hope of improved conditions. Giddens needs argument, because argument is the political equivalent of intimate dialogue. Argument guarantees autonomy, in the political context:

> Authority is justifiable to the degree that it recognises the principle of autonomy; in other words, to the extent to which defensible reasons can be given as to why compliance enhances autonomy, either now or in the future. Constitutional authority can be understood as an implicit contract which has the same form as conditions of association explicitly negotiated between equals. (*Intimacy*, p. 186)

Authority must argue, and so dialogue is essential, dialogue about reasons. Openness is the intimate virtue, and in politics openness means fair argument, honest self-defence, responding to objections:

> A forum for open debate has to be provided. Democracy means discussion, the chance for the 'force of the better argument' to count as against other means of determining decisions (of which the most important are policy decisions). (*Intimacy*, p. 186)

The forum is argumentative, a place where people seek the better argument. The theory is subtle. Private relationships are dialogic rather than argumentative; but the dialogue is about differences between autonomous individuals none the less. Public interaction is dialogic and argumentative, and it should preserve the rights of individuals to be autonomous. Every interaction must be open, but openness is different in different contexts, at different levels of private and public relations.

The problem of individuality, and of democracy, is learning to accommodate others, and argument is one technique for achieving this:

> The conduct of open discussion is itself a means of democratic education: participation in debate with others can lead to the emergence of a more enlightened citizenry. . . . A politically educated contributor to dialogue is able to channel her or his emotions in a

positive way: to reason from conviction rather than engage in ill thought through polemics or emotional diatribes. (*Intimacy*, pp. 186–7)

Giddens values 'the better argument' and 'open discussion'. But he returns to emotion quickly, emotions are fundamental: the role of debate is 'to channel ...emotions in a positive way'. However, Giddens goes further; he regards debate as general education, emotional growth. It is the personal growth which is the end, rather than the debate. Argument is not just an emotional entanglement: in a profound sense, argument has emotional results, and those results are just as important as the intellectual outcome in Giddens's view. In arguing, we learn to control emotions, to use feelings constructively, to be more creative, less destructive.

For Giddens, intellectual debate is not the model dialogue, and democracy does not model itself on pure intellectual discussion. Instead, the model for democratic procedure is intimate dialogue, a romantic paradigm of communication:

> The possibility of intimacy means the promise of democracy. . . . We can envisage the development of an ethical framework for a democratic personal order, which in sexual relationships and other personal domains conforms to a model of confluent love. . . . In the arena of personal life, autonomy means the successful realisation of the reflexive project of self – the condition of relating to others in an egalitarian way. (*Intimacy*, pp. 188–89)

Like Habermas, Giddens stresses 'egalitarian' interaction. But the true equals he has in mind are intimate companions, lovers who bring their standards into being citizens. Citizenship must be relearnt from intimate relationships, in which the partners are self-conscious agents, constructing their own projects together ('confluent') in a fair arena, so that their relationships are rationalised. That rationality may be in a romantic context, suggesting the description 'rationalised romanticism'; but love and trust are basic values in whose context reason makes sense. As in intimate relations, so in public affairs, the first factor in democracy is trust, not argument: arguments are creative in a climate of trust, but arguments do not create trust. Argument in a pure relationship will not be exploitative or compulsive; and argument will be fair in a democracy modelled on pure relationships, instead of a society expressing the addictions of power-seekers. Here Giddens converges with Habermas and his vision of unconstrained relationships in argument leading towards consensus. Giddens puts more emphasis on the emotional context of relationships, their psychological climate, than other rationalists: rational dialogue is not a primary value except where trust is reciprocated, where emotions are in balance. Rational dialogue is still an ideal, and Giddens endorses justification, and the better argument, open debate, the exchanging of reasons. But rational dialogue is part of a larger whole, and the central image is the pure relationship with its recognition of feelings and trust in the other.

Giddens raises important questions which advance the search for a dialogic rationalism. How would we relate argumentative dialogue and intimate colloquy? Should dialogic rationalism be part of a wider project? The only answer is to develop the conversation, the dialogue, about rationality just as we have to do when considering consensus-seeking argument and perpetual controversy, and recognising the points at which the interplay is creative. Such is the value, the intellectual and the human value, of dialogue between parties who disagree and are prepared to argue on equal terms.

Tannen's Linguistic Theory

A feminist theory, with elements of liberal and critical theories, is proposed by Deborah Tannen. She also values intimate dialogue, like Giddens, but sees women as more likely to conduct intimate dialogues, whereas men are more likely to have competitive dialogues:

> *Intimacy* is key in a world of connection where individuals negotiate complex networks of friendship, minimize differences, try to reach consensus, and avoid the appearance of superiority, which would highlight differences. In a world of status, *independence* is key, because a primary means of establishing status is to tell others what to do, and taking orders is a marker of low status. Though all humans need both intimacy and independence, women tend to focus on the first and men on the second. (*You Just Don't Understand*, p. 26)

Men also need intimacy, and women do compete: the distinction between them is fluid. But on the whole, Tannen distinguishes different dialogues towards which men and women are disposed, and different criteria for dialogues, and she sees the use of argument as one criterion of difference between men and women. In many contexts, argument is not appropriate:

> Women tend to show understanding of another woman's feelings. When men try to reassure women by telling them that their situation is not so bleak, the women hear their feelings being belittled or discounted. (*You Just Don't Understand*, p. 59)

Tannen contrasts empathy to argument and finds empathy to be most often a disposition of women. Her work cautions against overvaluing argumentative dialogue, particularly when emotion is the issue. Good dialogue can also seek similarity and connection:

> For most women, the language of conversation is primarily a language of rapport: a way of establishing connections and negotiating relationships. Emphasis is placed on displaying similarities and matching experiences. (*You Just Don't Understand*, p. 77)

In other words, to adopt and revise Habermas's terms, communicative rationality need not be critical. Consensus does not have to be won through conflict. Is there not another style of communication based on deeper empathy? Tannen warns against overrating particular ways of arguing:

> Many women's tendency to use personal experience and examples, rather than abstract argumentation, can be understood from the perspective of their orientation to language as it is used in private speaking. (*You Just Don't Understand*, p. 91)

Sociological questions arise. How are these differences constructed? How comprehensive are Tannen's observations? She herself qualifies the general claims about the differences between men and women. The suggestion remains: argument is only one model of the good dialogue, even of rational dialogue. There is also empathy. The problem is to connect different forms of communication, involving agreement and disagreement, empathy and argument.

Sheldon, Goodwin and Gender Differences in Argument.

Amy Sheldon considers 'Gender differences in dispute management' ('Pickle Fights', p. 83). The differences are complex. Using studies of children, Sheldon argues that 'Male speech can be characterized as competition oriented or adversarial' (p. 87). By contrast, 'female speech can be characterized as collaboration oriented, or affiliative'. The examples suggest the contrast is subtle, between different ways of pursuing both conflict and connection. Boys use 'more heavy-handed dispute tactics' (p. 98), girls have other ways 'to elaborate on their resistance to each other's opposition' (p. 97). The stereotypes are tricky. In the present context, though, it is notable that the question must arise: are men and women encouraged to handle disputes differently? And do the theories of argument inadvertently represent a bias?

Perhaps the most interesting move is to consider the models of argument proposed by the theories. Following Sheldon, Habermas's theory would be a complex blend of expectations associated with boys and with girls. The girls are more likely to seek agreement, Sheldon observes, following Gilligan ('Pickle Fights', p. 89). They seek 'understanding and communication'. The boys offer 'reasons from a principle to resolve conflict' (p. 90). Communicative action includes both facets. But the theory benefits from reflecting on the gender associations.

Gender studies show how the tactics of argument are various. Marjorie Harness Goodwin contrasts male and female teenagers in Chicago. The teenagers share a black cultural context, but it appears the boys and girls approach disputes differently. The boys confront each other directly, in sequences of 'challenge or threat' ('Tactical Uses of Stories', p. 113). They create consensus against one another (p. 118). The girls pursue more oblique tactics, 'reported deeds of absent parties' (p. 127). The result is a different 'trajectory of disputes'. The phrase illuminates the contrast between single-minded theories of argument and heterogeneous dialogue.

How could one model of argument be adequate, when in the world arguing is so diverse? In a Chicago neighbourhood, there thrive two modes: the boys 'engender disagreements that permit contesting in the immediate setting', the girls prepare the way with reports and plans, and they then use 'indirect, rather than direct, speech' in the conflict ('Tactical Uses of Stories', pp. 128–9). How could theory be uniform in a world so finely various? A dialogic theory cannot be narrower than the range of its dialogues.

Rhetorical Perspective: Towards 'Double Arguability'

There are many questions about dialogic rationalism. How far can dialogue be relied on to support reason? Will some dialogue not undermine reason? Is rational dialogue the best model of the good dialogue? There are also problems about the relationship between the different theories which might resource dialogic rationalism. Their diversity should be enabling, but it could be disruptive. Yet, in my view, dialogic rationalism has strong roots. It may be possible to reformulate reason. Dialogue may provide a new understanding of reason, one which connects reason with human communication. Science loses its exclusive dominion of-reason, without being rejected. A democratic vista appears within which many hopes and beliefs can flourish.

Different conceptions of argument involve varying kinds of personal involvement. These have already been shown to be multifarious and include personal reactions which overlap with those in intimate relationships, loving relationships and connections of trust. The emotional context may vary from aggression to empathy, and different backgrounds may influence the context. Many possible requirements have already been noted in passing: impartiality, the pursuit of agreement, mutual respect, self-control, imagination. The value and nature of argument is itself arguable, on any occasion as well as in theory. Double arguability is inescapable; argument itself can always be a subject of further debate and reinterpretation. On any occasion, the issue may arise: how much ill-feeling is permissible within the dialogue? How much anger can be absorbed? An emotion is constructive on one occasion, disruptive on another. Different parties interpret emotions differently, as well as ideas. The interaction is a field for further interpretation and judgement. The question even arises: when is arguability itself creative? When is it a distraction? Injustice may lead to arguments, or it may spark off reactions that hinder arguability. When it is assumed that double arguability is a constant potential in argument, the study of argument is enlarged, and the field of theory opened to include many ordinary occasions.

The central question is hope, the hope that rational progress is compatible with humane diversity. If reason is dialogic, then a rational society may also be dialogic. How far can a dialogic understanding of reason redeem the ideals of the good society, the good life? Does dialogue present a rational path to the good life? The conversation intensifies.

Notes

1 Habermas's reference to experience necessarily produces the type of response most effectively expressed by Richard Bernstein: 'However sympathetic one may be to the basic intuition that underlies Habermas's theory of communicative action, . . .' (Bernstein, *Beyond Objectivism and Relativism*, [Oxford: Basil Blackwell, 1983], p. 192).

2 'A problem with attempting to derive a universal ethic from these considerations, however, is that one's opponent may *not* claim that his ethical beliefs are rational. Indeed, if he is a "non-cognitivist", he may deny that *any* ethical beliefs are or could be rational' (Putnam, *The Many Faces of Realism* [La Salle, Illinois: Open Court, 1987], pp. 55–6).

3 Deanna Kuhn, *The Skills of Argument* (Cambridge: Cambridge University Press, 1991), p. 117.

4 The force of the claim appears in David Rasmussen's reformulation. He finds in Habermas the idea that 'One finds the very structure of communicative discourse to be emancipatory' (David M. Rasmussen, *Reading Habermas* [Oxford: Basil Blackwell, 1990], p. 6). So, oppression cannot be authentic communication.

5 A major influence is the hermeneutic philosophy of Hans-Georg Gadamer. In *Truth and Method* (London: Sheed and Ward, 1975), Gadamer is clearer about the power of necessity inside true exchange, though his necessity is more comprehensive (p. 345): 'We say that we "conduct" a conversation, but the more fundamental a conversation is, the less its conduct lies within the will of either partner.'

4

Arguing 'the Good Life'

Reason and 'the Good Life'

> Given two points greatly distant from each other . . . it is wished to establish railway
> communication . . . two other points also greatly distant from each other . . . [are]
> human happiness and human society. . . . The engineer for connecting human soci-
> ety with human happiness, otherwise called 'statesman' is nowhere to be had.

> (*Westminster Review* October 1848)

There have been many ideals of the good society and 'the good life', some rational, others anti-rational. Recently, reason has not seemed an obvious source for a
plan of the good life, the good society: rationalist blueprints for a better world are
discredited. *Dialogic* rationalism belongs to a search for new hope of a rational
ideal and a humane society. The wider context of these new hopes is given in
Seyla Benhabib's demand that: 'the stark opposition between political utopi-
anism and political realism . . . be rejected' (*Situating the Self*, p. 49): there must
be an idealistic basis for any constructive response to our problems. I will examine first how Habermas considers argument contributes to the good life in line
with his overall theory. Putnam also considers the good life a necessary aim, but
Habermas and Putnam diverge, as sources for dialogic rationalism, because they
put forward contrasting models of argument. Habermas links argument to agreement, which will lead to a better life; whereas Putnam considers many arguments
unresolvable, and looks for a way through dissension to the good life. Giddens
offers an alternative which is close to Habermas, an alternative critical theory with
overlapping concepts. I also consider other liberal theories, notably Rawls, theories which introduce other views regarding dialogue, reason and the good life. My
aim is to continue the conversation between theories, to extend the conversation
about reason, dialogue and the good life.

Habermas uses his idea of argument to address practical questions, questions
about how people live and about how societies are organised. 'Communicative
Action' is not ultimately about discussion, talk or language. The ultimate subjects
are society and human actions in their social context. Habermas does not merely
catalogue these actions and contexts, he evaluates them. His theory produces
criteria for judging a society, an activity, an institution, an ideology. Naturally, he
adds qualifications to the theory when applying it. He knows that standards for
judgements are complex when experience is targeted. He offers an approach for
judging society, but no easy mechanism for deciding what social requirements are
best. From one point of view, his approach opens on an extensive vista, which
indicates how compelling his visionary system can be, even if it is sometimes
self-denying as a dialogic venture:

> But the attempt to provide an equivalent for what was once intended by the idea of the good life should not mislead us into deriving this idea from the formal concept of reason which modernity's decentered understanding of the world has left us. (CA1, pp. 73–4)

Habermas is embracing reason for society, not reason as modern societies understand it, reason as abstract procedure, calculation or exclusively scientific method. He shifts reason into the context of living, living in communities. Here indeed Habermas's theory stakes its claim as 'the attempt to provide an equivalent for what was once intended by the idea of the good life'. Dialogic rationalism needs this energy of vision, the strong claim. This is the heart of a project: argument is central to this 'attempt' to identify the good life.

Once again we can see that Habermas is complex as a contributor towards dialogic rationalism. The form is elaborate, sometimes rigid, but the content draws on imagination and is powered by the thrust of imagination. For how can we picture the good life without a leap of imagination? The call on imagination is the stronger since Habermas presents no systematic blueprint for his ideal society; one might say no limiting blueprint which shores up the shapes of existing institutions. The good life is not a theme which belongs to abstract discussion. It has meaning only in terms of experience. The particular task of imagination will be to proceed from our experience, and particularly our experience of *argument*, to connect that experience with other worlds that come into view through argument and only through argument conducted in an appropriate fashion, new modes beyond the reach of a single understanding, or an isolated experience. In short, dialogic rationalism has to call upon the argumentative imagination in order to establish its ideas of the good life. But Habermas has elsewhere made clear his need to separate philosophy and literature, theory and narrative – a separation at odds with post-structuralist movements:

> Literary criticism and philosophy have a family resemblance to literature – and to this extent to one another as well – in their rhetorical achievements. But their family relationship stops right there, for in each of these enterprises the tools of rhetoric are subordinated to the discipline of a *distinct* form of argumentation. (PDM, p. 209–10)

Will that part of his theory not suppress the imaginative powers which are required for its necessary extension into life? The good life is an enriching and necessary theme for Habermas, but also a troubling one.

Putnam also tackles the good life as a fundamental issue, integral to his theory of reason. Whereas Habermas is systematic, Putnam is personal. He states his own position on the good life and it is a moral position:

> I shall try to show that our notion of rationality is, at bottom, just one part of our conception of human flourishing, our idea of the good. (RTH, p. xi)

Putnam is assertive. He does not use terms like 'equivalent to the good life' which distance us from it; he embraces the classical theme of the concept. But his requirements for the good life are also less definitive, because they do not integrate it into a comprehensive system. Which is more enriching – Habermas's visionary system or Putnam's personal perspective?

Habermas and Argumentative Hope

Societies

How does Habermas seek his 'equivalent' for the good life? This search is difficult, but he holds to the theoretical premise that he must pursue the human significance of reason. As we shall see, Putnam also recognises that reason must seek the good in lived experience. Habermas pursues a humane approach to reason because it accounts for people interacting, how they interact, and why they interact; and neither Habermas nor Putnam separates reason's arguments from the quality of life itself. And yet argument is ambiguous enough in its form and its outcomes to upset many plans for a better life. The good life shows how hard it is to harmonise reason with dialogue, how hard is the quest for foundations of dialogic rationalism.

Habermas begins his investigation of the good life with *society* and its potentialities for furthering human happiness. He contends that we can judge whether societies offer a good life, that we must judge them, and he urges us not to avoid this issue. He is aware that societies judge one another crudely, with brutal consequences. He is particularly aware that (so-called) advanced societies find other cultures wanting, with results that may be cruel and devastating. Too many judgements are pretexts for exploitation. He warns against false judgements which one society may make on an alien way of life, judgements on something taken out of its rightful context. But he believes that it is possible to judge whether and to what extent a society is rational, in its beliefs and practices. When it comes to rationality, the theme is behaviour, what people do, not just how they talk about their behaviour. Still, behaviour comes back to language, since acting rationally involves giving proper reasons for what is done, if required. Judging whether 'a group . . . behaves rationally in general is the same thing as asking whether 'they have good reasons for their expressions' (CA1, p. 43). What are 'good reasons'? Different types of reason are good in different discussions. If problem-solving is the point, then we use one type of reason; if moral choice, then another type; if aesthetic, another; if psychological, another; and so on, determining

> that these expressions are correct or successful in the cognitive dimension, reliable or insightful in the moral-practical dimension, discerning or illuminating in the evaluative dimension, or candid and self-critical in the expressive dimension. (CA1, p. 43)

Reasons act in diverse ways and are good in diverse ways. Martin Jay reminds us that Habermas is not an unsubtle universalist: he tries to incorporate diversity.[1] But Habermas insists that the diversity makes sense only in relation to the single ideal of the good reason. The stakes are high:

> When there appears a systematic effect in these respects, across various domains of interaction and over long periods (perhaps even over the space of a lifetime), we also speak of the rationality of a conduct of life. (CA1, p. 43)

Here is a start towards determining what is the good life for an individual. And the individual good life implies a context:

And in the sociocultural conditions for such a conduct of life there is reflected perhaps the rationality of a lifeworld shared not only by individuals but by collectives as well. (CA1, p. 43)

The context makes it easier for an individual to live a rational life, or more difficult, or impossible. A rational society is the sum of rational individual lives, and there is a binding inter-relationship between the form of the whole society and the lives of the individuals within it. Will a rational life be a good life? It will depend on how generous is the notion of rational.

But can we judge whole ways of life? And who are 'we' to do so? Habermas is aware of a poor record here, as earlier modern thinkers 'questioned neither the rationalism nor the universalism of the Enlightenment and were thus not yet sensitive to the dangers of Eurocentrism' (CA1, p. 153), dangers which are one of the major motives for putting rationalism on a new footing. It is one of the main claims of new rationalists to attention that they avoid the mistake of taking a local view of reason for a universal criterion. Hence Habermas warns us not to derive criteria for the good life from modernity's concept of reason, the efficient reason-power of Western bureaucracy and technology alone.

Mythic Worldviews

Habermas is aware universal claims may mask imperial ambitions. One way of fending off such encroachments is relativism: each society has its own criteria for living, including criteria for what is rational.[2] This moment is crucial in asserting the credentials of dialogic rationalism for doing the same, and allowing scope for difference, permitting cultures freedom from the prerogatives of scientific rationalism. The West is not entitled to impose its own practices under the sign of abstract reason: Habermas shows why a dialogic rationalism must recognise no such abstract reason. Habermas has more room for plurality in the exchange of opinions that leads to consensus, though consensus must be conceivable if the argument is to be rational. Moreover, he refuses to give the modern West credit for universal reason.

He insists there are different worlds in the proliferation of humanity, which offer wide vistas of different behaviour and independent standards, and we cannot judge them by narrow criteria stemming from a few.[3] But he still sets out decisively his own criteria for acceptable worldviews, criteria which follow from a particular sociological tradition to which he subscribes, and the tradition to which he opposes his own is that based on myth. A culture of myths will lack key distinctions, without which people have no basis for some reasoning:

> Myths do not permit a clear, basic, conceptual differentiation between things and persons, between objects that can be manipulated and agents – subjects capable of acting and speaking to whom we attribute linguistic utterances. (CA1, p. 48)

So, in some respects, having a modern worldview is better. Habermas prefers the refined distinctions which a modernised worldview makes. But his opposition to other worldviews, such as the mythical, is not complete and he complicates the judgement he has made on their limitations. He engages with various theorists, one of whom, Peter Winch, leads him to the idea that:

> Each culture establishes in its language a relation to reality. To this extent, 'real' and 'unreal', 'true' and 'untrue' are indeed concepts that are inherent in all languages and not ones that can, say, be present in this language and absent in that. But each culture draws this categorial distinction within its own language system. (CA1, p. 57)

Now he is moving towards plurality. Different cultures have their own definitions for what is truth and what is reality, and the integrity of language supports their views.

On the one hand, Habermas insists on the need to judge between ways of life, a judgement which leads to hierarchy. On the other hand, he accepts a degree of plurality, autonomy and diversity among ways of life. He is against the 'Eurocentrism' of the earlier Enlightenment, even while defending its legacy as the basis of a new beginning for a further period of enlightenment. Can he do the trick, keep the legacy and allow views to expand beyond it? He intensifies the case for plurality and difference by applying the notion of 'worldview', a basis for action, which governs the conduct of individuals, and has a particular coherence for each community. A worldview is not an assertion which claims to be true; therefore worldviews cannot be judged false. Worldviews support social practices, they are integral to individual experience and inseparable from the way people behave in their communities: they serve practical purposes. Worldviews are creations, not propositions. They need to be habitable.

Habermas is categorical that worldviews establish their own validity in (or through) action. But he also reasserts that comparative judgements on them are possible. For this balancing act, he uses his model of argument:

> Owing to their reference to totality, worldviews are indeed removed from the dimension in which a judgment of them according to criteria of truth makes sense; even the choice of criteria according to which the truth of statements is to be judged may depend on the basic conceptual context of a worldview. But this does not mean that the idea of truth might itself be understood in a particularistic way. (CA1, p. 58)

To an extent, cultures make their own contexts within which actions and values can be assessed. Habermas concedes that a worldview is a specific context for establishing propositions about truth, a local context. Has he not accepted in that case that truth claims are relative to cultures? Cultural relativity seems implicit in this scheme, but in fact, Habermas subordinates the potential for cultural relativity to a different principle: *the principle that truth claims are universal.* Context affects the formulation and expression of claims for validity, but the claims themselves are universal, not local. And indeed people rarely *say*: 'I think this is true, from the point of view of my context or community'; usually, they insist 'This is true, because . . .'.[4]

Habermas takes our assertions about what we hold to be true seriously:

> Whatever language system we choose, we always start intuitively from the presupposition that truth is a universal validity claim. (CA1, p. 58)

We should not bracket claims to truth made by speakers with their context. Are we not required by language itself to take them literally, to accord them the dignity of a proper claim, which extends into the whole domain of human understanding and experience? Here we feel the pull towards dialogic rationalism.

Habermas *is* qualifying scientific definitions of reason and 'calculative' truth, definitions which were too rigid and exclusive for all uses. However, he opposes relativism. While acknowledging contemporary reservations that there are no absolute truths, Habermas proposes a strong definition of truth: 'If a statement is true, it merits universal assent, no matter in which language it is formulated' (CA1, p. 58). Has Habermas reconciled the limitations of an individual claim arising within a specific context with its universal reference and status? While we are not entitled to judge a worldview in totality, we are required to evaluate critically any particular claim to truth that may arise from it, as a universal claim that applies to everyone, everywhere, not merely a local assumption. If it's true for you, it's true for us.

There are different ways of inflecting this idea of reason and truth. It could be oppressive, if the emphasis fell on the unified outcome. But if we emphasise the *process*, the theory is democratic, ensuring that everyone has the same rights to be heard in the argument about truth. Ultimately, there is only one arena for assessing truth, a single world arena, though claims emerge into it from many contexts. The potentially oppressive effects of unity in assent to truth claims are offset by Habermas's view of how claims are arbitrated: *only by good reasons, in a shared process.* He is not envisaging losers and winners, since the discussion about truth is a collective experience of reaching agreement which potentially satisfies all parties. Such is the consensual goal of argument, when the process of arguing is rational!

Habermasian arbitration depends on an interpretation of argument which tends towards consensus. Habermas's theory is broad and far-reaching, and covers the formulation of truths and other claims leading to the good life out of the differentiated contexts of varying cultures, but every aspect of this theory requires his definition of argument, which explains further why he is so definitive about argument and reluctant to accept debate on its nature. Argument *must* lead to unity and agreement if we entrust cultural differences about truth to it, or one culture will impose itself on another, one society defeating other societies. Yet these defensive strategies are discouraging. Should *dialogic* rationalism be a theory integrated throughout so that every part must support every other part depending on the influence of a single view of argument? Does Habermas take dialogue seriously enough in practice?

Habermas constructs a unified system of definitions. As a result, conceptual tensions are also logical inconsistencies, or weak links. An inquiry into human reason and society must inevitably raise more questions than it resolves, such is the scope for further problems to arise. In a closed *system*, these unresolved questions become flaws, areas needing constant repair. Specifically, it is doubtful if this theory squares the particular and the universal, the diverse and the unitary. Habermas allows each worldview its own space, while insisting that every claim to truth enters into the universal dialogue about truth. How much would be achieved by a really convincing model of argument in this enterprise when argument connects such a wide range of factors? But has Habermas established such a model by including consensus orientation among the requirements of proper argument in his definition? These are questions which merit discussion, indeed they *demand* it. But the centripetal form of the whole theory frustrates these

demands. Habermas has not applied appropriately imaginative criteria for dialogue to his own enterprise. He needed a theory as dialogic as it is rational. Such
a dialogue would integrate unresolved questions into further discussion. But the
system turns away from unanswered questions for they lead to logical dilemmas.
The theory lacks an argumentative imagination commensurate with principles of
dialogic rationalism.

Habermas is also concerned with the interconnecting problems of scientific
reason and the good life. The role of science is a major problem in the cultural
field. Habermas does not bar science from the interaction among worldviews
leading to truths. On the contrary, the defence of reason continues to need science.
But science is a knotty topic for the theory of different cultures and the good life.
If science has privileged access to truth, then are scientific societies also privileged over others? Habermas accepts that science discovers truths which are
universal, not limited to one context, one host culture:

> Scientific rationality belongs to a complex of cognitive-instrumental rationality that can
> certainly claim validity beyond the context of particular cultures. (CA1, p. 65)

Habermas has acknowledged that mythic worldviews cannot be outmoded by science, not as a whole; but their individual claims to provide the truth can be
contested in the universal debate, where science operates. But then truth is not the
only issue at stake in the cultural debate, nor is truth simple, and science encounters criteria which are alien to it.

Argument is never one-sided, given the commitment to dialogue which has
been built in. Therefore dialogue can rescue the theory from a one-sided view of
truth which might favour science exclusively:

> Can't we who belong to modern societies learn something from understanding alter-
> native, particularly premodern forms of life? Shouldn't we, beyond all romanticizing of
> superseded stages of development, beyond exotic stimulation from the contents of
> alien cultures, recall *the losses required by our own path to the modern world*? (CA1,
> p. 65; emphasis added)

And here Habermas turns round and looks at science from another viewpoint. He
strengthens the fundamental position which I interpret as dialogic rationalism, the
position that science is not the whole of reason, or necessarily the best of reason,
but makes its contribution to truth in an argument with other views. Furthermore,
truth is not the only subject of argument, since the applications of criticisable
claims extend to questions such as rightness, appropriateness or usefulness.
Habermas takes truth as the archetypal case in the debate for universal validity,
but 'forms of life' have other things to teach beside the forms of truth. Truth provides the model, not the sole instance of subjects for rational dialogues.

Modern Worldviews

Habermas gives a critical account of the place of science in modern societies:

> . . . a pattern of cultural and societal rationalization that helps cognitive-instrumental
> rationality to achieve a one-sided dominance not only in our dealings with external
> nature, but also in our understanding of the world and in the communicative practice of
> everyday life. (CA1, p. 66)

'Cognitive-instrumental rationality' is the way of science: it solves problems; it is about means and ends, causes and effects. Modern society represents the triumph of this form of rationality. Although there is much to be said for it, however, a good life needs other types of rationality, particularly *mutual understanding between people*. Indeed Habermas's theory privileges such communicative rationality as interaction leading to understanding. In short, Habermas does not say that the modern, the Western, is comprehensively more rational than other contexts or cultures. His criteria for rationality are too complex to give such a one-sided impression, though he himself does not always welcome the complexity! Science *is* persuasive in certain discussions, those about some kinds of truth and falsehood, but it does not cancel out other worldviews which apply to a general human experience, and human requirements. Science is not the whole of reason. Furthermore, in modern societies science and scientific attitudes have weakened these other types of reason which should play an important part in the good life. A scientifically-based society should learn from other cultures, in the most profound respect, concerning the requirements of the good life.

Habermas responds to problems by adding concepts. He enriches the idea of different kinds of knowledge proceeding from different worldviews with the concept of the lifeworld. White identifies the sociological imperatives behind the introduction of the lifeworld: 'The notion of the lifeworld (*Lebenswelt*) must be introduced in order to link action theory more convincingly with rationalization processes.'[5] For White, Habermas needs the lifeworld to integrate his larger view of social change with his emphasis on action and the co-ordination of actions by groups and individuals. The concept of the lifeworld is fundamental further to Habermas's balancing act in which he tries both to recognise differences between contexts and to integrate these differences. Lifeworlds are the settings for all exchanges, all people's attempts to understand each other's words and actions: 'Subjects acting communicatively always come to an understanding in the horizon of a lifeworld' (CA1, p. 70). What is this enclosing 'horizon' which determines understanding? It consists of 'unproblematic, background convictions', shared by all participants. The lifeworld makes people feel secure. Such existential security is essential for communicative action to be tolerable. But cognitive-instrumental rationality does not favour a strong lifeworld. It is not a secure context of shared 'unproblematic background convictions': so it is necessary to recognise other social forms, other different cultures and alternative models of life with more humane horizons in order to provide the sense of a secure world.

The systematic form of the theory is costly. Whenever Habermas adds a new concept, previous commitments must adjust for the system to remain stable. This adjustment is dynamic but inward-looking. The lifeworld surely is another extension where Habermas should have *thought* more dialogically. Hitherto rational argument has been the foundation of the good life, but the lifeworld complicates the requirements of the good life. The crucial problem is whether the lifeworld is itself rational, and rational by the criteria of communicative rationality. Or is it a residue of non-rational traditions, associations and habits, which structure on life, but are not arguable? In my view, the lifeworld as Habermas presents it has some features which devalue rational argument:

> The lifeworld also stores the interpretive work of preceding generations. It is the conservative counterweight to the risk of disagreement. (CA1, p. 70)

Given the cohesion of the whole theory, and considering the Habermasian view of reason and the good life, this passage ought to be disturbing. Suddenly, different views are a 'risk', a risk so great that it justifies conservatism and the 'dead' weight of the past. Rational argument is insufficient; we also need a 'conservative counterweight'. The good life as Habermas now perceives it has two foundations: critical discussion and inherited order. Surely these principles conflict?

Is this additional category, 'a conservative counterweight to the risk of disagreement', not the wrong *kind* of solution? When resolving the competing rights of different cultures, Habermas has acknowledged that 'wisdom' is as important as 'science' to human happiness; he has conceded that primitive societies have traditional virtues as well as limitations. Now he tries to integrate that insight with the theoretical structure that revolved round resolution through argument. The dominant metaphors that emerge are revealing, metaphors of counterbalance and equilibrium required by the theory, to keep itself intact, as much as they are required by society. The deep contradiction is between closed structure and open process. Dialogue suggests an open process; but Habermas still understands reason to demand closed structures. Consequently, he 'solves' problems in theory by complicating the structure, instead of inviting dialogue. Why *should* one theory solve all the problems that its author can envisage?

Risk and the Lifeworld

Habermas tries to reconcile stability with dynamism, both in his theory and in society. Critical discussion to decide claims presupposes a dynamic way of life. Would such a way of life, which leaves judgement open, not be too insecure? White captures the ambivalence with which Habermas regards this rationalisation of the lifeworld, when he remarks of Habermas's theory: 'With this progressive shift in the way actions are sociated, there is, however, an increase in the potential for dissensus and instability.'[6] In response to the 'danger', Habermas defines a 'counterweight', the lifeworld. In taking on the lifeworld, Habermas never truly affirms tradition in its own variable terms. He presents the inherited past as a comfort to those facing the dilemma of choice; a comfort and, so far as rationality is concerned, at best, a residue of rational work. In both form and substance, he is conceding to human limitations like a simple rationalist. A wholeheartedly *dialogic* rationalist could regard 'the interpretive work of preceding generations' differently, not as a stored object but as a continuing process. The theory itself could become a dialogue covering present and past. Instead Habermas defines the past cautiously and uniformly, erecting his structure of counterbalances:

> It is the conservative counterweight to the risk of disagreement that arises with every actual process of understanding; for communicative actors can achieve an understanding only by way of taking yes/no positions on criticizable validity claims. (CA1, p. 70)

This is a concession. Previously, the yes/no moment was a hopeful moment in which it was possible to reach agreement. Here the yes/no moment is threatening: it threatens endless disagreement.[7]

One reason for caution is that Habermas is talking about 'every *actual* process of reaching understanding'. People often don't actually reach an understanding in their exchanges; and he realises how painful those experiences of difference can be. In short, he is considering experience again, and experience tells us that discussion is a mixed bag. Even with the best will in the world, disagreement is hard to resolve. It is hard to understand the actions of others and the differing expressions they use to explain them and justify them. The disagreement may be explicit: their reasons for their actions may conflict with our reasoning. Or disagreement may be implicit in actions which imply conflicting reasons among different parties. Habermas sees that people are afraid to begin discussions because they know how hard it is to end them constructively. And he offers them an inherited lifeworld to support them against the prospect of disagreement! The need for this support conflicts with the Habermasian hope of reaching consensus through argument when the form of the argument is regulated and right. As a structure, this theory of the uses of consensus will require continuous overhaul, a requirement which is energising but also diversionary. Had Habermas conceived his work as a dialogic process, the contradictions in his theory would have been moments in a debate, ironically closer to the spirit of a dialogic approach. But his exposition of reason makes dialogue support reason, without redefining it radically, as his own practice indicates: for in the pursuit of a single version of reason dialogue is lost.

Repair work on the theory continues immediately! Not surprisingly, he returns to the modern and the mythical, to redress the balance before concessions to the past are too damaging to reason, and goes on to explain the *value* of the modernising process. For all its problems, modernity expands the territory of argument. Sadly a modern lifeworld is, therefore, far less secure than a lifeworld supported by mythical views. Modern worldviews are 'decentered' (CA1, p. 70), they lack the unifying power of myths. Modern lifeworlds are less stable than mythical lifeworlds. They draw upon more diverse sources for understanding. And, more important, people are more likely to be critical of the sources which they inherit, which are also the support for the lifeworld. Modern lifeworlds provide more scope to argue and this places greater strain on the accomplishments of individuals, and their ability to exchange views and argue coherently. The outcome can be perpetual disagreement – but it is also a challenge to the acquisition of proper argumentation, which ultimately would give greater scope to 'rational action orientations'. Traditional lifeworlds give more support to individuals, but they present fewer opportunities for these rational orientations, since critical discussion is a precondition for a rational orientation.

What could better provoke a debate about reason and the good life than these oppositions between past and present, between risk and achievement? No doubt, Habermas is influential partly because he stimulates discussion of these themes. But is he not influential also because he proposes solutions to the intractable problems which his theories embrace? Yet the answers he gives are unconvincing in proportion to the profundity of the questions he raises. Instead of yet more definitions of social factors needed to prop up the tottering edifice of theory, there needs to be a debate about security and the good life. Risks are sometimes worthwhile: they may be liberating. Why should every person require the same degree of security? Why should every culture have the same need for a 'counterweight'? Why should the past always be supportive, never challenging in itself? Could not achievements of the past challenge any complacency of present generations? Perhaps the present does not require a dead tradition to shore it up but the opposite of a dead tradition: an inextinguishable critique from other times? What is a risk is questionable.[8] Does not risk vary according to different criteria, both individual and cultural criteria? Why then enforce a single reaction to risk that leads to a definitive conclusion about 'the risk of disagreement', instead of inquiring what risk means and how it functions, and how far it is acceptable in different circumstances? The good life is a topos for debate, not simply the site of a structure. Yet it is Habermas's own approach to theory, and the constricting effects of structure, which point to the necessity for critical dialogue.

Arguable Worlds

Habermas cannot completely repair his structure. Specifically, his general theory depends on a model which makes impossible demands of argument. This model is not rich enough to face the problems of the lifeworld, modernity and tradition. An alternative vocabulary to be proposed for widening the perception of argument would start with the concept of 'arguability' – a word that expresses the potential for both discussion and difference. Through the accommodation of discussion and difference, we soon reach 'double arguability', because arguability is twofold: issue and also interaction. The issue is what is being debated, and the interaction is what happens to the people arguing, both of which contribute equally to the process and outcome of argument. Double arguability includes what is said and spontaneous reactions to what is said, the way it is said, the form in which it is said, and the situation in which it is said: reactions due to feelings, ideas, personality factors and past experience which are beyond the control of the participant in argument, and often beyond her or his perception of understanding. All these factors alter the course of an argument and determine to some extent the outcome of an argument in which the recorded linguistic content may appear autonomous and coherent. Transposing from Habermas's own terms, modern worldviews create more arguable spaces, and in those spaces we experience intensely the force of *double* arguability: the participants have to take more responsibility for the interactive dimension of argument. Habermas himself sees a double threat to the lifeworld. As well as perpetual difference, there is the danger from 'one-sided dominance' of a specialised rationality which is scientific and end-oriented rather than fully communicative, a rationality that is good at the universal argument about true and false, but poor at maintaining human relations. This instrumental rationality will not help us to develop creative interactions with each other, or settings for such interactions. Both to accommodate differences, and to forestall the tyranny of scientific reason in areas outside science, of strategic calculation where it is inappropriate, it is rational to promote humane relations. Double arguability emphasises the rational need for creativity in human relations, as a precondition for constructive discussion.

Habermas proceeds beyond the balance between past and present required to make risk acceptable to expand the analysis of myth and modernity more and more comprehensively. He sketches the lifeworlds of a mythic worldview:

> To the degree that the lifeworld of a social group is interpreted through a mythical worldview, the burden of interpretation is removed from the individual member, as well as the chance for him to bring about an agreement open to criticism. (CA1, p. 71)

A mythical worldview offers the individual more support, and less scope. Argument between individuals is less likely, less an opportunity for individual expression and less a threat to everyone, because mythical formulations cover many eventualities, so that there is less need to seek agreement. What would we lose if we did not need to seek such agreements with each other? We would lose a way to resolve differences between ourselves, and the power to argue. But we might have fewer differences to resolve in a mythical universe, since the myths would, according to Habermas, bind us together. In a myth-supported realm, there would be less need for agreement over personal orientations, agreements which Habermas himself regards as provisional.

In a modern worldview, agreement is provisional because *what we secure by reason, reason can undo*. Could a defender of myth not say that it is useful to need fewer negotiated agreements, when those agreements are only pauses in disagreement?[9] Habermas equivocates about the usefulness of argument; having defined arguing in purely rational terms, he fears that it may be too divisive for the requirements of the good life because people need emotional support. But he has diminished the role of emotion in argument: how then can argument perform its function in emotional situations? He needs to look outside of argument for existential security and elects myth as a source of security. But myth is supplanted by rational criticism in the Habermasian system, when the need for progress conflicts with the need for security. There is a radical contradiction between the means of pursuing the good life, which rely on rational discussion, and the ends, which include emotional security.

As an agenda for discussion, what could be richer? But as a structure, these 'balances' between different definitions are fragile! In a reconciling move, Habermas accepts that mythic lifeworlds are neither inferior nor superior to modern lifeworlds. Myth-based worlds perform a different function for their inhabitants from rationalised worlds. He is not being relativistic, at least not simply so. He does list the features of the lifeworld most likely to enhance 'a rational conduct of life' and he values them. These features include: distinctions between objective, social and subjective; distinctions between claims to truth, rightness and subjective truthfulness; scope to criticise the tradition itself; scope for the development of specialised areas of argument; and scope for the appropriate use of 'purposive-rational action'. The modernised order of society, then, is closer in many ways to Habermas's ideal, despite the anxieties that result from modernisation, and the loss of security. However supportive it may be, the

myth-dominated lifeworld does not offer scope for criticising its own traditions
and for differentiating claims to truth, rightness and other applications of knowledge – that is the judgement which Habermas encourages. But as Benhabib
implies, Habermas's significance is that he values modernity without accepting
the prevailing forms of modern society: 'We owe it to the work of Jürgen
Habermas that it has enriched our understanding of the social and cultural possibilities of modernity' (*Situating the Self*, p. 82).

In the Habermasian approach to the good life, scope for argument is our active
criterion, on which depends rational progress. A properly modernised society
would afford variegated claims to truth, more scope to criticise, more contexts in
which to develop arguments:

> The cultural tradition must permit a reflective relation to itself; it must be so far stripped
> of its dogmatism as to permit in principle that interpretations stored in tradition be
> placed in question and subjected to critical revision. . . . In its cognitive, moral, and
> evaluative components the cultural tradition must permit a feedback connection with
> specialized forms of argumentation to such an extent that the corresponding learning
> processes can be socially institutionalized. In this way, cultural subsystems can arise –
> for science, law and morality, music, art, and literature – in which traditions take shape
> that are supported by arguments rendered fluid through permanent criticism but at the
> same time professionally secured. (CA1, p. 71)

According to Habermas, modern traditions arise out of argument; and so they are
open to future argument; indeed, their function is to develop arguments. But he
has also framed a 'counterbalance' to this progression: tradition which is 'the conservative counterweight to the risk of disagreement', a risk he discerns in efforts
to reach understanding between people. This unstable balance between argument
and tradition generates the need for yet other further checks, and so Habermas
requires institutions which make sure arguments are 'professionally secured'.
White brings out clearly the sociological imperatives behind Habermas's emphasis on 'the institutional anchoring of specialized forms of argumentation'.[10] But,
as sympathetic commentators such as White also acknowledge, professional prerogatives create another problem: they limit the scope for argument. Has
argument not become more specialised? Who gets to participate in the arguments? And what happens to the rights of the others? Is the *individual* really more
able to frame criticisms and reach agreements in a society when arguability
becomes the property of specialists? These sociological questions raise imaginative and emotional doubts. Does Habermas trust argument? How far does he
trust argument, and do we wish to go as far as he takes argument, or further?

The discussion of the good life leads to a dystopian vision, in which the modern lifeworld will be the worst of both worlds: lacking the support of myths and
deprived of the scope for argument, which belongs to specialised institutions in
many areas of the culture. Habermas clearly wishes to democratise the arguments, to return them to the prevailing lifeworld in some form. But he is anxious
that the lifeworld would then be uninhabitable. Such constraints lead Habermas
to reaffirm that, where ways of living are concerned,

> It would be senseless to want to judge such a conglomeration as a whole, the totality of
> a form of life, under individual aspects of rationality. (CA1, p. 73)

He moves to other terms for judging society, which avoid prejudicing the outcome in favour of modernity in its prevailing forms, 'the model of sickness and health' (CA1, p. 73). Here the judgement on modern societies can be at least as critical as the judgements on others, in some ways more so. Modernity emerges as a necessary move, providing space for the individual, but a dangerous move, which can run in positive or negative directions. Modernity develops necessary practices, particularly in the realms of argument; but at huge cost, a cost which may yet become heavier. Promise and risk: that is the problem of modernity for Habermas.

In my view, any account of modernity that Habermas gives is bound to be unstable because it is underpinned by argument and replicates the tensions in his idea that argument, when properly conducted, leads towards agreement. *He welcomes the expansion of arguability, but only as a prelude to the expansion of agreement.* However, the theory does not require people to develop forms of relationship which will turn arguability into agreement. By repair and re-repair, he half-resolves and half-represses difficult questions about responsibility for the emotional contexts of rational discussion. Having made individuals responsible for the outcome of arguments, Habermas refuses them a truly creative role in establishing rational exchanges. He does not ask how individuals *create* interactions which support communicative rationality. Instead he assumes that individuals need fixed contexts to perform rationally. Therefore, his solutions are institutional: the support of myths is replaced by the authority of institutions. The theory searches for balances where it could have considered processes, ongoing processes and relationships, emotional as well as rational. Habermas does not perceive that emotion can play a *creative* role of establishing contexts for rational argument and action. He hopes that rational institutions can stabilise the lifeworld, and that tradition may sustain people while this is happening.

Yes and No

But Habermas has courage, and makes the bold 'attempt to provide an equivalent for what was once intended by the idea of the good life'. There is no retreat from the point we have reached, no returning to mythically supported lifeworlds; Habermas proposes a less fragmented world, a world where specialised arguments will re-connect, to achieve something like the old supportive coherence of myth. This enterprise is inspirational, but ultimately disappointing for the acceptable solution is a self-contained construction, where dynamism is frozen into a static pattern:

> Perhaps we should talk instead of a balance among non-self-sufficient moments, an equilibriated interplay of the cognitive with the moral and the aesthetic-practical. (CA1, p. 73)

Equilibriated interplay: the outcome of arguments will be dynamic but also balanced. Why should all the cognitive, moral and aesthetic-practical parts be so evenly related? Such rigid metaphors foreclose the debate about the good life, just as it is beginning! The story is too neat. As society modernises, arguability expands; then different arguments become specialised: over the horizon is a future where these specialised arguments interconnect, stabilising the lifeworld again as if the old myths still functioned. In that future, arguments could be dynamic, but might proceed to unanimity and their outcomes would interlock as supportively as myths. Such a structure deprives individual arguments of autonomy; their outcomes are dictated by the supporting system.

There are many ways to study argument: by analysing devices; by examining topics; by assessing institutions. But the crucial requirement is to deepen our understanding of why argument *matters*. Habermas performs that service by linking argument to wider issues, in which we recognise our hopes and fears. How far *can* his approach enable dialogic rationalism, enable it to support a modern analogue to the good life of classic thought? Argument is essential to his model and argument remains ambiguous: a negative requirement with an affirmative goal, criticism promoting agreement. Although he is aware of this problem, Habermas makes argument a universal requirement for seeking truth which is the outcome of agreement. In this use of argument, he must emphasise the affirmative goal, the agreement, to which it can lead. His good society is a space for rich agreements. But such a space still reverberates with the 'no' of the critical voice in argument. A good society will be rich in new agreements; in the same society people must also say 'no' to the claims of others and disrupt agreement. One outcome of this variation might be a kind of stoical optimism: insofar as it relies on argument, and is open to argument, a good life will be possible in the future, and will be a goal towards which people co-operate in striving.

Habermas's central question about a society is how the people in it act *together*. He has categorised different ways in which they can co-ordinate their actions: through pre-set traditions, which determine the conduct of everyone in their society; through efficient systems, which organise people along planned lines; through the communicative exchange of reasons leading to agreement among them. The good life is one in which people can co-ordinate their actions openly through understandings. His ideal is 'a theory of communicative action that places understanding in language, as the medium for co-ordinating action, at the focal point of interest' (CA1, p. 274). But the ideal is marred by doubts about the effect of individual differences within the lifeworld: support systems are necessary to counteract these differences, and create a 'balance' in society, so that it retains coherence in case they undermine security.

Habermas's theory goes over and over this idea that people can reach understanding through the proper process of argument. Benhabib captures the significance of Habermas's move for the concept of reason: 'We do not search for what would be non-self-contradictory but for what would be mutually acceptable for all' (*Situating the Self*, p. 28). Each time argument returns as the source of new *understanding* between people; but the process of argument remains ambiguous for it leads both to understanding and misunderstanding, agreement and dissension. The ambiguity affects the other themes to which argument is central, particularly the theme of the good life. The good life as Habermas perceives it develops through the agreements which are the potential outcome of rational exchanges. But Habermas has had to imply different senses of 'agreement' to sustain the good life: some agreements precede new understandings, agreements rooted in the inherited lifeworld. Other sources of authoritative opinion sustain agreement, specialised opinion ratified by specialist institutions. But I doubt that he has solved the problem of argument and agreement by introducing the life-world and specialisation. Given his assumptions about the need for emotional security, his problem remains: how is it possible to prevent argument's 'no' from undermining the lifeworld? His good life is viable only if there are secure contexts for achieving the new, the expanded, the richer 'yes'. Secure contexts should not be imposed by force, so what is to be done about the undying 'no'?

> Agreement can indeed be objectively obtained by force; but what comes to pass manifestly through outside influence or the use of violence cannot count subjectively as agreement. Agreement rests on common *convictions*. The speech act of one person succeeds only if the other accepts the offer contained in it by taking (however implicitly) a 'yes' or 'no' position on a validity claim that is in principle criticizable. (CA1, p. 287)

Is there not a difficulty about what 'no' means in Habermas's theory? The problem is that 'no' means so many different things, and Habermas attempts to narrow this range of meanings in order to reduce the importance of what is left out and stabilise his whole construction. There is the 'no' of disagreement about an issue. But 'no' can also be a refusal to respond, a refusal to argue, or argue further, if we think in terms of double arguability, and there is no clear divide between the 'no' which actively contradicts an argument and the 'no' which is a refusal to argue. Where these two 'no's overlap, there is a problem in Habermas's ideas, including his ideas of how argument supports the good life. Individuals within a scheme vary and individuality may require a wider 'no' than he allows, especially the 'no' of refusing to respond on someone else's terms! It seems to me he is trying to contain the power of the argumentative 'no' within a single concept of arguability, in order to contain the ambiguity of argument, and avoids the questions which focus through double arguability, the intermeshing of issue with interaction.

These questions of double arguability will recur in the discussion of the impact of dialogic relativism, for relativism exploits these problems of individual reaction in formulating its theory of differences. But at this stage, we can see both the power of Habermasian thought as a basis for dialogic rationalism and its limitations. The strength and the weakness have the same cause: all concepts are interconnected into one continuous and unified system. Such a system attempts to resolve problems internally, instead of reinterpreting them in a dialogue with other opinions. Yet dialogue is the central criterion in Habermas's system, the scene of reasoning. This problem is a handicap in realising the good life itself. For Habermas's conception of the good life is at odds with his own theoretical requirements. On the one hand, the good life derives from the exchange of opinion; on the other hand, the theory is self-contained and comprehensive, repairing flaws in its own terms from within.

This systematic tendency is consistent throughout Habermas's expositions of his theory. Subsequent developments in his work confirm both the strength and the limitations of Habermas's theory. In recent defences, he maintains his vision. For instance, he endows the lifeworld with 'a form of practical knowledge that is undoubtedly secured from within' ('Lawrence Kohlberg and Neo-Aristotelianism', in *Justification*, pp. 113–32, 124), an innate knowledge which helps people to decide practical issues rationally. This knowledge is ethical as

well as being rational: it also outreaches the lifeworld, 'points beyond its horizon'.
A lovely image follows: 'The horizon of every form of life is fluid, its boundaries
permeable.' Habermas shows a world in movement, in which everything is connected, everything interacts, or potentially interacts. The preconceived boundaries
are there to be crossed, the gaps are there to be leapt. Recently, Habermas risks
exhortation, alongside analysis. We must 'expand our local knowledge and ethnocentric outlook'. Yet tensions always arise: how is it possible to expand on an
outlook which remains ethnocentric? Does the metaphor work? Habermas's
method is vulnerable as he turns his definitions into practical exhortations. So the
virtue is urgency, vividness, deep seriousness; the limitation is impatience of
tension, a tendency to suppress strains rather than open them up for dialogue. For,
as ever, his attitude to dialogue, in practice, is ambiguous.

He knows that many thinkers are more cautious about interconnection, understanding across boundaries. And so, courageously, Habermas demands dialogue,
the widest dialogue: 'it is far from obvious why this practical knowledge should
not be extended in an intercultural direction' (*Justification*, p.124). But what is the
meaning of extending one lifeworld, one cultural context, towards an 'intercultural' space? Whose space will it be? It seems to me that when he says it is 'far
from obvious' why he should not carry his point, he pre-empts questions about
this 'intercultural' space which are honourable and relevant. Yet Habermas challenges the conscience of the times when he asks why dialogue should cease at
certain borders, and preserves the hope of exchange which gave value to his theory of communicative action.

In his discourse ethics, Habermas re-addresses the good life and imposes
another grid of distinctions. There are 'questions of the good life', which are 'ethical' (*Justification*, p. 126). There are also 'moral questions', which are more
general. Ethics is about how to live rightly, morality is about questions of judgement in general. In some intricate 'Remarks on Discourse Ethics', Habermas
defines the 'moral point of view' as a set of rules rather than a perspective, since
the moral view 'requires that maxims and contested interests be generalized' and
it 'compels the participants' to rise above the particulars, and to adopt an inclusive view (*Justification*, pp. 19–112, 124). The tensions arise between generalised
rules about procedure and particular situations. These tensions animate the theory
and also disturb it, and Habermas is well aware of them. Discourse ethics supplements communicative action by offering new rules, rules for regulating the
tension and ambiguity which reside in the communication of differences.

Morality is about justification, rational justification for judgement. Morality is
general, and justification must apply across contexts, it must be valid intercul-
turally: 'moral justifications resolve disputes concerning rights and duties'
(*Justification*, p. 32). But situations vary, and so do norms, whereas the central
problem continues as before. So Habermas supplements justification by application, 'the principle of appropriateness' (p. 37). It is application which counts in
particular contexts. Justification is about universality, whereas application is
about being appropriate in the context. On the one hand, Habermas continues alert
to complexities; on the other hand, he responds by making distinctions finer and
finer to deal with complexity. A rhetorical irony or paradox ensues: more rules

appear more flexible than one rule or a few rules. But oddly, the effect is the reverse: the more rules develop, the less flexible the system becomes.

The problem really lies in talking about rules and requirements, rather than telling the story in a different way. Discourse ethics signals a greater emphasis on particulars, anomalies, differences. Habermas is still maintaining his whole theory, communicative action, but is adapting to pressures from specific situations. Curiously, the adaptation feels more rigid than the basic theory, because Habermas is so concerned to keep everything under control. For example, his theory depended on the analogy between claims about truth and claims about rightness. Argumentation has the same form for the different claims. Now he notes 'an unsettling asymmetry' (*Justification*, p. 38). There are two levels in argument about moral and ethical problems, justification and application; and there is only one level in arguments about facts and theories in science. The insight is offered in fairness: Habermas never shrinks from complexity, he epitomises intellectual courage to inquire further. But why must asymmetry in life and in theory be disturbing, why not interesting, fascinating, even beautiful? If it is disturbing, asymmetry must be solved, prevented from damaging conclusions; if it is interesting, it could be explored, discussed, debated further.

To apply communicative action as discourse ethics, Habermas raises a problem which involves the good life and morality, 'the abortion question' (*Justification*, p. 59). Habermas is exercising his distinction between procedures and situations, between moral generality and ethical particulars. The approach is consistent with the whole of communicative action: there are linking forms of argument, which are general, and there are specific situations to which these apply, ways of life, norms. It is proper to raise a topical concern like abortion, and it extends his treatment of the good life. But Habermas becomes brisk, he notes that: 'At this stage of the debate, both sides in this dispute appear to have good, perhaps even equally good, arguments' (p. 59). At the level of the good life, the 'abortion question' hangs in the balance. How does he know? There is no assessment of particular arguments. It is hard to imagine either side accepting such equalisation. Habermas is too quick to take the heat out of the question, and his reconciling gesture is likely to fuel the flames, not resolve the dispute by being categorical and definitive. He believes that, as a 'moral matter', the issue must be resolvable, because, 'in the long run', the better reasons prevail. But, he wonders, is it a moral matter at all, or an ethical question, and is it open to justification or just to application? The example seems to illustrate how profoundly ambiguous are the categories which apply to morality and ethics. The ambiguities could connote a creative moment, a moment of reassessment. But Habermas proceeds to resolve the question in the terms he has established. If the matter is ethical, it is about different views of the good life in practice, and: 'Then the question would be how the integrity and the coexistence of ways of life and worldviews that generate different ethical conceptions of abortion can be secured under conditions of equal rights' (p. 60). Morally, reasons will emerge to decide who is right; ethically, rules will be required to mediate between worldviews that are different. But who decides which is relevant, morality or ethics? And is that a moral or an ethical decision? Or neither? And if neither, if it is, say, a philosophical matter, then has

the debate not been passed over for adjudication to a higher tribunal of specialists? An alternative is to consider double arguability, the way argument rebounds
between procedure and issue, between arguers and topics, between criteria and
judgement. Who decides the level of the issue? That decision must be part of the
dispute.

As with the paradigmatic Habermasian theory, I suggest that discourse ethics
is caught in contradictions between system and dialogue: indeed I think the tension that follows from these contradictions is less creative, more muffled in the
later work, which lacks the sweeping flow of thought in the great founding
process. Habermas has a knack for raising precisely the question which his system finds difficult. The knack is also a profound virtue, an intellectual honesty.
Yet he makes limited use of insights into his difficulties, defensive use. He continues defending his definitions of the good life from the full force of his own
recognition that modern life engenders 'pluralism', many ways of living, many
attitudes, many styles both personal and collective. He realises that modern life
implies 'a corresponding multiplicity of ideas of the good life' (*Justification*, p.
122), and defines the dilemma in multiplicity. We may proceed in either of two
ways: by classifying all claims of the good life 'in a hierarchy', or by invoking the
'modern principle of tolerance'. But we cannot do both. If we demand a superior
idea of the good life, then we cannot be tolerant; if we are tolerant, no idea is
superior. Habermas pleads for active tolerance towards multiplicity, tolerance to
enter into dialogue, oriented towards 'what is equally good for all' (p. 124), but
imposing no solutions in advance. The appeal is moving, and cogent. But is the
original dilemma plausible in the way he defines it? Is the choice between hierarchy and tolerance when confronted by diverse tendencies? Does tolerance
imply no hierarchies? Are there not more and less tolerant hierarchies?
Conversely, are there no examples of intolerance which are against hierarchy?
The good life seems to slip through the net, the questions will not stay in the right
shape for the system to address them.

In his recent work, Habermas is constantly addressing objections to his theory,
some by specific critics, others hypothetical. The effect is dynamic, engaged, but
this leads to an increasing split between moments of visionary power that encom-
passes unsurpassed complexity, and a driving closure, an intent resolution as the
theory imposes itself through definitions and forecloses on events. Confronting
doubters, Habermas is sometimes more systematic than dialogic: 'Here I take up
some of these objections and discuss them in a metacritical fashion, by way of
explicating once again' (*Justification*, p. 19). I suggest a different kind of conversation, a hypothetical play of other voices to recognise ambiguities, not for the
purpose of defusing them, but so as to promote a dialogue that enhances reason.

Putnam, Reason and Human Flourishing

Conflicting Realities

Putnam conceives different versions of the good life and imagines societies which
disagree with each other over requirements for a better world. For these purposes

he invents settings and characters in a typically spontaneous and imaginative way: the tone is light and unpretentious, in an almost postmodern idiom, but the subjects are basic to philosophy and the intentions serious. One imagined disagreement is about reality. One society dismisses all normal ways of knowing what is real, one does not. The former society holds that all our concepts of reality arise as illusions; we are in fact 'Brains in a Vat', but all these brains together are subject to a comprehensive illusion concerning what is real, an inescapable restriction depending on the nature of thinking. The other society holds that it is possible through scientific and other methods to arrive at a verifiable view of what is real. 'Ours' is this latter kind of society, in Putnam's view (a questionable assumption!). The 'Vat' society exists somewhere else:

> Imagine that in Australia only a small minority of the people believe what we do and the great majority believe that we are Brains in a Vat. Perhaps the Australians believe this because they are all disciples of a Guru, the Guru of Sydney, perhaps. Perhaps when we talk to them they say, 'Oh if you could talk to the Guru of Sydney and look into his eyes and see what a good, kind, wise man he is, you too would be convinced'. (RTH, p. 131)

Putnam rejects the view that it is not possible to get to grips with what is real. His argument is complex but the main point is that the concept that 'we are Brains in a Vat' is self-contradictory: if people were subject to a comprehensive delusion, they could not be aware of the fact. They could not formulate the thesis that they were 'in a vat' because they are inside the vat; if the delusion were 'true', they could not see that they were deluded so as to form the view that all conceptions of reality are an illusion. It looks as though Putnam is making distinctions in favour of the modern society which are going to resolve the problem of the good life on the basis that one society is right and one is wrong . . . but he takes the disagreement in an unexpected direction.

'We' confront the vatists. We ask how they know that everyone is deceived – they reply that the Guru tells them. We then ask how *he* knows, if the illusion is as perfect as they say; they reply that he is that sort of authority, by definition: 'Oh, the Guru of Sydney just knows' (RTH, p. 131). The disagreement is radical, a difference between two worldviews, each validated by its own context. Putnam makes two judgements. First, the vatists are profoundly wrong: 'their worldview is crazy' (RTH, p. 132). This is a much more intolerant view about the nature of a worldview than that of Habermas, who might even condone the existence of such a worldview, though each must submit its claim for validity to the universal debate. Putnam seems more categorical: one view is truer than the other view. But the debate between opposing views may be intractable. Putnam reconciles the idea that some views are more rational with the idea that debates may be unresolvable.

Immediately after recognising that the argument is unresolvable, he suggests some ways to argue:

> One of the things that we aim at is that we should be able to give an account of how we know our statements to be true. . . . it is an important and extremely useful constraint on our theory itself that our developing theory of the world taken as a whole should include an account of the very activity and processes by which we are able to know that that theory is correct. (RTH, p. 132)

How could the 'Australians' account for their knowledge? They believe in a perfect illusion. The only glimpse of truth comes from the Guru, but how does *he* know? In sum, the fact of knowing about the illusion falsifies the theory! Putnam is confident he has the better argument:

> The Australians, remember, have themselves postulated an illusion so perfect that there is no rational way in which the Guru of Sydney can possibly know that the belief system which he has adopted and persuaded all the others to adopt is correct. (RTH, p. 133)

Why is the encounter unresolvable? Putnam describes the victory of one system over another in a way which explains why *agreement* may not follow: 'Judged by our standards of coherence, their belief system is totally incoherent' (RTH, p. 133). Habermas does not judge the rationality of a whole worldview, only individual propositions from within it, which are submitted for universal assent. Putnam is more decisive about whole worldviews. But his decision does not imply a neutral, universal criterion for resolving disputes, a criterion called rationality which applies to both sides. Rationality is always a particular rationality. The outcome of the dialogue will satisfy 'us', or 'them', but not necessarily both.

Is Putnam saying that rationality is relative to context? In fact, he rejects that proposition, because the relation 'relative to' implies an absolute viewpoint:

> The idea, in a natural first formulation is that every person (or, in a modern 'sociological' formulation, every culture, or sometimes every 'discourse') has his (its) own views, standards, presuppositions, and that truth (and also justification) are relative to these. One takes it for granted, of course, that whether X is true (or justified) relative to these is itself something 'absolute'. (RTH, p. 121)

It does not follow that the vatists are wrong merely relative to 'our' standards of rationality. Who defines 'relative to' if relative relations are absolute?[11] To maintain the comparison, Putnam introduces the good life to justify 'our' worldview against the vatist view. It is the good life in a specific sense. He allows the vatists to appear as good as 'us' in practical enterprises:

> We can imagine that the Australians are just as good as we are at anticipating experiences, at building bridges that stay up (or seem to stay up). (RTH, p. 131)

Their way of life is as effective as 'ours' in material matters. Putnam prefers 'our' version of the world because it implies a better idea of the good life:

> I would answer that the reason we want this sort of representation, and not the 'sick' sort of notional world possessed by the Australians, possessed by the Brain-in-a-Vatists, is that having this sort of representation system is *part of our idea of human cognitive flourishing*, and hence part of our idea of total human flourishing, of Eudaemonia. (RTH, p. 134)

Putnam connects rationality with human flourishing.[12] He judges rationality by these standards of betterment and the ideals implicit in them, rather than judging the rationality itself, in its own exclusive terms. 'Our' version says we are rational when we respond constructively to critical questions, and there is a further requirement for rationalists: 'One of the things we aim at is that we should be able to give an account of how we know our statements to be true' (RTH, p. 132).

Therefore a dialogic criterion is relevant in judging these competing views and their versions of rationality. The vatist view precludes meaningful dialogue and discussion: 'the Guru of Sydney just knows'. But open dialogue is essential to a good ideal of human flourishing.

Different Values, Different Facts

Putnam invents another disagreement, about the good life. There is a society of 'Super-Benthamites', who measure the good life by 'hedonic tone', a unit of pleasure (+) and pain (−). The Super-Benthamites 'believe that one should always act so as to maximize hedonic tone (taking that to mean the greatest hedonic tone of the greatest number)' (RTH, p. 140). Their good life *is* 'the greatest happiness of the greatest number'. They are uncompromising, 'willing to perform the most horrible actions . . . if the result of these actions would be to increase the general satisfaction level in the long run'. What happens if 'we' argue with this society about a requirement for the good life? Surely we might present some facts concerning what is good, which both sides might accept. Might the facts settle the dispute?

> The disagreement between us and the Super-Benthamites is just the sort of disagreement that is ordinarily imagined in order to make the point that two groups of people might agree on all the facts and still disagree about the 'values'. (RTH, p. 140)

Even if the facts are agreed, Putnam thinks facts will *not* settle the disagreement. He considers the role of lying in a situation when 'values' differ. Super-Benthamites must lie if convinced that the result will be to maximise hedonic tone. Consequently in their world 'it is not counted as dishonest in the pejorative sense to tell lies out of the motive of maximizing the general pleasure level'. Therefore 'we' and they will not mean the same thing by the word 'honest'. Assume that we all start with the same language; they will evolve new meanings for words which are justified by their hedonic perspective:

> So after a while the use of the description 'honest' among the Super-Benthamites would be extremely different from the use of that same descriptive term among us. And the same will go for 'considerate', 'good citizen' etc. (RTH, p. 140)

The words for facts will change; it will be impossible to agree about the facts, let alone about the values. There is no neutral language that will preserve the facts. The differences between our discourses will be total, leaving no common ground of perception and basic experience:

> The texture of the human world will begin to change. In the course of time the Super-Benthamites and we will end up living in different human worlds. (RTH, p. 141)

When two parties differ about the good life, they will differ about everyday experience and present the facts differently. There are no neutral facts with which they can negotiate.

> And just as the Brain-in-a-Vatists' inability to get the way the world is right is a direct result of their sick standards of rationality – their sick standards of theoretical rationality – so the inability of the Super-Benthamites to get the way the human world is right is a direct result of their sick conception of human flourishing. (RTH, p. 141)

Putnam emphasises division, how difficult it is to bridge gulfs between people. On the other hand, Putnam is much less *anxious* about the ill effects of dissension than is Habermas. He robustly endorses his ideal of the good life, while recognising irreconcilable divisions exist within it. 'We' and they do not share facts. But facts exist and 'we' should continue to assert those facts which our view discloses and their view denies.

But Putnam does not grant truth to one culture and allocate error to the others. He does not mean that 'the West' is the home of universal truth, and other cultures are mistaken. On the contrary, truth is no-one's property, it changes, grows, leaps and bounds. Further, Putnam believes that relativism is not a form of toleration but 'cultural imperialism', because relativists have no means of criticising their own tradition, their own context. Here Putnam coincides with Habermas: both are against ethnocentrism, the privileging of 'our culture', though Putnam does satirise some conceivable worldviews, and he does advocate other views. Sometimes, he seems to favour 'us', a nebulous and provoking concept. But elsewhere he opposes imperialism of thought, as well as other imperialisms.

Consider a relativist, he says in 'Why reason can't be naturalized', starting with Richard Rorty, but aiming to generalise. The relativist believes every idea is culture-specific, and culture-bound. But then the relativist gives examples, for instance the German sentence 'Schnee ist weiss', which the relativist says means 'Snow is white' in the context of German culture. Putnam considers that a consistent relativist, say an American, should add: the German sentence means snow is white in a German context seen from an American perspective (R&R, p. 237)! But relativists do not acknowledge their own viewpoint when interpreting others. Relativists interpret other cultures, and then disregard the difference between their own idea and the original culture. Relativists reconstruct the world out of their own idea of other cultures, define cultural differences, and then emphasise diversity. But the diversity is framed in their own terms, narcissistically. Relativism appropriates otherness to corroborate its own belief. In the instance of the American, 'Other cultures become, so to speak, logical constructions out of the procedures and practices of American culture.' All the diversity confirms that we are right to be relativists, and so 'we' are the new centre from which otherness is judged: 'the cultural relativist can become a cultural imperialist' (p. 238). Relativism has its own replies to such criticisms, as we shall see. But the argument shows how Putnam sees his own thought. He does not think truth is the property of one culture. Eudaemonia is not code for the American way!

Rational Ends

Putnam does not require agreement to underwrite truth in the way that Habermas does. On the contrary, in his view the error of one side reveals the truth of the other and heightens the impact of that truth. The good life plays a central part in defining such differences between truth and non-truth in worldview and rationality. Putnam places the good life in a different perspective from Habermas and has different requirements for it. In Habermas's work, argument defines the good life, because consensus is always the potential outcome of argument, and the basis of rationality, on which the good life depends, but scope for argument also threatens the lifeworld, without which the good life cannot be *a lived experience*. Putnam sees arguments about the good life ending in *disagreement*, for different conceptions of the good life are supported by differing versions of the world and conflicting standards of rationality, but this disagreement is not necessarily threatening. On the one hand, the good life accentuates divisions. But on the other, there must be ways of coping with these divisions. To begin with, such coping requires a complex view of rationality. The good life is a matrix of everyday experience and facts. Every rationality includes a definition of the good life, and is interrelated with this definition. What is rational proceeds from the requirements of the good life, but rationality results in assertions about fact and experience, so that a preferred rationality may produce errors of fact and misinterpretations of experience. When people have a distorted view of life, their rational standards are open to criticism. Their idea of the good life has failed to yield a durable rationality. So long as they stick to their standards, and judge by what they consider rational, they *will be wrong*, not just in the limited sense that their standards of rationality are wrong, but in the wider sense that their grasp of the facts is wrong. Nevertheless, there should be a *dialogue* between us, because rational dialogue is necessary to test notions of the good life, although it need not produce agreement. If the views remain polarised, we should reconsider our standards of rationality to decide whether we are confronting a powerful critique or just a set of errors in someone else's view.

In considering the selection of rational standards, there is one that Putnam rejects, and that is the purely instrumental. We have examined previously some instrumental theories, and the next chapter considers further new instrumentalist refinements. Putnam's criticisms apply to a basic model of instrumentality, a model which, as we shall see, has been much refined recently. To demonstrate his objections to the instrumental version of rationality, Putnam next considers the case of a committed Nazi and explains why 'modern instrumental rationalism' is inadequate in refuting such a person. Instrumental rationalists equate rationality with correct calculation, following a loose analogy with science (an analogy Putnam has already contested). Putnam diagnoses that:

> The core of this notion is a deceptively simple dichotomy: the idea is that the choice of 'ends' or 'goals' is neither rational nor irrational (provided some minimal consistency requirements are met); while the choice of means is rational to the extent that it is efficient. Rationality is a predicate of means, not ends, and it is totally conflated with efficiency. (RTH, p. 168)

In Putnam's understanding – which is only partly applicable to contemporary developments – instrumental rationalism is a form of scientific rationalism, based on a narrow definition of scientific objectivity and method. If rationalism works within such narrow limits and is so rigid, the stimulus to anti-rationalism is powerful. How could we give up the judgement of ends? If ends were simply a starting assumption to set means going, and the means took over, would ends remain outside the discussion of rationality? Surely, in that case, rationalism is impotent to make strong judgements. It has no determining object in human good. This is where Putnam refers to the classic case of 'the rational Nazi', 'rational' in the ironic sense that a purely instrumental approach will labour painfully to refute that title, try as it undoubtedly will in good hands to endorse humane judgements. In Putnam's view, this case presents a modern paradox, a contradiction in the thought of those instrumental rationalists, who attempt to defend humane values but fail to see how their instrumental rationality offers such weak refutations of the Nazi. Although Putnam underestimates contemporary instrumental thinking, the case illustrates his dialogic approach, his power of imagining antithetical views, and his courage in confronting difficulties in dialogue.

The issue which decides what is rational and not in the case of the Nazi is the good life, an issue which clearly concerns ends not just means. If ends are beyond rational dispute, then we have an insoluble problem:

> We don't see how we can say that it is rational to choose the better life and irrational to choose the worse. Yet not saying some such things seems precisely to be saying that 'it's all relative'; the ground crumbles beneath our feet. (RTH, p. 172)

To find an outcome between rational and irrational potentialities in these circumstances dialogue is necessary, and dialogic rationalism emerges as a vital concern, through Putnam's perspective, a rationalism enlarged to include emotion and imagination. Rationality need not decide all judgements. The good life does not require us to desert some pure rationality judgement and rely on non-rational preference because good reasons already imply notions of the good life. Putnam accuses instrumental rationalists, whom I would call 'scientific rationalists', of impoverishing modern culture:

> We have lost the ability to see how the goodness of an end can make it rational to choose that end. (RTH, p. 173)

He proposes that choosing ends requires a compound of reason and imagination. To imagine the goal is as important as to analyse statements about truth and falsehood which support the goal: imagination does not conflict with analysis. On the contrary, without imagination, analysis does not engage with the living issues of the good life.

However, the complexity of ends and means is compatible with strong, simple judgements. In pursuit of these, Putnam imagines a dialogue with a Nazi. He begins this consideration with a decisive judgement:

> . . . it does seem odd to diagnose the situation by saying 'Karl has irrational goals.' Even if this is part of what we conclude in the end, surely the first thing we want to say is that Karl has monstrous goals, not that he has irrational ones. (RTH, p. 212)

The first criterion by which we repudiate Karl's viewpoint is human flourishing, the holistic concept of the good life. The Nazi is evil, because he has a perverted ideal of happiness and a distorted view of facts. But a secondary criterion for dismissing his project is 'the irrationality of his *beliefs and arguments*' (RTH, p. 212). The imaginary dialogue begins with Karl's viewpoint, and a quick riposte:

> Suppose, first, that Karl claims Nazi goals are morally right and good (as Nazis, in fact if not in philosophers' examples, generally did). Then, *in fact*, he will talk rubbish. (RTH, p. 212)

Karl makes absurd assertions because his ideals are distorted and his aims evil. Putnam believes that corrupt goals induce fallacious arguments. Rational dialogue discredits both the general idea and the specific proposition to which a bad goal gives rise. Wicked ideals cause false assertions:

> He will assert all kinds of false 'factual' propositions, e.g. that the democracies are run by a 'Jewish conspiracy'; and he will advance moral propositions (e.g. that if one is an 'Aryan', one has a duty to subjugate non-Aryan races to the 'master race') for which he has no good arguments. (RTH, p. 212)

What are 'good arguments'? There is no universal criterion for them; instead Putnam deduces his standard of the good argument from everyday instances of successful arguing:

> The notion of a 'good argument' I am appealing to is internal to ordinary moral discourse; but that is the appropriate notion, if the Nazi tries to justify himself within ordinary moral discourse. (RTH, p. 212)

We should trust our ordinary criteria for what is right: our intuition tells us when arguments succeed and fail. Often these intuitions are powerful and valid. We should judge the good life by our usual criteria for convincing and unconvincing arguments, intuitive criteria that proceed from our everyday experience.

The Nazi will resist these judgements. He may even denounce the prevailing rationality. Is he then beyond judgement? We may never convince him that he is wrong: there are too many evasive tactics open to him. But Putnam insists that dialogue will find him out:

> Suppose, on the other hand, that the Nazi repudiates ordinary moral notions altogether (as our hypothetical Super-Benthamite did). I argued that a culture which repudiated ordinary moral notions, or substituted notions derived from a different ideology or moral outlook for them, would lose the ability to describe ordinary interpersonal relations, social events and political events adequately and perspicuously by our present lights. (RTH, p. 212)

Of course, in theory any new outlook might be an improvement on our own. How can we tell which is the superior point of view? The answer is circular but strong. We apply existing standards to the innovation, rationally *and* imaginatively. We talk; we interact; we consider rationally and imaginatively from both points of view. If we sense something better in a fresh outlook, we explore its potentialities; if it seems worse than our habitual view, we should reject the 'new' outlook, not merely accept it as a different possibility:

> Of course, if the different ideology and moral outlook are superior to our present moral system then this substitution may be good and wise; but if the different ideology and moral outlook are bad, especially if they are warped and monstrous, then the result will be simply an inadequate, unperspicuous, repulsive representation of interpersonal and social facts. (RTH, p. 212)

Rational dialogue discredits any view which does not represent the world plausibly. There must be dialogue; but also judgement, and we need no 'absolute' standards to make the judgements which are urgent.

The Conversation about the Rational 'Good Life'

The Conversation between Habermas and Putnam

The moral is powerful. We must not *fear* dialogue. We do not surrender our standards when we enter a dialogue with an opposing view. Though no standards are absolute, in the sense of being neutral, some standards are superior, others pernicious. The task of dialogic reason is to differentiate: to endorse the better, expose the worse:

> Of course, 'inadequate, unperspicuous, repulsive' reflect value judgments; but I have argued that the choice of a conceptual scheme necessarily reflects value judgments, and the choice of a conceptual scheme is what cognitive rationality is all about. (RTH, p. 212)

Putnam cautions us against absolute opinion. We can trust judgements without having absolute grounds. We must trust in our judgement without having absolute authority for doing so: that is the nature of the human condition. We make suitable judgements because our preferences are deeply rooted in our own nature. Values derived from experience contribute to a total picture of the world. Knowledge derives in turn from this world picture. We discover facts by applying our world picture to experience and to theories. We apply values when differentiating one fact from another. Therefore, facts are inseparable from values: without values, we have no world picture, and without a world picture there can be no knowledge. Values thus enter factual disputes; equally, facts are relevant in value disputes. The good life is a question of values, but arguments about the good life necessarily include questions of fact. The Nazi fails the dialogic test, because he denies facts, he lies. The larger conclusion is that his way of arguing discredits his view of life, and exposes his end or ideal of the good life to scorn, fear and loathing.

Rational dialogue can disprove Nazi facts and rule out Nazi 'ideals' of the good life. Putnam leaves no space for any 'pluralistic' hedging, and surely he is right! Of course, the Nazi may not be convinced by the argument, but the dialogue is still an important *construct*. Putnam asserts that our 'conceptions' of fact and value 'define a kind of objectivity, *objectivity for us*, even if it is not the metaphysical objectivity of the God's Eye view' (RTH, p. 55). Putnam believes in rational judgement, in the context of dialogue and of hypothetical dialogue.

In his view there is no *universal* rationality or any absolute criterion for what is credible or valid: agreement is often insubstantial and even irrelevant to the proper conduct of affairs; rational judgement (properly) requires imagination, and rational dialogue takes emotion into account. But, though both patience and fortitude may be required, there are still rational outcomes to arguments and there are ideals of the good life which favour rational outcomes!

Putnam has no equivalent to Habermas's overarching theoretical structure. His ideas connect by leaps and bounds rather than through careful building and repair. The two projects are not commensurate. Habermas offers an all-embracing theory of society and of human development; Putnam lights on, in the sense that he leaps among, specific problems of knowledge and ethics. But each provides ideas to extend dialogic rationalism into the sphere of the good life. Habermas is both grander and more frustrating than Putnam. There is a deeper sense of contradiction in his project, and also an immense potential. Putnam makes imaginative discoveries and revelations of a different kind, in keeping with his greater emphasis on imagination. But together, they make a powerful, and diverse, case for connecting reason to the good life, and for seeing argumentative dialogue as the link. Set in the context of current doubts and fears, this case requires a hearing and a scrupulous answer.

When we reflect on these problems of reason and the good life, the urgent question is not, 'what shall we decide?' but 'how shall we decide?' In what directions should we move the discussion? Seyla Benhabib offers a criterion in the context of ethical theories, a criterion which we may extend to the discussion of reason itself: 'what would be allowed and perhaps even necessary from the standpoint of continuing and sustaining the practice of the moral conversation among us?' (*Situating the Self*, p. 38). Benhabib's criterion suggests the need to think further about the *nature* of the viewpoints as interventions in a wider discussion. In the next chapter, I consider more fully the contradiction encountered in this chapter, that Habermas both legislates for dialogue and resists a dialogue with others. How has the contradiction arisen? What is the connection between Habermas's profound creativity and the contradiction of form and content? What is the cost of avoiding this contradiction of form and content?

Rawls and Liberal Society

Besides Putnam, other liberals connect dialogue and the good life: neutral liberals. We saw that Rawls advocates 'political liberalism', which 'tries to answer the question: how is it possible that there can be a stable and just society whose free and equal citizens are deeply divided by conflicting and even incommensurable religious, philosophical, and moral doctrines?' (*Political Liberalism*, p. 133). Each doctrine aims at the good life, but each promotes a different understanding of the 'good': 'there are many conflicting reasonable comprehensive doctrines with their conceptions of the good' (*Political Liberalism*, p. 135). The crucial word is 'reasonable' which means for Rawls that they apply basic standards and are open to consideration. There are also unreasonable doctrines. But Rawls is interested exclusively in reasonable doctrines, because, although 'reasonable, comprehensive doctrines' differ about 'the good', their ideas are 'each compatible with the full rationality of human persons'. It remains a conundrum for him: 'this reasonable plurality of conflicting and incommensurable doctrines'. Neither Habermas nor Putnam settles for a society based on common ground between views which are accepted as equally reasonable.

Rawls believes in 'public reason', which is a neutral outcome of reasonable views that transcends differences about 'the good':

> . . . political liberalism says: our exercise of political power is fully proper only when it is exercised in accordance with a constitution the essentials of which all citizens as free and equal may reasonably be expected to endorse in the light of principles and ideals acceptable to their common human reason. (*Political Liberalism*, p. 137)

Citizens differ. But if they are reasonable, they also agree. Rawls balances difference and agreement carefully. Reasoning produces different results. But all reasoning is potentially a common bond. Public discussion should concentrate on the links that reason provides, leaving the differences to be taken up in private life:

> Only a political conception of justice that all citizens might be reasonably expected to endorse can serve as a basis of public reason and justification. (*Political Liberalism*, p. 137)

The language is tricky: citizens 'might be reasonably expected to endorse' an idea of what is just. Does 'expected' mean assumed, so that we can predict they would agree? Or does 'expected' mean required, we would require them to agree? The ambiguity is pointed, not merely careless.

Rawls wants to fix the ground rules for public discussion in a fair society. He is not in favour of spontaneity, improvisation, unexpected twists and turns in public deliberation. He wants clear rules:

> . . . an agreement on a political conception of justice is to no effect without a companion agreement on guidelines of public inquiry and rules for assessing evidence. The values of public reason not only include the appropriate use of the fundamental concepts of judgment, inference, and evidence, but also the virtues of reasonableness, and fair-mindedeness as shown in abiding by the criteria and procedures of commonsense knowledge and accepting the methods and conclusions of science when not controversial. We owe respect to the precepts governing reasonable political discussion. (*Political Liberalism*, p. 139)

Putnam also endorses virtues, but he does not legislate their content or application. He does not believe virtues are fixed, and he does not expect virtue to be the standard by which disputes are settled. Rawls uses virtue to limit the play of differences, Putnam commits virtue to the search for improved rationality through conflict. Putnam's virtues are also more colourful and they generate anecdotes which it is easy to supplement.

The Cultural Politics of Argument: Nancy Fraser and 'Struggle over Needs'

A good society is central to a good life. Central to good society is good dialogue – to the rationality of a good society as conceived by dialogic rationalism. But good dialogue is understood in many ways, with different applications to ethics and society. In this context of social applications, an important contribution towards dialogic rationalism is made by Nancy Fraser with a 'model of social discourse' which she develops fully in an essay on 'Struggle over Needs: Outline of a Socialist-Feminist Theory of Late Capitalist Political Culture' (*Unruly Practices*, pp. 161–90, 164). The issue is need, and the ways people and groups debate it. What do people need? How can society meet the needs? Whose needs are most important? Fraser's model 'foregrounds the multivalent and contested character of needs talk', in a way that gives a perspective on argument, arguability. Society shapes talk: 'in welfare state societies we encounter a plurality of competing ways of talking about people's needs' (*Unruly Practices*, p. 164). And so argument arises, but it is not an argument in straightforward terms, because need incites different ways of talking. One result is argument, and other results are the suppression, deflection and manipulation of demands for satisfaction.

Fraser theorises 'the sociocultural means of interpretation and communication' (MIC), which both define and express need (*Unruly Practices*, pp. 164–5). She refers to 'means' at a moment, in a place. Not all means of communicating need are socially equal, or equally accessible:

> 1. The officially recognized idioms in which one can press claims; for example, needs talk, rights talk, interests talk.

Talk appears spontaneous, personal. But it is not. Culture presents resources, ways of talking about need which are enabling and also restrictive. Some voices are 'officially recognized': power determines what is effective talk, according to the status and value accorded. Fraser argues that officially recognised talk disadvantages some groups where some issues are concerned. OK: you are free to argue. Have your say. But when you try, the ground is not even. There is a bias, a communicative bias. The way is prepared for some arguments, not for other arguments. It's not just that the arguments are treated unequally. The resources available to advocates favour some arguments:

> 2. The vocabularies available for instantiating claims in these recognized idioms; thus, with respect to needs talk, What are the vocabularies available for interpreting and communicating one's needs? For example, therapeutic vocabularies, administrative vocabularies, religious vocabularies, feminist vocabularies, socialist vocabularies.

Recognition is more likely for some presentations, within accepted definitions. But it takes work to create new vocabularies which challenge new respect. Arguing is part of the work, to promote vocabularies. Fraser reveals the cultural politics of argument:

> 3. The paradigms of argumentation accepted as authoritative in adjudicating conflicting claims; thus, with respect to needs talk, How are conflicts over the interpretation of needs resolved? By appeals to scientific experts? By brokered compromises? By voting according to majority rule? By privileging the interpretations of those whose needs are in question?

Some arguing is 'authoritative', a term which refers to both knowledge and power, rational authority and political authority. She recognises paradigms of argumentation, as does Habermas in his 'new paradigm of mutual understanding'. Fraser is interested in the plurality of paradigms, which are socially constructed, and she is especially concerned with the favoured ways of constructing shared opinions and the less high-status ways. Her target is unequal pluralism. The crucial point is that rules are included in argument which predetermine the resolution, the interaction, the consequences. Argument means the whole story, including the rules which affect the outcome, so think where the rules come from, whose rules they are, why those rules were made: why resolve the conflict like this, not like that? 'The sociocultural means of interpretation and communication' are an important factor in achieving reason through dialogue, or inhibiting reason and dialogue in sectional interests.

Fraser also finds other sociocultural pressures affecting argument:

4. The narrative conventions available for constructing the individual and collective stories that are constitutive of people's social identities.
5. Modes of subjectification; the ways in which various discourses position the people to whom they are addressed as specific sorts of subjects endowed with specific sorts of capacities for action; for example, as 'normal' or 'deviant', as causally conditioned or freely self-determining, as victims or as potential activists, as unique individuals or as members of social groups.

People use language to argue, to press claims. But language also shapes people, language and other media of communication and the way we respond to each other. We argue using language as a medium; but language also makes us a medium; we are absorbed by media of ideas, identities, images. A dialectic cuts across arguing and the dialogue, a dialectic of identity. Both Habermas and Putnam see that society shapes individuals, who then argue in the terms society makes available. Habermas is strong on the shaping effect of norms, prior consensus, and on social construction of lifeworld, system in lifeworld. Putnam is strong on social values shaping the language of individuals. But Fraser embeds arguing more deeply, she embeds it profoundly in culture, and culture in politics, and politics in economics, though these processes are not simple. She contributes scepticism to dialogic rationalism, scepticism about access to argument, about the effects of context on outcome. People and groups do not start equal in an argument, particularly where cultural, political and economic considerations enter – and how could pure reason alone achieve equality? Here is a different attitude, a different orientation from other thinkers aligned with dialogic rationalism: we must not presume fairness, or simply accept the story of how an argument arises, as if it were a neutral story. How did these voices get into this arena? How did this voice get to sound so confident, that voice so defensive? Why are the audience listening to that person, not this one? The questions can apply to any argument that might lead to consensus in Habermas, and to Putnam's ongoing arguments leading to improved standards. But the scepticism is deeper, the critique more demanding, and the need for vigilance greater if argument is to have an equitable outcome, particularly in public affairs.

These inequalities arise because 'late capitalist societies are not simply pluralist' (*Unruly Practices*, p. 165). There are pervasive distinctions between the powerful and the disempowered. Some resources, paradigms, identities, 'are hegemonic, authorized and officially sanctioned' and others are 'nonhegemonic, disqualified and discounted'. Arguments are rigged, arguing is not free or fair. Fraser wonders about the potential for freeing argument, since the whole process is so biased. Often, discussions are almost a parody of argument. Argument belongs ambiguously in the struggle for power: from one perspective, prevailing power appropriates argument; from another perspective, the argument contests inequity.

Fraser conveys a deep sense of conflict. Certainly mutual understanding is hard to envisage. Even when argument leads to understanding, you need to ask: in whose interests is this agreement? Who has gained from this understanding? Insights may be apparent, but whose cognitive virtues are these? Whose impartiality? In whose interests are the facts being regarded in this way? But like Habermas and Putnam, she has standards of rationality, she prefers some views and rejects others. And there are reasons for the choice:

> I claim that we can distinguish better from worse interpretations of people's needs. To say that needs are culturally constructed and discursively interpreted is not to say that any need interpretation is as good as any other. (*Unruly Practices*, p. 181)

It is not purely a power struggle. We can assess critically. Fraser then complements Putnam further:

> I do not think justification can be understood in traditional objectivist terms as correspondence, as if it were a matter of finding the interpretation that matches the true nature of the need as it really is in itself, independent of any interpretation. (pp. 181–2)

You never get to reality, if by reality you mean something independent of your views of it. The facts exist, but they exist in terms of values and vocabularies that are already available to you. From here, Fraser introduces dialogue:

> . . . how exclusive or inclusive are various rival needs discourses? How hierarchical or egalitarian are the relations among the interlocutors? (p. 182)

Look at the dialogue, the interaction. The more rational view is also more dialogic, more involved in the interplay, less repressive, more enabling to the exchange as a whole. How a view is argued demonstrates how rational it is, how true it is:

> In general, procedural considerations dictate that, all other things being equal, the best need interpretations are those reached by means of communicative processes that most closely approximate ideals of democracy, equality and fairness. (p. 182)

But when are 'all things . . .equal'? The tone is reserved: 'In general'. Fraser does not apply the model directly: she wants a gap, a gap between ideals and occasions. The theory is less ambitious than Habermas's, less comprehensive, more open to circumstances though she overlaps with Habermas ('communicative practices'). Putnam is too liberal, but Fraser's tone resembles his in one inflection: endlessly sceptical, endlessly inventive, not satisfied with a formulation for long, always looking ahead to other considerations. Her contribution applies urgently in any situation where the style of argument hides a particular interest. Only by exposing the whole story can the effect of such social injustice be recognised and dealt with so that arguments have a more equitable outcome.

Giddens and the Hope of Transformation

Like Habermas, Giddens tells a development story:

> There were experts in pre-modern societies but few technical systems, particularly in the smaller societies; hence it was often possible for the individual members of such societies to carry on their lives, if they so wished, almost solely in terms of their local knowledge, or that of the immediate kinship group. No such disengagement is possible in modern times. (*Modernity and Self-Identity*, p. 30)

Systems channel individuals, experts influence our lives. Neither Giddens nor Habermas sees system as evil, and neither believes systems are the answer to human problems. Systems are necessary, experts are essential for technical reasons associated with the complexity of modern society and knowledge. But for the good life, Giddens trusts 'reflexivity', the individual consciousness-of-self:

> The reflexivity of modernity extends into the core of the self. Put in another way, in the context of a post-traditional order, the self becomes a reflexive project. (*Modernity and Self-Identity*, pp. 32–33)

Individuals are experts on themselves and so reflexivity is the everyday equivalent of expertise! The interaction is internal: consciousness in dialogue with itself guides us towards life choices. People pursue life plans, they take decisions:

> The backdrop here is the existential terrain of late modern life. . . . On the level of the self, a fundamental component of day-to-day activity is simply that of choice . . . by definition, tradition or established habit orders life within relatively set channels. Modernity confronts the individual with a complex diversity of choices and, because it is non-foundational, at the same time offers little help as to which options should be selected. (*Modernity and Self-Identity*, p. 80)

Self-understanding is a primary factor, a precondition for interaction and social roles. Although what we know about our potentialities is learnt, and we learn it socially, from copying systems in society, so our choices are social and cultural as well as personal, and the distinction between self and system is not absolute. The theory is individualised to contain the self, stories of the self and its choices.

Personal choice enters politics: for Giddens, the search for a better life is also political, and promotes autonomy, in a quest which is shared, social, collective. Autonomy is a social good, a political objective, because there are two kinds of politics: emancipatory politics and life politics. Emancipatory politics is about liberation, from tradition, inequality and injustice. Life politics is a new politics which is about choice, in the way we live:

> Life politics . . . is a politics of life decisions. What are these decisions, and how should we seek to conceptualise them? First and foremost, there are those affecting self-identity itself. . . . A reflexively ordered narrative of self-identity provides the means of giving coherence to the finite lifespan, given changing external circumstances. Life politics from this perspective concerns debates and contestations deriving from the reflexive project of the self. (*Modernity and Self-Identity*, p. 215)

Giddens believes that in our time 'moral issues return to the centre of the agenda of life politics'. Debates multiply. The terms are rational: 'decisions', 'reflexively ordered', 'coherence'. The effect is necessarily dialogic: for we get 'contestations'. But the focus from which dialogue derives is internal, the forum for making opinion is the self.

Giddens writes about the self and self-identity in such a way that relationships evolve from self-identities. The approach is sympathetic, but a little claustrophobic, as each self becomes enclosed in its own concerns. One antidote to the claustrophobia is dialogue, debate between people. Giddens recognises the need and he wants better debates about value, about morality, as he terms lived value:

> Life-political issues cannot be debated outside the scope of abstract systems: information drawn from various kinds of expertise is central to their definition. Yet because they centre on questions of how we should live our lives in emancipated social

circumstances they cannot but bring to the fore problems and questions of a moral and existential type. Life-political issues supply the central agenda for the return of the institutionally repressed. They call for a remoralising of social life and they demand a renewed sensitivity to questions that the institutions of modernity systematically dissolve. (*Modernity and Self-Identity*, p. 224)

Debate is necessary, open and lively debate. Institutions will try to suppress discussion. But expertise also encourages discussion, by provoking arguments, and Giddens also sees people being able to debate the problems, despite all distractions and censorship. The harder institutions try, the less they suppress the questions. People respond to the suppression by asking new questions:

The tremendous extension of human control over nature (which, as in other areas of control, yields new unpredictabilities) comes up against its limits, however. These consist not so much in the environmental degradation and disruption that is thus brought about, as in the stimulus to reintroduce parameters of debate external to modernity's abstract systems. . . . The process is not an automatic one: on the level of everyday life, as well as in collective struggles, moral/existential problems are actively recovered and brought forward into public debate. (*Modernity and Self-Identity*, p. 224)

In this way, along a route very different from that taken by other thinkers, Giddens arrives at argument, at a point close enough to Habermas and Putnam and also different enough to allow for a conversation. Giddens, too, opts in the end for rational dialogue, but rationality in his view develops through personal choices made in search of a strong identity in the unstable world of late modernity. In this way, he is closest to Putnam, who likewise assumes a wide variety of interests in his theory, which develop through interaction facilitating an improved argument. Indeed Giddens complements Putnam with a deeper sense of individuality and its place in the ongoing debate. Like Putnam, too, Giddens is strong on good qualities which might help debates to flourish. Putnam connects favourable feelings with cognitive virtues; Giddens moves in a more romantic direction, but there is surely something in common, a regard for psychological context. On the whole, Habermas takes a different tack, placing more emphasis for resolving disagreement on the function of language, which, properly understood, must lead towards consensus. Both Habermas and Giddens start from critical theory and leave a place in their discourse for system and institution. There is another affinity between them, a deeper community. Just as Habermas added communicative rationality to enlightenment, so Giddens adds to enlightenment his own version of life politics:

Life-political issues are likely to assume greater and greater importance in the public and juridical arenas of states. Demands for emancipatory rights . . . do not thereby become any less important. Attempts to extend and sustain citizenship rights, for example, remain fundamental; such rights provide the arenas within which life-political issues can be openly debated. (*Modernity and Self-Identity*, p. 226)

The conversation is animated. Like all good conversations, it does not proceed in a straight line. On one point, Giddens is closer to Putnam, on another closer to Habermas, and always he contrasts with both, throwing into relief their vital characteristics along with his own.

Unbounded Dialogue

Dialogic rationalism is itself a dialogue, and the good life is a central theme. As this chapter indicates, the dialogue is unbounded, and ideas enter it from many points of view. Sometimes the contributions are hopeful about modern society, sometimes they are critical, or sceptical. The dialogue expresses feelings which vary as widely as the ideas: determination, excitement, anxiety, anger, sympathy. At the centre of the conflict is a question: how much potential for a good life is left inside modernity? The question resonates through the many conversations that constitute the whole dialogue on the good life.

Dialogic rationalism proposes no blueprint for modernising the good life. A kind of plan is conceivable, but a plan to ensure that discussion continues and widens, and that new ideas are forthcoming. In fact, at a practical level, in social and urban planning, dialogic rationalism is also represented: in the words of Fischer and Forester, some theorists advocate 'the argumentative turn in policy analysis and planning' ('Editors' Introduction', *Arg. Turn*, pp. 1–17, 14). Considering public policy decisions, John S. Dryzek advocates 'a rational commitment to free democratic discourse' instead of 'the automatic application of rules' ('Policy Analysis', p. 214). Dryzek suggests the following approach to specific decisions:

> ... there should be as few restrictions as possible on competent participation in policy discourse and the kinds of arguments that can be advanced. ... Anything less would be untrue to the analysts' and planners' claims to rationality, scientific or otherwise. ('Policy Analysis', p. 230)

Planners are rational because they encourage discussion, not because they devise blueprints: locally, the good life is a theme for dialogue, and the dialogue is unbounded.

It is not rational to require definitive answers to complex questions. Instead, it is rational to widen the dialogue, to encourage ideas, to let new conversations evolve. The next chapter widens the dialogue about reason to consider alternatives outside dialogic rationalism itself, alternative models of reason and alternative views of the modern world. Paradoxically, to be authentic, dialogic rationalism must recognise other voices.

Notes

1 Martin Jay, 'Habermas and Modernity', in Jay, *Fin-de-Siècle Socialism* (New York: Routledge, 1988), pp. 127–8. Jay emphasises Habermas's sympathy for Walter Benjamin in particular as evidence of a more subtle and qualified theory of 'universal communication' than often assumed by opponents of Habermas.

2 The importance of separating universal claims and imperial ambitions is, of course, that it attempts to include intuitions which otherwise lead to relativism. Compare Feyerabend (*Farewell*, p. 77): 'Relativism is a popular doctrine. Repelled by the presumption of those who think they know the truth and having witnessed the disasters created by attempts to enforce a uniform way of life many people now believe that what is true for one person, or one group, or one culture need not be true for another.'

3 Bernstein (*Beyond Objectivism and Relativism*, p. 196) makes such moments central: 'The read-

ing of Habermas that I am advocating . . . shows how he contributes to the movement beyond objectivism and relativism.'

4 Putnam (*The Many Faces of Realism*, p. 70) is even more forceful: 'What is wrong with relativist views (apart from their horrifying irresponsibility) is that they do not at all correspond to how we think and how we shall continue to think.'

5 White, *The Recent Work of Jürgen Habermas*, p. 97.

6 Ibid., p. 106.

7 Gadamer (*Truth and Method*, p. 331) goes further to avoid the risk. He promotes an interpretation of dialectic as the true art of argument. And this art would reduce these dangers: 'Dialectic consists not in trying to discover the weakness of what is said, but in bringing out its real strength.' Here indeed Gadamer is giving primacy to 'yes' and taking a more rigid view than Habermas of what is meant by being 'oriented toward understanding'.

8 Anthony Giddens gives a complex account of the *different* meanings of 'risk' in a modern context. These senses of risk vary from 'the sense of intensity' to 'the expanding number of contingent events' to 'Awareness of the limitations of expertise' (*Consequences*, pp. 124–5).

9 Alasdair MacIntyre, *Whose Justice? Which Rationality?* (London: Duckworth, 1988), p. 2 argues that modern society frequently *pretends* that agreements have been achieved, when there is really no agreement at all: 'The facts of disagreement themselves frequently go unacknowledged, disguised by a rhetoric of consensus.'

10 White, *The Recent Work of Jürgen Habermas*, p. 96.

11 Putnam here veers away from the alternative formulation of contextualism, eloquently exemplified by MacIntyre, *Whose Justice?*, p. 76: 'And, that is to say, when desires and emotions are understood in the context of interaction and interpretation which are constituted by particular cultures, it becomes evident that they can only function as they do if characterized in terms provided by one specific set of norms and justifications.'

12 Martha Nussbaum gives a rich account of the origins and complexity of eudaemonia in *Fragility*. Particularly apposite to Putnam is her interpretation of Sophocles (p. 52): 'The *Antigone* . . . ends with the assertion that practical wisdom (to phronein) is the most important constituent of human good living (eudaemonia).'

5

Landscapes of Rationalism and Postmodernism

Rationalisms and Postmodernisms

Beyond the ideas I interpret as contributions towards dialogic rationalism, there are alternative rationalisms, and there are postmodern views, relativist and sceptical. Some contrasts to dialogic rationalism have already been examined briefly, in the form of instrumental rationalism and scientific rationalism, and several bordering rationalisms have also been explored. A fuller perspective will show how complex are the relations between reason and dialogue conceived by contemporary thought, given the fundamental contrasts between different rationalisms and their attitudes towards dialogue. *Dialogic rationalism has to develop the conversation about alternative rationalisms, and also relate to relativism.* There is a particular onus on any dialogic approach to engage with alternatives. There are many rationalist challenges which do not endorse dialogic reason. Postmodernism also challenges dialogue in a demanding way: some postmodern ideas which are not rationalist can still only be expressed in a dialogic way. So this chapter explores a double challenge to dialogic rationalism, from different rationalisms and different conceptions of dialogue.

Non-Dialogic Reason

Habermas on Strategic Action

The perspective opens from Habermas's dialogic critique of reason which is independent of dialogue, particularly strategic and instrumental reason. We have considered his basic claims on behalf of reason which is part of an interactive process leading towards consensus, but he has a complex overview of reason in society. Habermas contrasts the needs of communication and strategy. The contrast is fundamental when he defines strategy, calculation and purposive action. To find a basis for co-ordinating action through agreement, Habermas distinguishes contrasting models of action, each with its own relevance to an aspect of society, and particularly to different stages of social development. First, there is the 'teleological model of action' which derives from Aristotle:

> The actor attains an end or brings about the occurrence of a desired state by choosing means that have promise of being successful in the given situation and applying them in a suitable manner. (CA1, p. 85)

This teleological model 'is expanded to a *strategic* model when there can enter into the agent's calculations of success the anticipation of decisions on the part of at least one additional actor' (CA1, p. 85). Strategic action is action which refers to other people without being truly social: others are present only as objects of calculation. Then there is *normatively regulated* action, governed by social criteria, shared values and requirements of behaviour. In normatively regulated action, actors move within the framework of 'an agreement that obtains in a social group' (CA1, p. 85). Next comes *dramaturgical action*, where other people are present to the actor as 'a public' and so the basis of interaction is 'stylizing the expression of one's own experiences with a view to the audience' (CA1, p. 86). *Communicative action* is then reintroduced as the fourth, and superior, model, both more inclusive and more advanced. It is communicative action which is the source of new agreements, agreements on which people can then act together. Habermas has already required that, in order to associate for the purpose of seeking agreement, people need some prior agreements: these are 'norms' which regulate action in society. Other agreements proceed beyond the vouchsafed agreements and are achieved agreements: these are free understandings between people. Only these achieved understandings testify to the rational power of communication. Others merely signify that people belong to groups.

Only in communicative action do the actors *achieve* consensus. To stress this advantage and sharpen the distinction between communicative action and other kinds of action, Habermas redefines the relations of each type of action to surrounding contexts. In teleological action, he sees the actor trying to change 'a world of existing states of affairs' (CA1, p. 87). Actors have aims in the first place; they try to impose these aims on the world outside themselves. Such actors are rational insofar as they try to fit their ideas to the world, or the world to their ideas. Here any 'agreement' is metaphorical, a good fit between the actor and a world, not an understanding achieved between two actors *in* a world. Only an outside observer can decide whether the actor and the world 'agree'. The next step is 'strategic action', where actors treat *each other* just as if they were part of an external world. Each has an aim; each tries to manipulate the other to achieve their aim. Not only is understanding unnecessary, if they did understand one another, they could not be manipulated. Strategic actors need to avoid being understood by others. They have not reached the threshold of consensus, any kind of consensus.

Habermas believes that purposive calculations, or teleological action and strategic action, imply 'a one-world concept' (CA1, p. 88). These actors interact only with an objective world, a world in which they are not represented, in which their own interpretation of themselves and their participation is repressed. They perceive only the outside world and the actions in it. They judge such actions in relation to that world. Did the actors achieve their aims? Was the world consistent with the actor's plans? Consensus is meaningless: the world outside cannot enter into reciprocal understanding with them to produce a consensus, even a world outside consisting of manipulable people as well as manipulable things. The 'one-world' is a measurable space; we measure success and failure in that world's space. If that world were all, life would be simple but impoverished.

Habermas accepts that we inhabit this space of measured actions. But he claims that we also inhabit other spaces: two-world spaces. The next step into another space produces the model of normatively regulated action, a two-world model of action. Actors now deal with a social world as well as with the objective world. Meanings and values matter. The actor is now an insider as well as an outsider, an insider who shares norms with other actors:

> A social world consists of a normative context that lays down which interactions belong to the totality of legitimate personal relations. (CA1, p. 88)

These norms are shared by all the people within that social world. Actors succeed when they align their actions successfully with the requirements of the social world, as well as with the objective world. The norms precede the actions; we measure the deed by the norm. To succeed in the social world is to belong fully; to fail is to be alien, to fail the norms, to misunderstand them or forget them or ignore them or fail to do what is normative. Again, the space for action is measurable, only the measurement is more subtle, including the 'objective world of existing states of affairs' and the 'social world' (CA1, p. 88). To decide whether an act succeeds, we need to know what norms and expectations society has for what the actor is doing as well as the interaction with 'states of affairs'. The model is founded on the depth of belonging to a social world.[1]

The 'dramaturgical' model of action is also a 'two-world' model. The two worlds are internal and external, the subjective experience of the actor and the world of an outside audience.[2] There is more scope for individuality and there is also an interesting ambiguity:

> . . . dramaturgical action can take on latently strategic qualities to the extent that the actor treats his audience as opponents rather than as a public. The scale of self-presentations ranges from sincere communication of one's own intentions, desires, moods, etc., to cynical management of the impressions an actor arouses in others. (CA1, p. 93)

Habermas is so aware that actors manipulate audiences that he tends to reduce the creative relationships of the actor with an audience. In particular, the distinction between sincere and manipulative expression seems almost arbitrary: is that the *main* criterion when it comes to emotional expression? The pressure of his own system limits the treatment mainly to concepts which seem appropriate to the design. When he returns to communicative action, after further defining the social and dramaturgical models, Habermas can now clinch its claim because it offers people a 'threefold relation to the world' (CA1, p. 96). Communicatively, people live in a triple world. The 'threefold relation' incorporates objective, social and subjective levels in life. So communicative action takes place on all these levels. Habermas reviews the other models in terms of language and world:

> . . . first, the indirect communication of those who have only their own ends in view [strategic, teleological]; *second*, the consensual action of those who simply actualize an already existing normative agreement [normatively regulated]; and *third*, presentation of self in relation to an audience [dramaturgical]. (CA1, p. 95)

By contrast, 'the communicative model of action . . . takes all the functions of language equally into consideration'. But the implication is that communicative action is not just a mixture of the other three ways of acting: it is also distinct. Above all, communicative action uses the whole scope of language: action is communicative when the whole of language is alive, which is qualitatively different from the use of any one dimension of language and not merely a synthesis of all the limited uses.

Norm-regulated action also depends fundamentally on language: more so even than strategic or dramaturgical actions, because language transmits the norms to which people must adjust their actions. Without language there can be no normative criteria for action. So norm-regulated action needs words, but uses them in a different way from communicative action, as Habermas specifies:

> The normative model of action presupposes language as a medium that transmits cultural values and carries a consensus that is merely reproduced with each additional act of understanding. (CA1, p. 95)

Language conveys the norms to the people, but its effects are then fixed and not negotiable; in the normative context, language establishes us in groups and societies, but only within strict limits. In Habermas's vision, the use of words is most dynamic in communicative action: it is an action that *creates* consensus through understanding; and such new understanding is possible through the fullest use of words. Further, the full use of language provides a paradigm for all cases of genuine understanding and communication. The argument is powerful, gripping and energising. Can there be any debate, any real exchange? I think so: non-dialogic rationalists have contributions to the conversation about reason, about reconstructing humane reason, though the basic criticisms are potent. I think Habermas strikes home against basic instrumental reason, as discussed earlier. But there are refinements. I propose 'the new instrumentalism' as a term for developments almost complementary to dialogic approaches, developments capable of meeting Habermas's criticisms and making new contributions to the study of reason in society.

Elster, Sen and New Instrumentalism

Jon Elster is a major innovator within instrumental theory and rational choice. As we saw earlier, Elster starts from the standard instrumental model of knowing and acting. The knowing is scientific – scientific and logical, tightly logical.

> The action should be the best way of satisfying the agent's desires, given his beliefs. Moreover, we must demand that these desires and beliefs be themselves rational. . . . With respect to beliefs, we must also impose a more substantive requirement of rationality: they should be optimally related to the evidence available to the agent. . . . In forming their beliefs, the agents should consider all and only the relevant evidence, with no element being unduly weighted. As a logical extension of this requirement, we also demand that the collection of evidence itself be subject to the canons of rationality. (*Solomonic Judgments*, p. 4)

Elster propounds a theory of rational choice:

1   there is a rational agent, the individual (methodological individualism);
2   the individual seeks to implement aims, to achieve goals.

Here he is vulnerable to dialogic criticism: he presupposes isolated agents acting for their own purposes, little interaction with others, little depth to human relations – as if individuals act on their beliefs in isolation, as abstracted units! Such rationality only makes sense in the absence of other people! So a critique emerges from Habermas's deep sense of social being, and another from Putnam's socialised rationality which is moral and livable and widely acceptable.

In his later work, Elster shows many exceptions to rational choice made along the lines of simple individualism. He tests the model, so that his instrumentalism becomes subtle, flexible and even self-mocking. For instance, he acknowledges aims which can only be achieved if you are not trying to achieve them: sleep, participation, prosperity through democracy. Dialogue and argument can be reviewed from an equivalent perspective: perhaps agreement can be best attained by not trying to agree, but just letting differences find their place in the world. There might be an ironic map of reason, showing exceptions to reason and reason's limitations, proceeding to a conversation about the limits of rationality involving both dialogic and instrumental models.

The later Elster identifies ambiguities effectively, particularly ambiguities about what is rational. His new instrumentalism tells complex stories examining ambiguities of reason, reason's boundaries. A key case that Elster examines is that of revolution: 'I shall try to separate out what is rational from what is irrational in revolutionary movements' (*Political Psychology*, p. 15). Why do people support revolution? Particularly, why before the revolutionaries are winning? The revolution wins – then people benefit even if they weren't revolutionaries: 'A successful revolution would establish a public good, that is, a good that could not be restricted solely to the militants themselves' (p. 16). If revolution fails, there is 'severe punishment for those supporting it': 'The rational conclusion seems obvious: There would be everything to gain and nothing to lose by abstaining from any revolutionary strategy.' Yet people do join revolutions before the outcome is certain. Is it 'on the basis of "irrationality and madness"'? Or are there 'other explanations still falling within the bounds of rational behaviour'? Perhaps such support is rational if people have 'nothing to lose'. But few have 'nothing'. So Elster proposes 'a further rationalistic interpretation which holds that revolutionaries are prompted by selective incentives in the form of either rewards or punishments' (p. 17). For instance, the fun of joining is 'its own selective incentive' (p. 18). He extends rationality:

> So far I have limited myself to rational, self-interested motivations. Contrary to widespread misunderstanding, however, rationality does not rule out altruism. If the revolutionary takes the consequences of his action for other people into account, the large number of such people may make up for the limited effect on each of them. (p. 19)

But why begin the revolution at first, when the risk is great and the benefits remote, whether motivated by self-interest or altruism? Who begins the revolution, and are they rational? Rationality will not explain their actions entirely, but they can still demonstrate admirable values, to endorse as necessary in human history:

> If we rely on the idea that rationality is defined by instrumental efficacy and orientation toward the future, we can distinguish between two types of nonrational behaviour. (p. 19)

Elster defines rationality in practical terms: a rational person asks what effects actions will have, whether aims will be achieved, altruistic or self-interested. Beyond rationality are people who ignore consequences, they just act directly:

> First there are the unconditional participants who do their duty without worrying about the efficacy of their action. . . . Although they take no account of consequences, their behaviour can nevertheless have very desirable consequences. Such frequently admirable behaviour must, however, be considered irrational, partly because it has its roots in magical thinking (everyday Calvinism) and partly because it may work against its own ends. (pp. 19–20)

The key phrase is 'Such frequently admirable behaviour', which indicates these are historically necessary, good acts. Then, 'we have to take into account that some participants may be motivated by a norm of fairness' (p. 20). Doubts are raised about their rationality, though they are also necessary: 'The essential fact is their commitment to a non-instrumental value' (p. 22). Ironically, they serve a rational function, since:

> Later, they are the only ones that can act effectively as leaders, because their proven integrity means that they can make promises or utter threats which in the mouth of others would lack credibility. (p. 22)[3]

Elster exposes reason's ambiguities: what was once irrational can become rational later, what was irrational can have constructive consequences. Rationality may emerge only in retrospect, or its limits may appear in time. Putnam comes closest to this sense of indeterminacy, which justifies the search for what is rational rather than definitions of rational behaviour. Elster can teach us to enlarge dialogic approaches to reason, even though he himself is monologic. The monologic view is not final, but can enter into a wider dialogue which is alert to ambiguities and ironies.

Elster also scrutinises social norms. He believes that instrumentalism has reduced norms to individual self-interest:

> There is a norm of fair division of the surplus between capital and labour. Employers will appeal to this norm when the firm does badly, workers when it does well. There is a norm of equal pay for equal work. Workers will appeal to this norm when they earn less than workers in similar firms, but not when they earn more. The norm of preservation of status, or wage differences, can also be exploited for bargaining purposes. ('Economic Order', p. 361)

One might question whether these are norms at all! The 'norm' of 'fair division' is not evident. But Elster's point is more general: basic instrumentalism always discerns self-interest in normative behaviour, as if people only follow norms which suit their purposes and social norms were an aggregate expression of individual requirements. But Elster recognises that norms are different from other self-interested tactics:

> Some argue that this is all there is to norms: they are tools of manipulation, used to dress up self-interest in more acceptable garbs. But this cannot be true. Some norms, like the norm of vengeance, obviously override self-interest. ('Economic Order', p. 361)

Norms are social expressions, they cannot be reduced to individual motives and personal goals. Indeed there is an irony, because individuals can exploit norms for their purposes, only because others conform at the cost of their interest:

> A more general argument against the cynical view is that if nobody believed in norms, there would be nothing to manipulate. . . . If some people successfully exploit norms for self-interested purposes, it can only be because others are willing to let norms take precedence over self-interest. ('Economic Order', p. 361)

Elster concludes that 'norm-guided behaviour is not outcome oriented' (p. 362). But is such behaviour rational at all, then? The problem is analogous to the problem Habermas has because norms do not fit his main model of rationality. Clearly norms are prior to communicative understandings, and so Habermas tells complex stories about how norms arise, linking them back to rational communication. He also has to allow norms a space next door to communicative action, so that they are part of the context of rational behaviour but do not derive directly from consensual argument. Similarly Elster has to accommodate norms to instrumental rationality. Habermas sees norms contributing towards communicative reason, Elster sees them contributing towards instrumental reason. But neither can quite demonstrate that norms are consistent with communicative or instrumental reason, so norms remain separate from the main body of their theories.

Elster has something further to contribute to the conversation about reason and norms. First, he considers that reason inhabits a normative world, yet norms do not reduce to reason. He allows norms to remain problematic:

> Rules of etiquette, norms of dress and the like do not seem to have any useful consequences. Some writers argue that they serve the useful function of confirming one's identity or membership of a social group. Since the notion of social identity is pretty elusive, the argument is hard to evaluate. A weakness is that it does not explain why these rules are as complicated as they often are. ('Economic Order', p. 363)

Norms exceed need, they are pure sociality, and they have no specific purpose or function in some cases, so norms are ambiguous in relation to reason: they may serve rational ends, they may not:

> Norms regulating the role of money are also ambiguous. I don't think the norm against buying places in the cinema queue has useful consequences, although, of course, it might have. (p. 363)

Norms invite many interpretations but they are essential expressions of social existence. But what kind of interaction do they facilitate? The answer varies, because there is no comprehensive theory of norms. Norms remain an enigma, a permanent challenge to any theory of rationality. Norms, Elster argues, are neither reducible to rationality, nor separable from it. Dialogic rationalism has a clearer approach to norms than this: since its rationality arises in interaction, dialogic rationalism does not have an inherent problem with sociality. But Elster also has a point: it is not necessary to resolve the problem of norms comprehensively. Particular cases remain ambiguous.

Other thinkers develop instrumentality in ways which resonate with dialogic rationalism, and illuminate any theory of rationality, whether dialogic or mono-logic. Another new instrumentalist is Amartya Sen, who concentrates on the arguability of reason itself. He surveys conventional theories of rational choice as consistent and self-interested:

> There are, it can be argued, two dominant approaches to rational choice extensively used in decision theory and economics:
>
> (1) *Internal consistency*: Rational choice is seen, in this approach, simply in terms of internal consistency of choice.
> (2) *Self-interest pursuit*: The rationality of choice is identified here with the unfailing pursuit of self-interest. ('Rationality and Uncertainty', p. 109)

Sen defines the basic models. He also argues that

> an objectively founded theory can give an important role to what people actually do value and to their ability to get those things. (*On Ethics*, p. 42)

Further, he advocates that:

> The advantages of consequential reasoning involving interdependence and instrumen-tal accounting, can be . . . combined not only with intrinsic valuation, but also with position rationality and agent sensitivity of moral assessment. (*On Ethics*, p. 77)

Therefore, Sen is serious about instrumental reason, and he starts with purpose-ful agents. But his approach is subtle, and he distances himself from both 'internal consistency' and 'self-interest' when he surveys rationality:

> I would like to argue that neither approach adequately captures the content of rational-ity. . . . It is arguable that what goes wrong with these two standard approaches to rationality is their failure to pay adequate and explicit attention to the role of reasoning in distinguishing the rational from the irrational. ('Rationality and Uncertainty', p. 110)

Reasoning makes its own rules and finds its own limits: it is reflexive. This is close to Putnam, for whom rationality appears in a search that is open-ended. But ironically, rational choice theory may be more open-ended than dialogic theories of reason. Sen's idea links to double arguability, and the communicative processes which make rational dialogues self-defining and self-creating. Sen's view of rational choice is worth considering for analogous applications to dialogic reason. Although not formulated dialogically, his view of rationality has vital implications for dialogue, in general, and the dialogic forms of rationality. If reason is self-identifying and self-limiting, if it creates the boundaries within which it functions, then it is unpredictable. Starting within rational choice, Sen restores spontaneity to reason, spontaneity and ambiguity. His theory even allows reason to have arbi-trary areas, borders which will shift around on occasion. Yet he also endorses efficiency and methical accounting. While recognising freedom of self-defin-ition, Sen also recommends efficiency, without which society is weakened and left open to exploitation.

Sen is a profound critic of oppression. He is deeply conscious of inequality, of injustice, of global distortion. He has a rich idea about particularity, difference, the whole person. Sen also recognises inter-relation, interdependence:

> Behaviour is ultimately a social matter as well, and thinking in terms of what 'we'
> should do, or what should be 'our' strategy, may reflect a sense of identity involving
> recognition of other people's goals and the mutual interdependencies involved. (*On
> Ethics*, p. 85)

The 'we' seems secondary still, oddly additional to individual requirements. Yet the language is rich: identity is discovered through co-operation, we are approaching communicative action and shared ideals of human flourishing; moreover, Sen's regard for the particular is perhaps sharper than that of Habermas.

Other instrumentalist thinkers make sociological qualifications. They apply a basic model, but they are aware of other factors that impinge on rationality, especially emotion – for instance, Randall Collins, who writes on 'Emotional Energy as the Common Denominator of Rational Action':

> The rational actor perspective has several appealing qualities for sociological theory. It
> begins with a motivated actor and avoids reifying macroentities such as culture or
> structure; these are valid concepts only to the extent that they can be derived from the
> action of individuals. It also has a general explanatory strategy: All social action is
> explainable in terms of individuals attempting to optimize their expected benefits rel-
> ative to costs of their actions.[4]

The approach is less subtle: 'all social action' reduces to one person's motive, to one-track units. But there is an effort to link reason and emotion and so the way is open for a more complex discussion of the rational basis of what people do together.

Nussbaum and Ethical Deliberation

Closely connected to rational choice in the new instrumentalism of Elster and Sen is a deliberative theory of ethics and rationality. Shelly Kagan observes that theories of rationality 'can come not only in "instrumental" versions . . . but also in "deliberative" versions that assign weight only to desires that survive some rational process of reflection'.[5] A leading innovator in deliberative ethics is Martha Nussbaum, who criticises instrumentalism which is quantitative, mechanistic and formulaic. She stresses experience, and the need for imagination, but, like Sen, she also considers that judgement may require a qualitative calculation. Within rational choice theory, she promotes sensitivity above method.

Writing on non-scientific deliberation, Nussbaum adds a profound historical perspective in advocating an Aristotelian style of ethical deliberation. An Aristotelian approach 'will ask who the person of practical wisdom is and how he deliberates' (*Fragility*, p. 291). An Aristotelian will question 'the Platonic aspiration to universality, precision, and stable control' and favour 'Aristotle's more "yielding" and flexible conception of responsive perception'. Founding principles will be:

> Aristotle's claims that practical deliberation must be anthropocentric, concerned with
> human good simpliciter. . . . Aristotle's attack on the notion that the major human val-
> ues are commensurable by a single standard. (*Fragility*, p. 291)

This concerns the choosing individual, estimates of value, making decisions and choices by reasoning. Reasoning is a party in the choice of action, as in Sen, but rational choice is even more integral to character and situation:

> . . . we must insist . . . that the 'perception' that is the most valuable manifestation of our practical rationality, and an end in itself, is not merely motivated and informed by the desires. Perception is a complex response of the entire personality, an appropriate acknowledgement of the features of the situation on which action is to be based, a recognition of the particular. As such, it has in itself non-intellectual components. (*Fragility*, p. 309)

Rational choice links to psychology generally. In 'The Discernment of Perception: An Aristotelian Conception of Private and Public Rationality', Nussbaum offers 'a defence of the emotions and the imagination as essential to rational choice' (*Love's Knowledge*, pp. 54–105, 55). It is possible to choose the right thing to do: by reason employing sensitive comparison. Motives for choice are complex, and attached to incommensurable values:

> By reducing music and friendship to matters of efficiency, for example, I will be failing to attend properly to what they themselves are. (*Love's Knowledge*, p. 59)

People make rational choices when they are attuned to the relevant value in the specific situation:

> 'The discernment rests with perception.' This phrase . . . is used by Aristotle in connection with his attack on another feature of pseudo-scientific pictures of rationality: the insistence that rational choice can be captured in a system of general rules or principles which can then simply be applied to each new case. (*Love's Knowledge*, p. 66)

Therefore ethical deliberation is rational but not scientific; though it complements science, ethics itself resists scientific method. The term 'new instrumentalism' is not meant ironically, for it sees instrumentalism transformed by recognising new motives and goals, rich ways of choosing. Nussbaum's deliberation promotes this transformation, by trying to correct rigidity, to link reason and experience, to humanise rationalism in the defence of reason. 'Deliberation' is internal, but also social; it occurs within the self and also in public life. Internally, rational deliberation is an interior dialogue analogous to formal debate between parties with different motives. Individual deliberation strikes a judicious balance just like social deliberation and so Nussbaum's deliberating self is complementary to rational dialogue between people and groups.

Like Elster and Sen, Nussbaum is open-ended, patient about uncertainty, ironic and responsive to spontaneous circumstances. Deliberative theory results in a dialogue, a dialogue about choice, between choices, towards choices. Indeed Nussbaum analyses actual dialogues, literary and philosophical dialogues. Her work is, therefore, a vital ingredient in any new consideration of reason and dialogue, even though she does not begin with dialogue but with the discriminating individual. The interesting feature of new instrumentalism is that it is so aware of indeterminacy and circumstances; the possible limitation is that interaction is a secondary consideration, though important. The conversation about reason requires the thinkers I have called 'new instrumentalists', because they have a refined model which is a necessary rival and complement to rational dialogue models.

Bookchin's Scientific Hope

Scientific rationalism is also rich and complex. Earlier I introduced Murray
Bookchin as a rival to dialogic reason within critical theory who deserves recognition further for his reinterpretation of reason and science, supplying an
alternative which is also humane and committed. Here he is presented as an eco-
rationalist, with an approach which is both scientific and political:

> ... nearly all our present-day ecological dislocations have their basic sources in social
> dislocations. Hence my conviction that a serious environmental movement must be
> based on social ecology. ('Twenty Years Later', *Ecology of Freedom*, pp. xiii–lxi,
> p. xxx)

He defends ecology as science, against what he sees as anti-rationalism:

> I say this provocatively at a time when a huge literature has surfaced that tries to refo-
> cus public attention away from social issues and toward socially neutral phenomena
> like technology as such, rather than the social matrix of technics; toward science as
> such, rather than the social abuses of science; and toward reason as such, rather than the
> reduction of reason largely to a means–ends 'skill' to be used for instrumental ends. (p.
> xxx)

Bookchin is aware of public attention and the need to refocus it expresses an
implicit requirement for public dialogue about the uses of modern rationality
and science. The outcome must be new arguments subtle enough to recognise the
damage done by modern technology and also the need to retain science:

> Because greater reason, science, technology, even knowledge and talent have been
> historically yoked to the service of hierarchical rule, it seems to follow for many eco-
> logically oriented people that they are antithetical to freedom, care, and an ecological
> outlook. (p. xxxiii)

The new argument will also be scientific, a scientific argument about reason
itself:

> ... its species-distinctiveness and its uniqueness. .... I speak of humanity's ability to
> reason, to foresee, to will and to act insightfully on behalf of directiveness within
> nature and enhance nature's own development. (*Social Ecology*, p. 116)

There are wonderful human potentialities which we must understand scientifically
to make them effective:

> We are grimly in need of a 're-enchantment of humanity' – not only of the world – by
> a fluid, organismic, and dialectical rationality. .... There is nothing more natural than
> humanity's capacity to conceptualize, generalize, relate ideas, and engage in symbolic
> communication. (*Social Ecology*, pp. 160–1)

It is this symbolic communication which brings Bookchin into the area of reason
and dialogue. Rationality is inseparable from communication; indeed, in practice,
Bookchin recognises the need to communicate what he sees as a more rational
idea of science and reason. Though his main focus is science rather than reason
in general, Bookchin's is an urgent case for the reconsideration of argument and
reason, for the issues he raises are momentous and urgent. The conversation to
which Bookchin points other rationalists might be about how ecology should be

implemented, about the role of dialogue, about the dialogue which makes ecology relevant in the first place.

Haraway and Cyborg Society

Ecology is one way to reinterpret scientific rationalism, but there are others. From a feminist perspective, Donna Haraway reinterprets science in her 'Manifesto for Cyborgs' with an approach that overlaps scientific rationalism and dialogic rationalism: overlap is her theme! Haraway rejects 'universal, totalizing theory', which, she says, is 'certainly now' unable to encompass reality ('Cyborgs', p. 223). But she warns against rejecting science, because science is too effective. Instead she advocates 'taking responsibility for the social relations of science and technology' and 'refusing an anti-science metaphysics, a demonology of technology'. We need a context for science and technology, a new, progressive context. Despair follows if we accept that science *must* be oppressive; we must analyse *why* it is oppressive.

We are not free to shake off the effects of science and modernity. In Haraway's terminology, we are 'cyborgs'. Cyborgs are modern, they are both synthetic and natural: 'A cyborg is a cybernetic organism, a hybrid of machine and organism, a creature of social reality as well as a creature of fiction' ('Cyborgs', p. 191). We include machines, and we are still people: 'Modern medicine is also full of cyborgs, of couplings between organism and machine' (p. 191). Our actions presume machinery, and yet we are not dehumanised, not necessarily. To deny machines is to deny part of ourselves. The problem is how to be creative cyborgs, not mechanical ones. And here modernity fails, because too often human and machine interact destructively: war, devastation, surveillance. Hope lies beyond modernity, beyond the 'traditions of Western science and politics', beyond in the sense of on the other side, passing across. Some connections emerge with Giddens. The cyborg is 'utopian', though not naïve. The cyborg utopia is 'a technological polis', a new order beginning with 'a revolution of social relations in the oikos, the household' (p. 192). The cyborgs will re-make the public world, starting with the intimate world. Like Giddens, Haraway praises intimacy, but among 'partiality, irony, intimacy and perversity' (p. 192) in a postmodern reworking of liberty, equality, fraternity.

How do we reconstruct liberty in the context of science? How can we restructure the uses of technology and fulfil a better destiny as cyborgs? There is no panacea, no formula. A formula would be self-defeating, a rigid solution to rigidity. The remedy is a process, many processes. Haraway's manifesto 'means embracing the skillful task of reconstructing the boundaries of daily life, in partial connection with others, in communication with all of our parts' (p. 223). The skill is communicative, in a creative sense, which aligns it with dialogic rationalism. Communication is a positive term in her worldview, a hope, central to reconstructing science and the scientific society. Communication can be internal, interpersonal, social, global. Daily life needs to be communicative, more communicative, so that we are aware of what is happening and can ensure that science and technology are humane. Haraway is seeking humane modernity through communicative activity, but in her view we do not yet understand communication, and we will learn in practice, not by theory, so there is some tension with Habermas in particular. Communication is a craft, a creative craft. In Haraway's account, communication is enigmatic, its nature will unfold in the future, it persists as a vision.

The problem is not that science is evil, but that it is ambiguous: 'science and technology are possible means of great human satisfaction, as well as a matrix of complex dominations' (p. 223). To reconstruct science more creatively, we must reconstruct daily life as well. The aim is to shake off rigid categories, categories that confine life to artificial boundaries, 'the maze of dualisms'. Communication is both a tactic and an ideal. But again Haraway is careful to leave the content open, she does not want to define communication in advance. Ideal communication is 'a dream not of a common language, but of a powerful infidel heteroglossia' (p. 223) – the play of voices, the interplay of voices, contacts and disconnections, collisions and overlaps, inherently anti-authoritarian. From Haraway's perspective, Habermas's view of communication is too definitive, even Putnam's various rationalities are too restrictive. From either of their perspectives, Haraway is too ambiguous about communication. They require a more explicit formulation. But she is clearly aligned with dialogic rationalism in her stress on the role of communication in transforming the scientific society, the cyborg world. For Haraway, the role and nature of the new communication are still to be explored, but in her vision it will play a vital part in releasing the true potential of modernity and science.

Postmodernity and Postmodernism

The Postmodern Climate

So rationalism is alive, and inventive, and extends new forms that engage dialogic rationalism. Yet Anthony Giddens notes a generalised feeling, 'the sense many of us have of being caught up in a universe of events we do not fully understand and which seems in large part outside of our control' (*Consequences*, p. 2). He adds that knowledge itself is altered under contemporary conditions; knowledge seems to share the pervasive ambiguity and indeterminacy: 'No knowledge under conditions of modernity *is* knowledge in the "old" sense, where "to know" is to be certain' (p. 40). Since knowledge itself is uncertain, the claims of science cannot be absolute; hence the idea arises of 'a plurality of heterogeneous claims to knowledge, in which science does not have a privileged place' (p. 2). I now consider some thinkers who have taken radical views based on the heterogeneity of claims to knowledge: Paul Feyerabend, Jean-François Lyotard and Richard Rorty.

Feyerabend's Epistemological Relativism

Paul Feyerabend radically questions the value of both science and reason. He rejects completely the superiority of science over other modes of understanding:

> Knowledge is a local commodity designed to satisfy local needs and to solve local problems. . . . Orthodox 'science', in this view, is one institution among many, not the one and only repository of sound information. (*Farewell*, p. 28)

He goes beyond the critique of science to defend alternative models of knowledge, such as the classical paradigm of knowledge, which he defines as follows:

> Knowledge, in tradition and in Greek commonsense, was a collection of opinions, each of them obtained by procedures appropriate to the domain from which the opinions arose. (*Farewell*, p. 72)

Feyerabend has regard for opinion as against privileged knowledge; he endorses local procedures against officially validated methods. He bids 'farewell to reason' in the name of a utopian vision that includes other possibilities:

> This world is not a static entity populated by thinking ants who, crawling all over its crevices, gradually discover its features without affecting them in any way. It is a dynamic and multifaceted entity which affects and reflects the activity of its explorers. It was once a world full of gods; then it became a drab material world and it will, hopefully, change further into a more peaceful world where matter and life, thought and feelings, innovation and tradition collaborate for the benefit of all. (*Farewell*, p. 89)

So Feyerabend aims to rescue the world from reason as conceived in modern life, and indeed to rescue reason from itself. He proposes the re-enchantment of the world by recognising many values embodied in the practices of communities outside the demands of enlightenment and the surge towards modernity with its restricted view of rationality derived from science and technological consequences. Feyerabend extends the recognition of that plurality of worldviews further than Habermas and Putnam; he values local autonomy in knowledge. He does not consider the need for such views to answer to others, yet his evaluation could help to ensure that any debate is conducted with goodwill and open-mindedness.

Lyotard's Heterogeneous Universes

Lyotard considers each phrase to be a separate universe, and there are as many universes as there are phrases. Questions of coherence in the use of phrases address themselves pertinently to dialogic rationalism:

> But you say that there are families of instantial situations such as space and time . . .? Then, there are phrase universes that are at least analogous to one another? (*Differend*, p. 76)

Even if all phrases depict separate worlds, cannot some phrases from separate worlds connect? Do not some dominant patterns emerge among the connections words make? Lyotard suggests that interconnection between words and phrases involves the establishment of a superior language, a metalanguage, a kind of translation into another form at another level. He analyses the process by which the meaning of phrases is redefined by a metalanguage in terms which radically qualify the process:

> A metalinguistic phrase has several of these phrases as its referent, and it states their resemblance. This resemblance removes none of their heterogeneity. (*Differend*, p. 76)

There are local patterns among phrases, and some phrases preside above other phrases. Indeed Lyotard develops a complex theory of genres and regimens, by which one set of phrases is given precedence over others. But the elements over which any metalanguage presides are separate if examined closely with all the potentialities of a phrase in mind: heterogeneity is inescapable.

On these grounds, Lyotard is sceptical towards rationalism of any variety: no linkage of phrases is universally valid, or even generally stable. Not only are there limitless phrases and phrase universes, which challenges rationalism from one direction; but where phrases *are* grouped under rules, the rules need not be rational:

> ... but phrases can obey regimens other than the logical and the cognitive. They can have stakes other than the true. What prohibits a phrase from being a proposition does not prohibit it from being a phrase. (*Differend*, p. 65)

Logic regulates some phrases and their connections according to local criteria, but other phrases resist logical rules and are not bound by this test of truth. Indeed not only logical criteria, but even cognitive criteria are local at best; and cognitive is a much broader category than logical, involving any kind of coherence at all. Lyotard's phrases are disjunct and he allows no basis to formulations as general as rightness, or truthfulness, or truth: no procedures for reaching general conclusions apply to all phrases in their different universes. Furthermore, rules that do apply may be counter-logical, anti-rational, even non-cognitive. (Though it is not easy to imagine a rule which is not to some extent 'cognitive' in the lowest sense, possessing some coherent significance. How would such a regimen convey itself at all?)

Not only does Lyotard dismiss general requirements for coherent interpretation, he also dissolves stable contexts. Each linkage implies a different 'context', and in each context the speaker has a different role. Lyotard immediately denies the validity of putting phrases in context, if 'in context' is taken to have any finality. 'Context' is another deceptive 'metalanguage', no more absolute than or even superior to the phrases it locates:

> But doesn't the occurrence of these phrases depend, in turn, upon the context? – What you are calling the context is itself but the referent of cognitive phrases, those of the sociologist for example. (*Differend*, p. 82)

No rules are universal; but there are not even stable contexts to define local rules. Context is an external construct, the consequence of certain particular phrases, such as the phrases of sociology. Habermas constructs a careful structure in which contexts submit diverse proposals to universal rationality; Lyotard's theory overrides such a compromise. Validity and context remain intransigently heterogeneous; indeed Lyotard invalidates contexts as well as general rules which might be thought to apply to them.

Lyotard's *The Differend* is subtitled 'Phrases in Dispute'. Here then is a rival approach to dialogic rationalism as regards the specific question of argument and difference. From Lyotard comes the premise that there is no general rule for adjudicating disputes. Lyotard cites the sophist Protagoras: there is a series of *phrases*, then a series of debates, and 'the debate over the series of debates is part of this series' (p. 60). There is no higher language to establish the rules for lower languages: 'That only shows that metalanguage is part of ordinary language' (p. 76). No escape is visible. There is no resort to an objective universe as a way out of the tangle:

> No, I am not saying that this universe is reality, but only that it is the condition for the encounter of phrases, and therefore the condition for differends. . . . Regarding this universe, it can just as easily be said that it is the effect of the encounter as its condition. (*Differend*, pp. 28–9)

Yet Lyotard is closer to Habermas and Putnam than these basic differences at first suggest, for his approach is profoundly *dialogic*. He repeatedly presents cases of people interacting and trying to reach conclusions with each other, even though no unanimity results. In the specific sense, dialogue is one set of games in which people interact, one form of interaction among many others. For instance, 'agon' is an arrangement likely to rival dialogue: agonistics is a game with a judge outside the debate. But just as there is a disjunction between phrases, there is a disjunction between different games, and 'differend' is Lyotard's term for the disjunctions between rival regimens, genres and games:

> There is a differend, therefore, concerning the means of establishing reality between the partisans of agonistics and the partisans of dialogue. How can this differend be regulated? Through dialogue, say the latter; through the agon, say the former. (*Differend*, p. 26)

Dialogue is one game among many conflicting rivals, with differend the inevitable outcome between them. But the whole philosophical and cultural project which includes dialogue and agonistics is fundamentally 'dialogic' in a deeper sense. Lyotard *thinks* dialogically: his whole text is a play of different voices, voices which engage each other. Moreover, like Putnam, he invents many hypothetical encounters between differing parties. In the fundamental sense of 'interaction' between people and voices, dialogue is central to Lyotard's way of proposing his theories about life; it is the specific model of equal and open interplay between opponents which is only a local game. Therefore, we encounter the puzzle of a deeply interactive method and outlook which propounds the notion of disjunction, and hence the ironic overlap with the rationalist partisans of interaction and exchange. There is a common focus on discourse and in particular on discursive *interactions*, and a common need to judge those interactions, not merely to 'describe' them. The criteria of the judgements conflict, but the conflict is relevant to both sides because of the overlapping objectives.

The world is full of 'contacts' involving 'phrases of heterogeneous regimen' (*Differend*, p. 29). For Habermas, mutual evaluation resolves contact. Putnam thinks some views at least show understanding of other views: 'we' understand the 'vatists', we analyse their arguments, although they remain unconvinced by our analysis. Lyotard's gaps between differing views are wider: understanding does not occur, even to that extent. Yet life includes these impossible contacts. Exchange may be doomed, but exchanges happen, hence the theory is dialogic, however negatively, however frustratingly for more constructively dialogic theories! Adorno conceived of negative dialectics; Lyotard invents negative dialogics.

Lyotard is not detached about irreconcilability in differences. Apathy is not his ideal, far from it. He has other grounds for reacting to the human predicament apart from general rules supported by a generalisable reason:

> The plaintiff lodges his or her complaint before the tribunal, the accused argues in such a way as to show the inanity of the accusation. Litigation takes place. I would like to call a *differend* the case where the plaintiff is divested of the means to argue and becomes for that reason a victim. (*Differend*, p. 9)

'Victim' is deliberately emotive. When Lyotard judges situations, he does not need to resort to the impersonal authority of a general reason. Differend can be unjust; injustice matters and then the differend must be resisted. But it is noticeable in the above case that argument will not help the victim, for, by arguing, the victim allows the phrase offered in defence to be violated, and risks accepting the legality of a censored phrase universe.

Lyotard in the Perspective of Putnam and Habermas

Dialogic rationalism commits reason to dialogue. There are diverse models of the dialogic redemption of reason. Could dialogue also *betray* reason? Can a negative dialogics, such as Lyotard's, turn dialogue against reason, cracking the very centre of Habermas's construction? Lyotard suggests that dialogue, in the interactive sense, though without any bond of understanding, is pervasive in human affairs; but dialogue in the fully communicative sense required by Habermas is difficult, often impossible, a transient fluke when successful. For judgement in human relations, Lyotard sometimes seems to turn away from reason altogether.

Can arguments be reclaimed as rational dialogue? Lyotard's encounters are argumentative, but the interpretation can be extended to show no overall coherence. Lyotard considers it is possible to define argument tightly as structured exchange but the structuring is just one more game:

> Controversy belongs to a genre of discourse, the dialektike, the theses, arguments, objections, and refutations that the [Aristotelian] *Topics* and *Sophistical refutations* analyze. (*Differend*, p. 86)

But when argument is defined more loosely as conflicting views in contact, it covers much of Lyotard's theory, and in that theory the elements of the argument are polymorphous and do not elide in a necessary conclusion. What is the interpretative power of this model as against the rationalist model when applied in an imagined argument? Which meaning will *stick* to the argument?[6]

Consider an encounter between Lyotard and Putnam. Putnam considers the general claim of relativism that every viewpoint is autonomous. He attributes this view partly to Kuhn and also to Feyerabend and Foucault, rather than to Lyotard. But the principles on which he criticises the autonomous viewpoint apply to each relativist standpoint, including Lyotard's. Putnam believes that the relativist, or 'anarchist' (RTH, p. 113) case is self-refuting. He defines it as 'the thesis of incommensurability' (RTH, p. 114). He considers terminology in a way which applies to Lyotard's 'phrases'. He gives a historical example:

> The incommensurability thesis is the thesis that terms used in another culture, say, 'temperature' as used by a seventeenth-century scientist, cannot be equated in meaning or reference with any terms or expressions we possess. (RTH, p. 114)

Lyotard's theory is an extreme form of the incommensurability thesis, with every phrase potentially autonomous. Putnam believes that the view is unsustainable because how could we not know about differences between meanings unless we bridged gaps between meanings to *some* extent? The general conclusion is decisive:

> That conceptions differ does not prove the impossibility of ever translating anyone 'really correctly' as is sometimes supposed; on the contrary, we could not say that conceptions differ and how they differ if we couldn't translate. (RTH, p. 117)

Phrase universes cannot be completely disjunct, otherwise we would not even know that they were disjunct. To realise that different regimens apply to different phrases, we must connect the phrases.

Putnam believes that relativists underestimate the necessary coherence of our interactions:

> Not only do we share objects and concepts with others, to the extent that the interpretative exercise succeeds, but also conceptions of the reasonable, of the natural, and so on. (RTH, p. 119)

Without assuming meanings are universal, Putnam defends common ground for understanding. He adds tersely: 'The important point to notice is that if all is relative, then relative is relative too' (RTH, p. 120). Of course, Lyotard has replies to this line of criticism. He does not rule out connections that might *seem* to offer the prospect of mutual understanding:

> A genre of discourse determines what is at stake in linking phrases . . .: to persuade, to convince, to vanquish. (*Differend*, p. 84)

But the genres which suggest understanding are only linked phrases, nothing more. Putnam's 'the reasonable' and 'the natural' could be genres of phrases. But incommensurability exists within genres as well as between them, which makes incommensurability radical:

> A genre of discourse inspires a mode of linking phrases together, and these phrases come from different regimens. (*Differend*, p. 128)

Heterogeneity remains among the elements that are connected. Finally, it is not possible to assume an understanding of words and phrases; even the word 'phrase' comes under Lyotard's scrutiny. Lyotard inserts a demand into his text: 'Give a definition of what you understand by phrase' (*Differend*, p. 68). But definition is only one rule that might apply to the use of a phrase: why should Lyotard submit to this requirement? Moreover the command to 'Give a definition' is outside the rules of definition! An impasse results. Consider 'the phrase':

> you command me to link onto it with a metalinguistic definitional phrase. You have the right to do so. But know that you are making a command. (*Differend*, p. 69)

The gulf between a definition and the demand for definition is never automatically bridged. We may choose to try to agree upon a definition, but we don't have to make definitions:

> Lacking a definition of phrase, we will never know what we are talking about, or if we
> are talking about the same thing. (*Differend*, p. 69)

Putnam declares that such relativism in the use of words

> means that there is, in the end, no difference between asserting or thinking, on the one
> hand, and making noises (or producing mental images) on the other. . . . To hold such
> a view is to commit a sort of mental suicide. (RTH, p. 122)

Freedom for Lyotard, suicide for Putnam. Is *this* a differend? Or is it more like
Putnam's vision of Carnap meeting Newman: their views are unresolvable but
leave scope for further judgement and progress?

Consider an encounter between Lyotard and Habermas. At issue is Habermas's
commitment to a *unified* standard of rationality, the very starting-point for his theoretical considerations. These interpretations illuminate Habermas's project, and
are another way of evaluating his 'goal of formally analyzing the conditions of
rationality' (CA1, p. 2). When 'basing the rationality of an expression on its
being susceptible of criticism and grounding', it is necessary to locate for us
'that critical zone in which communicatively achieved agreement depends upon
autonomous yes/no responses to criticizable validity claims' (CA1, p. 71). How
clear-cut are such zones in practice? Lyotard's differend tests the applications of
Habermas's communicative rationality:

> As distinguished from a litigation, a differend would be a case of conflict between (at
> least) two parties, that cannot be equitably resolved for lack of a rule of judgment
> applicable to both arguments. (*Differend*, p. xi)

Following this definition, Lyotard collects stories where two disputants lack a rule
for resolving their disagreement. By the time he has finished, we realise that
there is no particular sort of dispute to which 'differend' applies: *any* dispute can
be interpreted as a differend because no rule for evaluating difference is absolute
or universal. (But is *that* an absolute rule . . .?):

> One side's legitimacy does not imply the other's lack of legitimacy. However, applying
> a single rule of judgment to both in order to settle their differend as though it were
> merely a litigation would wrong (at least) one of them (and both of them if neither side
> admits this rule). (*Differend*, p. xi)

Habermas grants that it is appropriate to judge the rationality of any claim to truth
within the context of its own worldview; for he accepts that 'even the choice of
criteria according to which the truth of statements is to be judged may depend on
the basic conceptual context of a worldview (CA1, p. 58). But the process of
truth-seeking does not end there, within the context of the worldview, for dialogic
rationalism requires each claim to be submitted for consideration in a wider dialogue as a universal claim to truth, since 'truth is a universal validity claim', and
then focuses on the *process* by which claims to truth are argued. Habermas could
accept the status of the two worldviews which harbour different theories, but then
he would consider the *way* in which each argued his or her case against the other
in the universal forum; he could read the exchange so that one view was more
rational about the procedure of discussion. A rational view encourages criticism
of proposals. An irrational view does not offer relevant criticism. Claims are true

if they survive in the universal dialogue, until they meet better critiques. That is the logic of dialogic rationalism. But Habermas does not propose that truth is fixed, absolute or final, only that it is possible to win an argument about truth and win it meaningfully. That truth is not absolute: it can be displaced by other versions of the truth in argument.

What does dialogic relativism propose? In human differences, Lyotard sees only 'encounters between phrases of heterogeneous regimen' (*Differend*, p. 29) – conflicts between parties on either side of an empty space, a space that no rule can bridge. Clearly this would indicate that one method of argument was not superior to another, not outside their respective contexts. Further, Lyotard brings in his concept of *genre*: 'A genre of discourse determines what is at stake in linking phrases' (p. 84). In this theory, we have seen that argument itself becomes a genre of discourse, or may contain several different genres. If phrases belong to an argumentative genre, they can be linked into an argumentative encounter. And Lyotard considers *science* a rival genre to one important genre of argumentation, 'dialektike' (p. 86), the formal disputation between systematically antithetical theories. Science is like other genres, more powerful than many but not above the fray.

At issue is the structure of argument. How dependable is that structure? Can the outcome of argument ever be trustworthy? Is it possible to maintain criticism based on argument? Lyotard questions the role of criticism. At a more basic level, he also contests the preferability of 'yes' over 'no', of agreement over dissonance. Why should it be right or necessary for people to agree? Such prevarication strikes at the very heart of the Habermasian project, proceeding as it does towards universal affirmation. Lyotard derives from Hegel the ideal of a 'speculative stage, or stage of positive reason' which 'apprehends the unity of determinations in their opposition' (*Differend*, p. 90). He argues that this speculative discourse still begins 'in the negative as a magical affirmative force'. Lyotard defends the power of 'no'. 'No' prevents people from being sucked into conformity but it also inflicts on philosophy 'the wound of nihilism'. Habermas would be a later instance of the tendency to weaken 'no' – he begins argument with the rational 'no' of the critical moment, and then subordinates it to the 'yes' which is the goal of understanding. Lyotard resists that *critical* suppression, and he further insists that any 'no' 'is only subordinated to "yes" by the rules of that genre of discourse which is speculative' (*Differend*, p. 91). In Lyotard's terms, Habermas is a descendant of the speculative genre: he applies a specific set of rules and attributes universal authority to a local genre. Out of these rules of discourse, Habermas is reconstituting his new enlightenment; Lyotard resists on behalf of a post-enlightenment awareness.

Rorty: A Postmodern Accommodation?

To conclude the survey of dialogic trends and developments in rationality, I want to consider a proposal for a mid-point between Habermas and Lyotard, a proposal sponsored by the philosophical approach of Richard Rorty, who has offered to mediate between Habermas and Lyotard in 'Habermas and Lyotard on

Postmodernity'. His standpoint is not neutral in the conflict. In effect, Rorty is closer to Habermas, while rejecting his complete theory. Rorty endorses the dialogic rationalist ideal of 'undistorted communication' ('Habermas and Lyotard', p. 88), but he endorses the uses of rational dialogue *only* when dialogue is part of a specific tradition, in a specific historical situation, and not as a method leading to generally applicable truths. He recommends certain values in dialogic rationalism, but he believes there are no universal criteria for truth and validity, and so he sees dialogue as an alternative to verification. Both Habermas and Putnam would find Rorty's proposition too limited, though Putnam shares Rorty's emphasis on some inescapable values:

> What is needed is a sort of intellectual analogue to civic virtue – tolerance, irony, and a willingness to let spheres of culture flourish without worrying too much about their 'common ground'. ('Habermas and Lyotard', p. 90)

Though more regional, Rorty's civic virtues resemble the cognitive virtues. What Rorty offers is one kind of 'meta-interpretation', an interpretation of theories in general, encouraging us to think more about *our* role as interpreters of dispute, including the dispute about rationality itself. He asks us to reflect on our identities, identities which determine our interpretations and are part of specific historical situations. To quote a line from Auden's great rhetorical vision of a commemoration in *The Orators*:

> What does it mean? What does it mean? Not what does it mean to them, there, then. What does it mean to us, here now?[7]

How do our interpretations of dialogue, reason and argument express our identities – the identities we perceive for ourselves, here, now in the situation we inhabit – and how did those identities come about historically?

Rorty has created a position which projects in both directions of an argument; which has implications for both parties to a contest, since it acknowledges where you happen to stand historically and the affinities and loyalties which shape all sides. In our time, this approach means that Rorty acknowledges the coherence of science, though he does not mistake science for universal reason. A modern interpreter of arguments is bound by an awareness of the theories of science, the role of science, and its pervasive effects. Rorty makes a clear separation between the advance of science within Western cultures and ethical progress:

> It does not greatly matter which way we see it, as long as we are clear that the change was not brought about by 'rational argument' in some sense of 'rational' in which, for example, the changes lately brought about in regard to society's attitude toward slavery, abstract art, homosexuals, or endangered species, would *not* count as 'rational'. (*Philosophy*, p. 332)

In social progress, changes in values *precede* argument, they are the precondition for argument. Rorty warns us not to judge ethical progress by scientific criteria, or criteria analogous to science. The changes involve tradition, and the evolution of tradition, but nevertheless Rorty favours 'a possible conversation', one 'where the hope of agreement is never lost so long as the conversation lasts' (*Philosophy*, p. 318). He is not a dialogic rationalist, despite his hopes for a possible conversation to encourage reasonable progress, because he gives priority to tradition and context in determining what we consider true, and is much more emphatic than Putnam or Habermas about these binding influences. Rorty urges 'continuing the conversation of the West' (*Philosophy*, p. 394) as a specific tradition: he is, in effect, a dialogic historicist. He challenges us to see every interpretation in *its* context of history, tradition and inheritance when examining present and past. But we may doubt Rorty's own histories: what authenticates these narratives, which are said to explain attitudes and arguments? Such endorsements are relatively uncritical, exempt from the characteristic questioning and plurality of Rorty, and these histories provide a fairly easy basis for excluding issues from serious consideration on grounds of 'history' or 'tradition'. Rorty sees modern rationality as the product of a specific history, the history of 'the West', as he calls it, and makes large assumptions about the unity and exclusivity of this entity. So some views become more rational because they are parts of a more rational society, a more humane way of life, as Rorty views values in 'the West'. But Rorty accepts that other views are rational in their context. We in 'the West' should choose between these different kinds of rationality and choose modern rationality, on the basis of our shared allegiance, not because of any universal principle of rationality. This division coincides with one made by Putnam, in which there is a rationality for different communities and groups. But despite the introduction of 'conversation', Rorty does not stress creative interaction between the groups in reasoning, from which a general improvement in reasoning and even the good life can follow.

Rorty's handling of tradition and opinion sucks some of the *life* out of the conflict about reason and dialogue. Perhaps this draining away comes partly from his preference for 'hermeneutics' over rhetoric. With all their contrasts, Habermas, Putnam and Lyotard conceive a world where real views and actions are at stake, hence their engagement with rhetoric and the need for people to confront and persuade each other. By contrast, Rorty's 'conversation' seems less dynamic, there is less urgency to change people's opinions, more stress on the historical route by which we inherit our opinions, and the context in which we find ourselves. Paradoxically, Habermasian argumentation and Lyotardian differend share a dramatic quality. We could reply to Rorty: who *is* this 'we' of which you speak so confidently? Are you sure 'we' all belong in the same category? Is that not what the argument is partly about? If there *is* an inheritance from the past which predetermines the present, it is an inheritance already full of conflict, as the next chapter shows.

Notes

1 Seyla Benhabib, *Critique, Norm and Utopia* (New York: Columbia University Press, 1986), p. 286 identifies Habermas's approach to norms as a 'consensus theory of normative validity' analogous to his 'consensus theory of truth'.

2 Erving Goffman, *Forms of Talk* (Oxford: Basil Blackwell, 1981) demonstrates that a 'dramaturgical' approach has more potential than Habermas recognises. The crucial point is that Goffman allows much more subtle interplay and reciprocity between performer and audience, including centrally the performer of familiar roles in everyday life. Exemplary is his analysis of the relation to audiences implied by 'spillage cries' (oops, whoops, etc.) in 'Response Cries' (pp. 78–123, notably pp. 99–113).

3 There is further consideration of rational choice and revolution in *Rationality and Society*, 6, 1 (January 1994), on the theme of 'Rationality, Revolution and 1989 in Eastern Europe'. A methodological survey is provided by Mark I. Lichbach, 'Rethinking Rationality and Rebellion', pp. 8–39.

4 In *Rationality and Society*, 5, 2 (April 1993), pp. 203–30, 203.

5 S. Kagan, 'The Present-Aim Theory of Rationality', *Ethics*, 96, 4 (July 1986) pp. 746–59, 747.

6 John B. Thompson, *Studies in the Theory of Ideology* (Cambridge: Polity Press, 1984), p. 132: 'Hence the meaning of what is said – what is *asserted* in spoken or written discourse as well as that *about which* one writes – is infused with forms of power; different individuals or groups have a differential capacity *to make a meaning stick*.'

7 W.H. Auden, 'Address for a Prize-Day', Book 1, section 1 of *The Orators* (1932), reprinted in Edward Mendelson, *The English Auden* (London: Faber and Faber, 1977).

6

Dialogic Rationalism and Dialogic Relativism

A Case for Interpretation: Galileo the Rational Hero

Science is a crux for dialogic rationalism. In Weber's story of enlightenment, the fundamental term for Habermas was 'modern natural science', because science 'puts theoretical knowledge in mathematical form and tests it with the help of controlled experiments' (CA1, p. 157). Habermas wishes to improve on Weber's story, subordinating its rationalism, and the old enlightenment, to *communicative* rationality and a new enlightenment, in the project which I call dialogic rationalism. But science remains a locus of value within the new project. Science must still have a large say in the dialogue about what is rational. And for Putnam, science is rational, though not rationality itself. Therefore Galileo's *Dialogue Concerning the Two Chief World Systems* seems an appropriate test case for dialogic rationalism, particularly the Habermasian variant!

Rorty examines Galileo, why he is central to reason. In *Philosophy and the Mirror of Nature*, Rorty specifically raises the case of Galileo when dealing with rational disagreement. Rorty is refining the thought of Thomas Kuhn, the historian of science, but his approach is more germane to argument, because he is concerned with rational disputes in general and not with the rationality of science in particular. He focuses on the opposition to Galileo by his contemporaries, the resistance by Cardinal Bellarmine which overlaps with the arguments of anti-scientific voices in the *Dialogue*. Rorty explains why the case of Galileo is so resonant:

> Much of the seventeenth century's notion of what it was to be a 'philosopher', and much of the Enlightenment's notion of what it was to be 'rational', turns on Galileo's being absolutely right and the church absolutely wrong. (*Philosophy*, p. 328)

He then highlights the theme of disagreement:

> To suggest that there is room for rational disagreement here – not simply for a black-and-white struggle between reason and superstition – is to endanger the very notion of 'philosophy'. (*Philosophy*, p. 328)

Rorty implies that the proper role of philosophy was to support Galileo and legitimate his method. To rule out that method would undermine the philosophical enterprise: to have opposed Galileo at that time cannot be rational, given the evolving perspective of the new philosophy. By comparison with Rorty, here Habermas is rich. He can supply a criterion which endorses an enlightenment view: if oponents did not argue properly, they were less rational, and the scientific view is more rational when it deals in criticism, not simply because it is scientific. We shall see how a Habermasian interpretation may apply to the sides in Galileo's own *Dialogue*. Unlike Rorty's view, nothing in this Habermasian verdict turns on Galileo's being viewed in this curiously absolute historical perspective. Habermas's reformulation of truth in terms of universal *claims* leaves scope for manoeuvre, while at the same time endorsing the enlightened voices.

Elsewhere, however, Rorty even speaks for the anti-Galilean viewpoint:

> What determines that Scripture is *not* an excellent source of evidence for the way the heavens are set up? (*Philosophy*, p. 329)

It looks as though admission of evidence depends on rules governing the dispute, in accordance with the provisions of Lyotard's differend. But Rorty does not concede that every view has its own context with its own procedures. He goes on to answer his question: 'Lots of things, notably the Enlightenment's decision that Christianity was mostly just priestcraft' (p. 329). Rorty's point is that *history* is a determining factor in evaluating authority. He asks what being rational meant at *that* time: 'But what were Bellarmine's contemporaries – who mostly thought Scripture to be indeed the word of God – supposed to say to Bellarmine?' Rorty is not arguing that the evaluation of truth is merely a matter of context, that what was rational then is simply not rational now. He argues for a more complex position. There has been an argument of historic importance about rationality. *Galileo is on the side which later thinkers have shared and endorsed as rational:*

> The notion of what it was to be 'scientific' was in the process of being formed. If one endorses the values – or, perhaps, the ranking of competing values – common to Galileo, and Kant, then indeed Bellarmine was being 'unscientific'. But, of course, almost all of us . . . are happy to endorse them. (*Philosophy*, p. 330)

We are 'the heirs' to this argument and should not pretend otherwise, even if we are more cautious about the meaning of the argument, as witness Rorty's own summary of our inheritance as 'three hundred years of rhetoric about the importance of distinguishing sharply between science and religion, science and politics, science and art, science and philosophy, and so on' (p. 330). We can modify our allegiance, but we cannot deny that we belong to the community which Galileo helped to found. We should be loyal to that community and its values, *because we belong to it*:

> We can just say that Galileo was *creating* the notion of 'scientific values' as he went along, that it was a splendid thing that he did so, and that the question of whether he was 'rational' in doing so is out of place. (*Philosophy*, p. 331)

This is nothing less than an appropriation of history itself, history granted its own objective reality, which is also present in our inheritance, and part of our very consciousness, since we do not have a random choice in selecting the integers of our thought and thinking. Rorty creates an interpretation that relies neither on communicative rationality nor on differend. For Rorty, we interpret the Galilean dialogue as inheritors of a tradition which Galileo was helping to found, the tradition of enlightenment. Our reading would be biased, in the sense that we have our own stake in the conflict. We could not endorse the other side without fudging our own identities.

I shall take a particular episode, since my concern is with interpreting the dynamic interaction, rather than unfolding Galileo's theory. The episode occurs early in the work, when the parties to a dispute are still working out how they can deliberate, a pivotal moment for the application of any dialogic model. The passages are given in the seventeenth-century English translation of Thomas Salusbury, because his idiom is consciously dramatic and interactive. There is another translation, Stillman Drake's modern version, used by historians of science, yet it is far less dramatic.[1] Two 'readings' will be counterposed: a dialogic rationalist reading, with a Habermasian accent, and a dialogic relativist reading, based on Lyotard's *differend*. The intention is to mediate a contemporary conversation using a previous conversation, and so to consider the scope for interaction between different viewpoints in contemporary intellectual culture.

Galileo's Dialogue in Rationalist and Relativist Perspective

Saying 'No' to Science

There are two main participants in the drama, Salviatus, a scientist, and Simplicius, a traditionalist and Aristotelian – together with Sagredo, a mixture of judge and audience, but, in fact, an ally of Salviatus. The background to their dispute is this. Salviatus has demonstrated mathematically that 'by the three perpendiculars . . . you have the three dimensions'. Simplicius replies:

> I will not say that this your argument may not be concludent; but yet this I say with Aristotle, that in things natural, it is not alwaies necessary, to bring mathematical demonstrations. (Salusbury, p. 6)

As onlooker and ally of Salviatus, Sagredo is frustrated:

> Grant that it were so where such proofs cannot be had, yet if this case admit of them, why do you not use them? (Salusbury, p. 6)

The disagreement has produced from one side a 'no', the crucial problem in the debate. The enlightenment model implies that when Simplicius says 'no' he is misinformed, unreasonable and, therefore, wrong. But what if we rooted rationality less in the possession of knowledge than in the conduct of discussion?

How should we account for such a negating construction as: 'I will not say that this your argument may not be concludent; but . . . '? Is it a relevant criticism? One interpretation would be that Simplicius is not arguing rationally because he is not giving critical reasons: he is not taking up the challenge of argument. He is also failing to join any search for better reasoning, improved rationality. He is fiddling to scrape through, by mixing up two negative constructions.

But Sagredo's answer on behalf of Salviatus is also double-edged, by these criteria. He appears to agree and fashions the agreement into a new challenge: 'Grant that it were so . . . why do you not . . .?' Simplicius considered mathematics irrelevant to an argument about life and faith; Salviatus' ally side-steps this approach, by granting that it might *sometimes* be so, *but* when mathematics *is* applicable . . . . Can Simplicius' point of view fairly be extended to take in the possibility that mathematics applies in the situation they are discussing? To interpret Simplicius' opposition in this way is convenient for the scientist, but ignores what his opponent meant.

Is the mathematician more rational in argument than the mystic? Is he the better arguer and more rational according to the structural requirements for argument? Does Simplicius seem less rational – not because he rejects science, but because his method of defence is evasive towards criticism and towards improvement in thinking? Salviatus is putting forward a criticisable claim; as Simplicius has failed to respond, Salviatus' ally Sagredo has *supplied* a response on his behalf, to provide some argumentative momentum and re-initiate Simplicius into the debate, in the hope of achieving further rational communication. He has set up a further case to which a 'no' move is relevant, if Simplicius will take it up. But perhaps Sagredo is being manipulative on behalf of Salviatus by substituting another answer for the one which Simplicius gave, making a monologue, in which case he has treated Simplicius as an awkward interruption to his own exposition.

There is another standpoint from which Simplicius is justified in taking the stance he does: he is refusing to play by the rules that suit the scientist, according to the requirements of a scientific rationality. He would be justified if there were no common grounds for matching their opinions. His is not an evasion, but open acknowledgement of incommensurable difference. This counter-interpretation suggests that Salviatus–Sagredo and Simplicius represent different sets of rules, rules about discussion itself. If Simplicius has his own rules governing a discourse for the world as he sees it, is he not rational in the way he applies those rules? Then how far could we say that Salviatus–Sagredo have a more rational *way* of approaching the discussion? Could we not just say that each is rational in his own terms? Or even that Salviatus–Sagredo are *less* rational because they fail to see the extent of the differences, and their irreconcilable terms when they threaten to appropriate the whole dialogue?

Reasonable Limits

Salviatus next introduces the concept of acceleration which seems straightforward enough, and not arguable. A body is moving fast; how did it reach that speed? Only by passing 'all degrees of less velocity' (Salusbury, p. 11). Using this innocuous opening, he proceeds to the conclusion that nature allows only circular motions – except where a body is moved out of place. Certainly, this is a criticisable claim which others can assess. Simplicius is *horrified* at the loss of straightness, which is implicit to his worldview:

> how can you ever rationally deny, that the parts of the Earth; or, if you will, that ponderous matters descend towards the Center, with a right motion . . .? (Salusbury, p. 22)

Is his reply a criticism – a relevant criticism? He means 'no' without any doubt! But perhaps his 'no' goes beyond the specific claim to circular motion? Perhaps Simplicius' 'no' means that Salviatus has not made a *comprehensible* claim.

When is someone being critical, and when are they being obstructive? It would be essential for Habermas that we distinguish absolutely between criticism and obstruction, otherwise, as we can see from this extract, the line blurs between rationality and traditionalism. *If* Simplicius is just being difficult, then he fails in the argument by Habermas's criterion of the right person for the argument, the rational participant, someone with 'a willingness to expose themselves to criticism and, if necessary, to participate properly in argumentation' (CA1, p. 18). But two objections may arise to this Habermasian line. First, his 'no' may be irreducibly ambiguous, hanging in the space between criticism and recalcitrance. In other words, it may not be *possible* to define his attitude, and, secondly, Simplicius may be defending his right to a different type of discussion in which an alternative vernacular and phraseology apply: a Lyotardian strategy.

Salviatus pushes ahead with his brazen reasoning from circular motions. He argues that the universe does not need one centre as it has in Simplicius' model: one single centre towards which everything would fall. Experience does not suggest that all bodies tend toward such a central point. Simplicius is more heated than before, but is he becoming more offensive or more exacting?

> This manner of argumentation tends to the subversion of all Natural Philosophy, and to the disorder and subversion of Heaven and Earth, and the whole Universe. (Salusbury, p. 25)

Is this a dialogic *criticism* of the claim that the universe has no centre? Or is Simplicius waiving Salviatus' right to submit this claim? Here is the crux. Is Simplicius suppressing criticism of his beliefs? And trying to end the search? We might ask whether *any* 'no' is ever purely critical, not at all obstructive. This question may produce answers favourable to Simplicius which run counter to the apparent intention of the dialogue-writer; the question may refer only to undercurrents in the dialogue. Simplicius is given a 'character' in the exchange which is not very engaging. But the questions that arise from the disagreement are necessary.

Clearly tensions arise in the course of the argument. Personalities intrude. There is unpleasantness. Consider in that perspective the 'risk of disagreement', or the fact that disagreement carries risks: this is a danger which Habermas recognises requires some 'conservative counterweight' for the sake of social stability (CA1, p. 70). (Here we move towards the contradiction in Habermas's thinking about consensus.) If Salviatus' claims *really* threaten the *framework* of all exchange, is it not better that Simplicius excludes them? Can we tolerate claims that undermine the whole structure within which all live and communicate? Salviatus is aware of the 'conservative counterweight' and mocks the need for it within the dialogue itself:

> Take no thought in this place for Heaven or the Earth, neither fear their subversion, or the ruine of Philosophy. (Salusbury, p. 25)

There is no real danger of total disorientation. Salviatus suggests that Simplicius is not in good faith: doom and gloom suit his purpose. He does not want a proper argument – an open pursuit.

But the story looks different if Simplicius has his own world, with its own rationality for expounding its sacred principles. Of course, the text is partisan, and favours the scientist, (as the names imply)! But *we* could see Simplicius as a victim, a victim of imperial reason advancing foreign terms under the guise of open debate. This latter reading focuses a challenge to any view of legitimacy in debate, a challenge to the meaning of 'no' and particularly to the 'no' which gives science its ascendancy in the Enlightenment. Simplicius is protesting against rules that apply to an 'experiment', and an 'observation' and mathematical analysis in defence of different presuppositions about the world.

Unacceptable Responses, Unacceptable Requirements?

Salviatus keeps on proposing, Simplicius goes on denying. Salviatus proposes that the heavens are not unchanging. He gives evidence for changes in the heavens: Tycho observed new comets in the sky. Simplicius denies that these observations establish *facts* about the heavens:

> *Salviatus*. . . . in the particular bodies, and in the universal expansion of Heaven, there have been and are continually, seen just such accidents as we call generations and corruptions; being that excellent Astronomers have observed many Comets generated and dissolved . . .
> *Simplicius*. As to the new Stars, Anti-Tycho extricates himself finely in three or four words; saying, That those modern new Stars are no certain parts of the Celestial bodies. (Salusbury, pp. 38–9)

Simplicius suggests that new stars may be illusions or misinterpretations or due to errors in the apparatus. On this logic, no observation ever settles a dispute. One side can always deny that there has *been* an observation – or that it is relevant, or reliable. Simplicius gives priority to the basic principles of the universe as conceived in his system. Anything contrary to his principles must be error – by definition – however the error arose. Salviatus gives priority to observation and experiment: in his system it is a mistake to ignore information from these sources. Simplicius fails to *enter the dialogue*; or he is refusing to be *absorbed* by it, or intimidated by its terms of reference. A contest between interpretations is possible. The contest is not between absolutism and nihilism, rather it is between two understandings of the relationship between reason and dialogue. Whereas *dialogic rationalism* proposes that dialogue can rationally arbitrate our differences, *dialogic relativism* warns that the process of dialogue is never impartial. On this model, Salviatus imposes the rules of science on a different genre, the dialektiké, where different rules apply; Salviatus has an imperial motive – the enclosing of controversy inside science. In that case, Simplicius represents traditional controversy, and its refusal to be enclosed in the higher genre of science. That would explain why he makes controversialist points in reply to experimental observations. Galileo intends to make that recalcitrance seem ridiculous; but a sympathetic reading endorses the refusal to be ruled by science. Simplicius represents a genre of traditional *disputation*, and, of course, within Lyotard's terms of reference, his own claims to truth do not have universal applications.

From a dialogic relativist perspective Simplicius makes more impact than the dialogue was designed to show. He keeps returning us to incompatibility. He makes us aware that the triumph of one genre over another is not a fair way to win an argument. But dialogic rationalisms maintain that claims to truth do not exist *only* as part of genres. They can be seen in a wider perspective, either where they are also universal or where they belong to a search evolving towards truth.

In the dialogue, Salviatus continues to pile up observations which support his argument. For instance, he says: consider the sun spots. Are they not signs of change in the heavenly bodies? Simplicius seems to waver:

> I, for my part, have not made either so long, or so exact observations, as to enable me to boast my self Master of the Quod est of this matter. (Salusbury. p. 42)

Is he about to concede the argument in the face of observation and evidence? He lacks a Lyotardian defence. He does not realise that rules of different genres are incompatible:

> . . . but I will more accurately consider the same, and make tryal my self for my own satisfaction, whether I can reconcile that which experience shews us, with that which Aristotle teacheth us; for it's a certain maxim, that two Truths cannot be contrary to one another. (Salusbury, p.42)

If he had known about incommensurability, Simplicius could have claimed that his rules work perfectly well in the sphere to which they apply, the sphere of systematic theology. But instead he hopes to reconcile two kinds of rule, one of which governs his thought and the other that of Salviatus. One could therefore claim that Simplicius has conceded that claims to truth are universal or the search for truth is interconnected. And in the universal debate he has not met opposing claims with responsive criticism; he has not argued in a spirit which could lead to ultimate agreement. A relativist reading must see that Simplicius has made a disastrous move for he here accepts the idea of an overriding genre and a unified truth, in the hope that it will be his genre of systematic theology which triumphs. But if his genre loses to science in a straight contest with common standards, then he will have lost the argument. Taking the dialogue as a whole, the trap has been sprung on the unenlightened past.

The conflict of interpretations focuses on 'no' and the way Simplicius negates scientific views. It seems this rejection is not sincerely critical, nor given in a spirit to permit understanding. Rational argument incorporates 'no' into understanding, as a stage in the meeting of opposing claims, but it is a rational 'no', a straightforward 'no', criticising the opposing view. Simplicius, therefore, falls below rational standards. But can he be so easily dismissed? Lyotard sees that move, that critical 'no' of Habermas leading towards agreement, as belonging to a particular genre, the genre of speculative philosophy, one going back to Hegel and the rise of modernity which gives authority to 'no' and negation. Lyotard leaves room for 'no' to be acceptable as a refusal to play: a person may say 'no' to interaction, being contradicted by rules implied by the interaction. For Lyotard, 'no' is neither rational nor not rational: the judgement on 'no' would depend on the rules invoked for interpreting it, and rules are open to conflict. According to Lyotard, 'no' cannot be divided into a properly critical negation and a merely obstructive refusal. The two 'readings' of the argument between Salviatus and Simplicius follow from these two different theories.

Salviatus gives his evidence that the heavens change. Simplicius resists, in a way which is open to different interpretations. Sagredo is listening, as an ally of Salviatus. He now defines the underlying situation, according to his vision:

> I cannot without great admiration, nay more, denial of my understanding, hear it to be attributed to natural bodies, for a great honour and perfection and they are impassile, immutable, inalterable, etc. And on the contrary, to hear it to be esteemed a great imperfection to be alterable, generable, mutable, etc. It is my opinion that the Earth is very noble and admirable by reason of so many and so different alterations, mutations, generations, etc. which are incessantly made therein. (Salusbury, pp. 44–5)

Sagredo adds that an unchanging world might as well be 'one vast heap of sand' or 'Globe of Christal'. Simplicius gives way under the force of these distinctions and accepts that the earth is indeed a place of changes and properly so. But he insists that the heavens must be different from the earth in these respects:

> There is not the least question to be made, but that the Earth is much more perfect, being as it is alterable, mutable, etc. than if it had been a masse of Stone; yea although it were one entire Diamond, most hard and impassile. But look how much these qualifications enoble the Earth, they render the Heavenly bodies again on the other side so much the more imperfect. (Salusbury, p. 45)

The dialogue is intense and even moving, a contrast of human visions.

Simplicius may be improving, trying to engage with the other side. Perhaps here he even offers a relevant criticism. But *as a criticism*, his point is weak. The same quality, mutability, can hardly be 'perfect' and 'imperfect': so he has failed to make a rational case (or appropriate case), and Sagredo has the better argument, in this exchange. But perhaps Simplicius only thinks he is participating freely: he is too *prejudiced*. He is not listening properly, or giving the terms of his adversary their proper due, so he does not respond pertinently.

From a relativist view, Simplicius has made a tactical error by accepting the terms of the other side. He is too generous or credulous because he insists there is only one universe, and is therefore vulnerable to the formulation of others for that universe. We might conclude that *both sides* are naïve to argue for one view which can explain all the phenomena of the universe in a unified conception. Sagredo's speech betrays ancient roots, for the new physics simply inherits a *weakness* in the old theology. The whole exchange is corrupted by delusions of power on either side, an interpretation which leaves both systems exposed to a future reading. Both science and religion will be discredited by the differend. The dialogue miscarries because the participants offer only a choice of absolutes. Sagredo may be even more to blame than the main parties for the impasse, and confusion, because he stood outside the argument, and did not have to deal with opposition: he was in a position to see the weaknesses and strengths of both sides and could have redirected the discussion, but was seduced by absolutes and opted for one side.

Double Arguability

Interpreting Argument

I have taken *interpretation* as a framework for juxtaposing dialogic rationalism with dialogic relativism. I want now to present a response to the conflict of interpretations: a rhetorical vocabulary which can take in meanings which derive from the ambiguities of 'no' itself. This rhetorical vocabulary also sustains *the theme of double arguability*. Both Habermas and Lyotard claim to appropriate rhetoric, Habermas as a part of the analysis of argumentation and Lyotard as a forerunner of scepticism about the adjudication of disputes. Habermas, as we saw, refers to Aristotle, but Lyotard refers beyond Aristotle to the rhetoric of the sophists, a rhetoric which he sees as emphasising that an absolute context is inconceivable, since 'the debate over the series of debates' (*Differend*, p. 60) is merely one more debate. In my usage, rhetoric is itself an ambiguous and self-divided inheritance of linguistic, discursive and argumentational analysis.[2] This use of rhetoric will lead to a position analogous, I hope, to that of Seyla Benhabib on the ethical divide between Habermas's universalism and supporters of local contexts: 'There is no incompatibility between the exercise of moral intuition guided by an egalitarian and universalist model of moral conversation and the exercise of contextual judgment' (*Situating the Self*, p.54). Indeed Benhabib herself proposes a remedy which involves the exercise of both imagination and narrative, precisely the powers which I hope this rhetorical approach serves to support:

> What I am suggesting so far then is that if we view discourses as moral conversations in which we exercise reversibility of perspectives either by actually listening to all involved or by representing to ourselves imaginatively the many perspectives of those involved, then this procedure is also an aspect of the skills of moral imagination and moral narrative which good judgment involves whatever else it might involve. (*Situating the Self*, p. 54)

It is not impossible to combine a Habermasian model of rational dialogue with considerable Lyotardian latitude: the crucial factor is to leave scope for individual interpretation and judgement.

The term 'contradiction' has many meanings. To 'contradict' can mean offering a critique, on the one hand, or being 'bloody-minded', on the other.[3] Contradiction points towards argument in a form which settles issues, and also towards conduct which blocks arguing, bars discussion, and makes it impossible to settle differences. Habermas should have distinguished clearly between these different senses of 'contradiction' to sustain his thesis, but he has not done so because, as we have seen, negation is not a homogeneous response – at least it is impossible to exclude alternative criteria for interpreting a 'no'; even the vulnerable Simplicius could forge a 'no' which is itself contestable, open to contending interpretations. Habermas requires that 'no' should proceed from a rational critique to resolve argument one way or another, but others resist his requirements and interpret negations as justifiable resistance to inauthentic authority. Even if the rationalist requirements are preferable, they can be maintained only through a contest of interpretations, as we have seen, and not as absolute requirements. 'No' is often ambiguous, that is surely part of its point and even its power.

Rationalism, Relativism and the Ambiguities of Contradiction

The OED defines 'contradiction' as 'Denial; opposition; statement contradicting another; inconsistency'. The range of possible interpretations *is* wide. One reason for this latitude is that 'contradiction' refers both to a way of behaving and to a way of speaking, to actions and to language. To say that a statement is contradictory is to make a *logical* judgement, though there may be different types of logic involved in different cases of contradiction; but to say that a person contradicts another is to make a *narrative* claim, to suggest a dramatic episode. There is a division at the heart of 'contradiction', reflecting the ambiguities of negation, the different dimensions of 'no'. In their different ways, dialogic rationalism and dialogic relativism privilege some senses of 'no' over others. The rationalist approach prefers to emphasise the dimension of logic, though incorporating that logic into a model of interaction. The relativist approach emphasises the dramatic 'no', the negative that enacts refusal and resistance. Where rationalism discovers the 'no' of refusal, it diagnoses irrationality; where relativism discovers the 'no' of critique, it discerns a particular genre, often with dangerously imperial ambitions, and it may *advise* resistance.

It may be pertinent to keep different possibilities when interpreting a given situation, not so as to keep them *equal* but so as to explore the difference before judging. The problem with the approaches of Habermas and Lyotard is that they pre-empt the exploration of 'no' and the way it acts in a given situation. These models pre-structure judgements by delivering them within either the terms of communicative rationality or the terms of differend. Rorty advises us to consider the implications of our own position. But is it possible to adopt more open-ended terms whose effect does not constrain judgement? We could exploit the ambiguities of terms such as 'contradiction' by accepting them, terms which acknowledge ambiguity, terms which will not submit to the definitions of either dialogic rationalism or dialogic relativism, and find other uses for them. I propose to supplement 'contradiction' with another term in order to enhance this sense of ambiguity and not suppress it. One reason for negotiating a new term is that the different meanings of 'contradiction' become confused and do not remain open-ended in effect. Different writers use the term in their own familiar and habitual way. 'Contradiction' gets taken for granted, particularly as a logical concept. History makes them or other terms available, terms which overlap with contradiction. The OED gives us:

Contraversion. rare n. of action.
   A turning in the opposite direction.

Controversion. n.
   1. A controversy: a dispute.
   2. The action of controverting.

Controvert. vb.
   1. To oppose by argument or action; to dispute or contest (a title, possession etc.).

2. To make the subject of controversy or verbal contention; to debate, discuss, dispute about.

3. To contend against or oppose in argument; to dispute, deny, contradict.

Both words and actions are included in these definitions of argument. The form 'contra-version' keeps alive the relation to 'contra-diction', allowing the two terms to support each other. But 'contraversion' avoids the possibility of becoming static implicit in 'contradiction', which refers to the sense of a fixed feature of a single text or utterance, a pure logical flaw. 'Contraversion' *always* applies both to an action, or, better still, an *interaction*, and to a relationship between statements. The focus, then, in the context of a dispute, would be on the action of 'contraverting'. On the one hand, to contravert may be a mode of communicative action, expressing the wish for communicative rationality: contraversion supplies criticism along the lines that dialogic rationalism requires. On the other hand, contraversion may also express a refusal to engage with the other side, the 'no' which establishes an impasse between two alien sets of criteria, on the model of dialogic relativism. The point is not to blur the differences, but to construct a vocabulary which discriminates actively on individual cases rather than giving absolute labels. Using 'contraversion' to discuss the negative moment in dispute, we can *explore* each case without pre-empting it. There is a helpful analogy here with Hilary Rose's proposal of 'common feminist project' where 'the realists and postmodernists handle the arguments about truth claims with exceeding care, not dismissing the other'.[4]

Once we use words which focus on an action, or interaction, it becomes possible in dynamic terms to discriminate, when analysing an argument, between criticism, which implies *the wish to engage*, and resistance, which implies a *refusal to engage*, which differentiates between a defence of autonomy and an avoidance of any development in the exchange of opinions. We will be allowing for two *interpretations* when using one vocabulary, labels signifying an underlying attitude, and we will be involved in a *process* of distinction, a process that *starts* from acknowledging the difficulty of giving effect to difference in dialogic positions categorically. Under the sign of 'contraversion', with its shared meanings, we can think systematically about the differences that being 'critical' and being 'resistant' make to the dynamism of an argument. The distinction between being 'critical' and being 'resistant' expands to cover the instances in Table 6.1.

The vocabulary is a rhetorical one because it applies in the interpretation of disputes which feature actions and interactions among people, an interpretation of rhetoric aligned particularly with Billig's notion of the 'rhetorical turn' as a renewed emphasis on the understanding of argument.[5] One effect of using this vocabulary is to bring the theories of dialogic rationalism and relativism closer, although they appear irreconcilable, and this convergence is one product of rhetoric's demands on both theories. The purchase on opposing theories is through interaction – the way people deal with rival speakers. This is tenable because Habermas asks the question: how do people orient themselves toward the other view, the alternative view, the antithesis? And it is relevant to Lyotard because he issues the challenge: is constructive engagement possible, let alone desirable, since it is *engagement* that is under consideration? The vocabulary

Table 6.1 *A rhetoric of contraversion*

Critical Action	Act of Resistance	
Dissent from (a view)	Recoil from (a view)	*Content*
Supplant (the criteria)	Balk at (the criteria)	*Framework*
Diagnose (the motives)	Expose (the motives)	*Agency*
Predict (the effects)	Prophesy (the effects)	*Consequence*

also covers requirements Rorty makes because he questions the apparent dichotomy between Habermas and Lyotard, questioning whether the contrast between them need be as absolute as their demands make it appear. Rorty asks: is it obligatory to choose categorically between the criteria of communicative rationality and the pure differend? But this vocabulary does not introduce a focus between two extremes, to balance them out, or synthesise them, or mediate between them, as Rorty does; the vocabulary supplies an interpretative framework for examining the differences between opposing parties in argument, case by case.

Criticism and resistance are separated in the proposed terms for analysing argument, but closer in application to a particular case. Philosophically, dialogic rationalism and dialogic relativism may still remain disjoint; nevertheless, rhetorically, their usefulness can overlap in application to particular arguments. The underlying theme of such usage is double arguability, the way in which arguments create, test and re-create their own dynamics. Whether an action counts as critical or as resistant will depend on how the action affects the exchange and how the whole exchange responds to it; whether an action is critical or resistant depends on how the interaction is referred by standards that are general and apply to any dispute. The interpreter's task is not to apply labels to the argument when considering the negation in the argument, but to explore the process by which the negation may tend towards one sense or the other, towards criticism or resistance, and for this purpose a particular vocabulary is necessary.[6] This vocabulary covers the applications of Habermas's and Lyotard's theory; but it can be applied to any *particular* argument without invoking the apparatus of either theory. In other words, the interpreter of an argument no longer uses *either* Habermas's approach, or Lyotard's approach, since both approaches carry within them a pre-selected outcome for interpretation, which focuses most crucially around 'no', whenever negation is encountered in argument. This vocabulary makes it possible to apply criteria to an argument which derives from *both* major theories; but the vocabulary is applied according to the situations encountered in the particular argument considered, so the outcome of analysis depends on the facts of the case, and not on a predisposition derived from a major theory to which the interpreter

subscribes. This enhances interpretative freedom and promises greater speci-
ficity, accuracy and detailed application to any argument. The vocabulary, further,
contains words that cover both the linguistic aspect of argument and the behav-
ioural features. Finally, the vocabulary suggests that the theories of Habermas and
Lyotard are not ultimately polarities without prospect of a meeting between them,
or reconciliation – since the single vocabulary in use covers requirements of both
major theories, and constitutes, in its derivation and use, a bridge between them,
and suggests further possible encounters between Lyotard and Habermas may be
envisaged in a spectrum of meanings and actions linking the two.

Applications

When the different dimensions of 'no' are constituted in a new, single vocabulary
and applied to what Simplicius says and does, the result is revealing and opens up
that episode in many ways which show how complex and symbolic it is. Consider
in these terms what Simplicius said and did:

> This manner of argumentation tends to the subversion of all Natural Philosophy, and to
> the disorder and subversion of Heaven and Earth, and the whole Universe. (Salusbury,
> p. 25)

Emphatically, he turns away from considering these possibilities! To call this a
critical rejection would be stretching the meaning of criticism: he is *resistant*. His
statement does not imply 'this is why you are wrong', but 'these views are not
worth considering'! He is *recoiling* from the exchange, rather than *dissenting* to
a proposal, to apply the rhetoric of contraversion. The advantage of this rhetoric
is to keep us aware of the disputants' alternatives as we interpret the dispute; we
are conscious that these are two routes down which the argument can go: criticism
or resistance, and that in this case the participant has chosen one. Neither communicative rationality nor differend performs this function. So Simplicius recoils
from the content of the argument. This remark shows a concern with the *consequences* of such controversy: the disastrous outcome implicit in the other side's
orientation. Here is a fine instance of '*prophesying*' the effects of the encounter.
He is prophesying, not simply predicting, because he is moved by a vision, and is
not quoting evidence for his doubts. From this prophetic vision he recoils and
becomes resistant rather than critical. He also has some doubts about his opponent's motives for adopting *subversive* views. At the level of *agency*, he is trying
to *expose* his adversaries' motives, though he proceeds subtly by suggesting they
are more naïve than deliberately harmful. Nevertheless, the implication is that if
they do persist in their argument, after his warning, their dangerous motives will
be clear. Salviatus responds to this comment as if it were a prophecy and unnec-
essarily lugubrious:

> Take no thought in this place for Heaven or the Earth, neither fear their subversion, or
> the ruine of Philosophy. (Salusbury, p. 25)

Salviatus ignores the subtext which impugns his motives for adopting a new
view of the universe, though he may be driven to a hint of self-justification.
When he says 'in this place' he may imply that no-one *here* intends subversion.

But his main point is that there is no risk of the new views being harmful. His original proposition might have contraverted religious principle, but now he contraverts doubts arising from that thrust. He tends towards a *critical* stance and logic: there is no *reason* to fear the consequences of his ideas. He is also implying a logical answer to doubts in the subtext: subversion has to be effected by active subversives, and there are none present! He *dissents* from the prophesy, and its effects. He *diagnoses* Simplicius' conditions, as over-anxious, obsessive, even paranoid.

Then Salviatus specifies his interest in the subject by introducing those comets, which change the order in the heavens. Simplicius reacts as if he understands the idea and the intention behind it

> As to the new stars, Anti-Tycho extricates himself finely in three or four words; saying, That those modern new Stars are no certain parts of the Celestial bodies. (Salusbury, p. 39)

The idiom is *resistant*: 'extricates himself' is still extricating himself from further discussion. At the level of content, he is *recoiling* with a shudder from the proposition. But he is also being *critical* at last – enlarging his repertoire of argument, by raising a question as to what is 'certain'. So he *recoils*, but stays close enough to lodge some critical *dissent* from Salviatus' claim concerning Tycho's evidence. Then Simplicius refers to higher authority, offering to

> make tryal my self for my own satisfaction, whether I can reconcile that which experience shews us, with that which Aristotle teacheth us, for it's a certain maxim, that two Truths cannot be contrary to one another. (Salusbury, p. 42)

Up to this point, Simplicius has been *balking* at the criteria of his adversary, particularly at the application of mathematics. But now he makes a more problematic gesture, and goes halfway to accepting scientific criteria into the argument, for he proposes to 'make tryal' which covers experimental testing; and then he re-introduces his own criteria into the 'tryal': the wisdom of the past and the principles of classical logic criteria which contravene all the applications of science. This contravention attempts to *supplant* the criteria of argument used by the other side with his own criteria, in other words, it is a *critical* contravention rather than a resistance. *Using the rhetoric of contraversion, Simplicius is shifting from wholehearted resistance to being semi-critical.* The contest of interpretations can be understood using a spectrum of rhetorical concepts that connects different theories of interpretation. Disjunct models for interpretation become alternatives within a connected scheme, an outcome which follows from linking Habermas and Lyotard through their rhetorical intentions and applications.

A rhetorical vocabulary does not provide us with neutral facts about the argument, thus the interpretation must point in one direction. The analysis is always contestable, and it always requires value judgements to apply the terms in use. But we can observe *how* the value judgements arise in the process of interpretation and see where they are operating in inclining the interpretation to one side or the other. We have an integrated contest with alternative outcomes, and we can see where the alternatives arise. The vocabulary gives interpretation more space, makes interpretation more self-reflective. Even in judging an argument, we retain the sense of ambiguity that always affects argument. We never forget the other possibility. In that sense, the rhetorical vocabulary complements Rorty's dialogic historicism, making the interpreter more conscious of the process of interpretation. But the rhetorical vocabulary derives its effect of self-consciousness by working from within the process of interpretation, rather than from a presumed external framework of historical process, which accommodates the argument.

In the latter stages of the episode, Sagredo has claimed that change is noble. Simplicius accepts half the proposal and controverts half:

> But look how much these qualifications enoble the Earth, they render the Heavenly bodies again on the other side so much the more imperfect. (Salusbury, p. 45)

Fundamentally, he *recoils* from continuing along this line which threatens Heaven by ennobling Earth which is the proposition's content, the effect being a startled movement away from Sagredo and Salviatus, an instinctive distancing from the possibilities inherent in their approach. His manner seems more composed than before, because he seems to be explaining his point of view and introduces a clear idea, a clear dichotomy between Heaven and Earth, but the impulse behind his argument is tactical and *resistant*. He cannot stomach the thought that the Heavens are capable of change: his statement implies that he will not tolerate that idea or consider it seriously, so he is *recoiling* from the argument. He is only pretending to offer critical dissent, he is wrapping up resistance in a thin skein of criticism as a deliberate ruse for appearing reasonable or even as systematic self-deception. That would be the dialogic rationalist interpretation. The dialogic relativist alternative is that he lured Salviatus into a critical discussion, to blunt the natural tactic of fierce resistance. But the whole performance is fully covered in the terms of 'contraversion', which uncovers a debate with alternative nuances and consequent judgements.

Salviatus continues to be confident, and to account for his views, but he finally inclines towards contempt, and it is difficult to see who could tolerate the terms he now heaps on his opponent:

> . . . though I have a thousand times rehearsed this which you at the very first have your self apprehended, yet could I not beat it into men's brains. (Salusbury, p. 53)

The dialogic relativist might point out the authoritarian tone: are these claims really criticisable? How are we to know whether he could or could not beat something into someone's brains? Is Salviatus not in fact demanding unconditional assent to his views from anyone who takes in what he says? He is not seeking a critical response. The relativist can now see clearly why Simplicius would be well advised to *resist* Salviatus, to recoil from his superior tone and balk at his grand manner, to prevent an engagement with this imperious power! The dialogic rationalist would counter that Salviatus is merely reacting to his adversary's refusal to take communication seriously, which we have seen for ourselves, and his incapacity to tolerate another viewpoint, and be enlightened.

By this stage Simplicius has developed a cooler style which suits an ambiguous response:

> If you mean by your not being able to persuade them to it, that you could not make
> them understand the same, I much wonder thereat. . . . but if you mean that you have
> not persuaded them, so as to make them believe it, I wonder not, in the least at this, for
> I confesse my self to be one of those who understand your discourse, but am not satis-
> fied therewith. (Salusbury, p. 53)

In other words, he has joined in the argument – he has thought about what
Salviatus said, and he has decided against it. He claims to be dissident, to dissent
from a critical point of view. The parties are interpreting the story in which they
have been placed. Salviatus has spotted that Simplicius is resisting – and he
derides him for offering mere resistance instead of critical argument. Simplicius
has not read Lyotard and Kuhn! Instead of defending his right to resist a takeover
by foreign standards, he claims the role of critic. The dialogue tells against him.
But then it would, wouldn't it, since Galileo wrote it?

Re-imagining Reason

The use of narrative was always implicit in the conceptual models of Habermas
and Lyotard. A rhetorical vocabulary makes us think about the narrative – about
the different stories which the rival theories will land on us. In this case, rhetoric
translates the conceptual conflict between Habermas and Lyotard into a contest
between stories derived from their way of thinking. These stories do not replace
the theoretical dispute. They show why the theories matter in practice and allow
for further exploration of roles immanent in their differing outlooks. This account
is not neutral. In my opinion, Habermas emerges strongly. But I hope to acknowledge the cost of preferring Habermas to Lyotard: the alternatives persist, because
they each have a place in the dimensions of 'no'. In the same way, each returns a
'no' of a kind to some cherished ideals of enlightenment. Habermas sees that the
historical Enlightenment was valid, but did not stretch far enough. It was too sci-
ence-oriented, and left no space for other worldviews, nor for communicative
action. Lyotard rules out the possibility of being enlightened, because the phrases
from which its dicta are composed do not meet in a truly contiguous and meaningful way: at best they fall within associated areas of genre. When the proposed
vocabulary is applied to *their* disagreement, Habermas shows a tendency for critical action: he dissents from pre-enlightenment theology and metaphysics; he
supplants these with the need for observation, and the interaction of different
experiences and opinions; he diagnoses resistance as backward-looking and
obstructive: and, above all, he looks forward to the applications of rational argument, and predicts a better life will follow. Lyotard is resistant: he recoils from the
view that science has an appropriate relationship to the facts of life, all of which
have an irrevocably separate nature, and are fundamentally different, and beyond
classification; he balks at the idea of meaningful exchange; he exposes culture as
ideological manoeuvre for power; and, above all, he prophesies continuing conflict but finds in this conflict the stirrings of human vitality.

   On the question of what argument *means* to us, we already see in the dialogic
theories the outlines of an *emotional* and *imaginative* contest which is part of
argument. Dialogic rationalists determine the nature of argument as: a sometimes

paradoxical foundation for progress; a sign of rationality; a resource of hope. But they recognise the pressure of other meanings on argument through experience: as a trouble; a risk, something to be feared; disintegration. I have been exploring the way these challenges already shape dialogic rationalist thinking, centrally in the case of Habermas and also with other thinkers, notably Putnam. My purpose has been to show that a responsible modern rationalism must already show strong signs of accommodating these challenges from emotion and experience, even though it may prefer to repudiate them or overcome them. At various points in Habermasian theory the existence of such factors is implicit, whether or not the theory was constructed to deal with them.

I have been suggesting throughout the account of dialogic rationalism a need to enhance the imaginative potential of the theory so as to take in all the human aspects of disagreeing and disputing which feature under argument. The same insistence on *argumentative imagination* continues when we consider dialogic relativism and the way it confronts the rationalist models. We are never more in need of an imaginative effort than in considering Lyotard's concepts of the dissociated universe in each phrase, the imperialistic motives of genres of phrases, and the oppression that follows from them. I suggest that whatever the power of these approaches, we are going to need voices which assert their imaginative potential, and fulfil it, voices which connect theory with experience, including experience as we imagine it to be. Indeed I think the expansive theories of Habermas, and the theories of Lyotard, Putnam and Rorty, already *possess* far more imaginative energies than are usually drawn from them; they can readily be shown to feature aspects of argumentative imagination, ideas which can only be grasped when they are represented concretely with a full complement of characters and settings, except that the terms of their proposals sometimes disguise the imaginative element in their discourse. I have previously indicated where those imaginative possibilities exist in dialogic rationalism, by generating a dialogic challenge between Habermas and Putnam and by my own dialogic interventions in portraying both. The same imaginative treatment characterises the account of Lyotard, and his opposition to Habermas, except that their two approaches are harder to bring into play together; but the only resource for mapping their contours in relation to each other, for aligning them, and comparing them, remains argumentative imagination: the play of images depicting us and our experience, and the areas where we differ.

Notes

1 Thomas Salusbury's version is entitled *Galileo: His Systeme of the World* and was included in his *Mathematical Collections and Demonstrations* published in London in 1661. Most copies were lost in the Great Fire. References are given in the text. There is a modernised adaptation of Salusbury by Georgio di Santillana published by University of Chicago Press, 1953. Stillman Drake's authoritative modern edition *Galileo: Dialogue Concerning the Two Chief World Systems* is published by University of California Press (2nd rev. edn), 1967, foreword by Albert Einstein.

2 For this account of rhetoric in relation to argument, see Dick Leith and George Myerson, *The Power of Address* (London: Routledge, 1989), specifically Chapter 3 on 'Argument' (pp. 79–113). A

further elaboration focusing on the complex overlap and tension between rhetoric and dialogue is presented in the Introduction to Myerson, *The Argumentative Imagination*.

3 Habermas (PDM, p. 112) cautions against reducing contradictions to what he regards as merely the desire to be different. He associates this development with the influence of Nietzsche, surely too specific an attribution!

4 Hilary Rose, 'Rhetoric, Feminism and Scientific knowledge' in J. Roberts and J.M.M. Good (eds), *The Recovery of Rhetoric in the Human Sciences* (Bristol: Bristol Classical Press, 1993) pp. 203–23, 219.

5 Michael Billig, *Ideology and Opinions*, p. 2 and passim, notably also p. 213: 'Under these circumstances, the recapture of past moments, or the new revival of the old, need not be purely nostalgic. It can convey a rhetoric which expresses hope, critique and, above all, argument.'

6 The vocabulary is also a responsive alternative to schemata devised in informal logic, notably by Douglas Walton in *Informal Logic* (Cambridge: Cambridge University Press, 1989). Walton offers a subtly sliding scale of exchanges, from quarrels through persuasion dialogues to inquiries and educational discussions.

Conclusion: A Culture of Intellectual Encouragement

Reason, dialogue and communication are aspects of human behaviour, they involve character and interaction. Throughout this book, character is important, character and attitude towards other people. The subject is not individual character in isolation: character is not self-generating, it has social contexts and cultural contexts. However we distinguish communicative character, and dialogic orientation, there are social and cultural conditions for them.

It is difficult to decide which character is suited to communicating ideas, which character is at home in a dialogue of ideas; and difficult to determine how society enhances communicative potential in ideas, how cultures make dialogue creative. Different thinkers approach character differently, as they approach truth, meaning and freedom differently. Notably, different characteristics are valued highly in different theories. Habermas applauds a critical orientation and being open to criticism, and he also requires emotional security. His communicative people are integrated with a lifeworld, not alienated. Yet they are also independent. Putnam recommends impartiality and balanced judgement, and also manageable ambivalence, liking and controlled dislike, respect and conviction, courage to denounce as well as tolerance to discuss. Giddens focuses on trust, to which he connects creativity, self-reflection, deep respect for the other, love, the courage to demand autonomy. Intellectual courage is also essential in Fraser's view, the courage to formulate need, and to keep solidarity. Empathy is important to reasoning in the view of Tannen and Sheldon, empathy as against aggression. Lloyd celebrates the power of reason to transcend stereotypes, to expose them. Postmoderns have other criteria for character in communication and dialogue. Haraway advocates irony, humour and originality. Rorty endorses tolerance, patience, and also rootedness, security within a tradition. Lyotard promotes committed scepticism, and refusal to accept definitions. Then there is efficiency, humane efficiency from Sen and Elster, who also acknowledge idealism. Nussbaum selects sensitivity, discernment of perception. Dialogic and rational characteristics are themselves arguable: they belong to debate, they cannot limit debate or regulate interaction. This has been represented throughout as *double arguability*.

When considering good dialogue and communication, especially significant problems are intercultural dialogues, interaction between different worldviews and different systems of value. It is a fundamental consideration of social thought how different societies approach intercultural dialogue, how different ideologies approach others, 'outsiders'. More than tolerance is involved, though this is important: these stretched dialogues between cultures and ideologies require creativity, respect, and also the courage to disagree. We need to include also issues of equity, of fairness within and between societies and cultures. Equality is seen as a precondition for dialogue by most thinkers in this book, from both a critical and liberal perspective. But equality is not uniformity, and contemporary ideas of equality stress difference strongly, notably in feminist work from Fraser, Tannen and Haraway.

Character does not replace truth as the criterion of good dialogue, rational communication. Throughout the book, we have considered different views of truth and rightness. It is misleading to isolate being 'good at communicating', in a technical sense. As we have seen, good communication means dialogue, and good dialogue involves reasons as well as other qualities. There is a strong case for connecting good reasons to improved knowledge, or understanding, or effectiveness, or creative thought. Good reasons are interpreted differently by different thinkers, and they hold different views about whether the outcome is truth or understanding, fairness or creativity. But dialogic rationalism connects communication to truth, fairness, meaning. Consider by contrast, prescriptions for educational efficiency or pronouncements about social efficiency in which communication skills are seen as a technique to be acquired.

Character and personality emerge, too, in the presentation of theories themselves. Theories are personal, as well as analytic, and they express personality strongly and directly. Personality is insufficiently acknowledged in discussions of theory, particularly personality as a positive factor: theory is not 'merely personal', but theories include the intellectual personality of the theorist. This personal element does not undermine rationality or objectivity: personality is involved in both, as Putnam demonstrates. Nor do I see the personal element as requiring moralistic judgements about personality and character. One of the main arguments in this book is against intellectual moralism, set requirements for character and personality, the exclusion of characters, the exclusive valuing of given characteristics. We should take personality into account without being moralistic.

Character involves language, the use of words. Some ways of using words conduce to rational dialogue, or creative interaction between ideas; others preclude dialogue, dilute rationality, suppress creativity and interaction between ideas. Habermas's major contribution is to connect language and rational communication. His concentration on language makes *The Theory of Communicative Action* in particular a great work. But there are many ways to look at language, and no one perspective will include them all. Billig's witcraft is important as well as Habermas's criticisable propositions.

There are also risks to concentrating on character, on social conduct, how people use words to interact. There is a danger of being prescriptive, or, as I remarked above, moralistic, producing too many prescriptions and proscriptions. We should not rely on labelled characteristics and virtues. Discourse ethics runs this risk of labelling, if it is too definitive, and so does liberalism, if it restricts virtues to a precise list, if it is dogmatic about what 'reasonable' means. We should resist too tight a language of values, and avoid converting values into rules too quickly.

Certain proposals are implicit in this book, and they can be presented in conclusion. The proposals are not a programme for dialogue and intellectual activity, they are not a formula for democratic conduct, since such formulae are self-defeating. Intellectually, I am in favour of gaps, gaps between values and rules, gaps between terminology and its applications. I also applaud gaps in theories, gaps for other ideas, gaps for other ways to put things, gaps for dialogue. I recommend theories which make leaps across their own gaps – as Putnam does sometimes, not always filling in the connections, leaving something to imagination. Theory can leave gaps also between examples and their point, a sense that there could be other examples which made the point differently, another strong aspect of Putnam.

Dialogic rationalism should relish gaps in its own presentation: of course, not just lapses, but opportunities for other perspectives to contribute. More generally, dialogic rationalism should elicit diverse responses. And wider conditions can promote intellectual interaction, or inhibit it! Dialogic rationalism implies a culture of intellectual encouragement and a society favourable to this end. Dialogue gets its ideas from the surrounding context, and its participants, too! Rational dialogue needs many ideas and diverse protagonists; a culture of encouragement describes the favourable setting for rational dialogue. Rational dialogue will always be open to critique from within, including radical scepticism about both reason and dialogue. The outcome of all dialogue is unpredictable, but the most creative outcomes are likely in an encouraging climate.

There are no rules for implementing this culture of encouragement, and I would not dignify encouragement as a virtue, or defend it as a norm, or embody it in an ethic. But the following conditions seem appropriate to wide dialogue:

1 people being disposed to communicate ideas, and therefore contexts in which it is safe and easy to do so;
2 ways of thinking which favour comparisons, which are relative in that sense, not necessarily relativistic;
3 creative forms of negation, which present new possibilities, or which supplement previous propositions;
4 active tolerance of difficult emotions involved in the exchange of ideas and opinions.

Communicative reason is a major stimulus towards a culture of intellectual encouragement, even though it has limitations as a whole theory. Rhetoric is also an ally in its creative modes, when it is not compiling catalogues.

There is implied a negative model, a culture of intellectual discouragement. The following are discouraging to ideas:

1 social unfairness, inequality, prejudicial stereotypes, threat and menace to identity;
2 the keeping of ideas in storage, intellectual stockpiling;
3 premature refutation, the assumption that it is necessary to negate ideas immediately, without seeing where they lead;
4 a single model of argument or conduct in argument.

A culture of intellectual encouragement does not disallow criticism – on the contrary. But real criticism is difficult, and not the same as gestures of criticism, the critical reflex which inhibits ideas. Encouragement means recognising imagination, the creativity which generates different ideas, a creativity openly acknowledged by Putnam, Giddens, Haraway, Billig. As Fraser warns, criticism can be a weapon of the powerful when it overlaps with institutionalised power.

Disciplines both offer intellectual encouragement and restrict it. Modernism consolidated disciplines, one reason why Habermas, a modernist, maintains distinctions between philosophy and literature. In this book, the approaches examined are informed by different disciplines: sociology, philosophy, linguistics, politics, psychology, literature. But the ideas also cross disciplines, and they do so radically: feminism, rhetoric, liberalism, critical theory – these movements are not confined to a discipline, they do not originate in a discipline. To insist on disciplines too tightly means duplicating ideas without recognising connections.

Ideas belong both to disciplinary cultures and to interdisciplinary cultures. We require new ways of representing ideas, the multiple identity of contemporary ideas and their many contexts, in different disciplines and also as applied by different theories. Ideas cannot be restricted to one theory, nor applied solely in the terms given by a particular theoretical definition. Habermas's work is an inspiring vision, discouraging as a bundle of definitions; Lyotard asks enabling questions, but his work is discouraging as a prohibition on coherence.

A culture of intellectual encouragement is not relativism. Relativism is a negative concept, the absence of unity and coherence. In practice, relativism can be either encouraging or discouraging – it depends on the relativist! Sometimes relativism discourages new ideas, if no progress seems possible. I think a culture of intellectual encouragement implies a search for truth, not a preconceived relativism; but it's an arguable proposal.

Index

Compiled by Jackie McDermott